FADING ADS OF

CINCINNATI

FADING ADS OF
CINCINNATI

RONNY SALERNO

THE
History
PRESS

Published by The History Press
Charleston, SC
www.historypress.net

First published 2015

Manufactured in the United States

ISBN 978.1.46711.872.9

Library of Congress Control Number: 2015953041

Notice: The information in this book is true and complete to the best of our knowledge. It is offered without guarantee on the part of the author or The History Press. The author and The History Press disclaim all liability in connection with the use of this book.

CONTENTS

FOREWORD

An excited sixteen-year-old student once came into my classroom and exclaimed, "Last night I snuck into the abandoned water park off 275! Look at the pictures I took!" My first instinct—being an adult in a position of authority—was to tell him what an idiot he was and how dangerous and illegal his actions were. Then I saw the pictures. Never before had I been forced to open my eyes to this place, now defunct and all but invisible to the urban landscape. How could I have driven past this place dozens of times and not noticed the enormous park? Ronny's photographs had somehow lifted the veil. All I could say was: "Do more of this."

This was the start of Ronny Salerno's love affair with the fading history of the places where we live, work and play; the history of places and things that are not all that noteworthy—water parks, shopping malls, suburbs. You won't find remnants of them in museums or history books. No scholarly articles will be written about them. They, even while alive, were not all that significant. Now dead or dying, they are becoming even more ghost-like, not connected to the visual information of what we allow ourselves to see.

With *Fading Ads of Cincinnati*, Ronny Salerno has trained his eye to see what is usually imperceptible to the rest of us. How does one train one's self to see the invisible—phantoms of signs that used to let us know what was where, who owned what and what was being advertised? For Ronny Salerno, it started with an honest love for his city. "Infatuation" is the best word I can think of to describe his love affair with Cincinnati. Like people who travel the world to photograph foreign landscapes or exotic wildlife, Ronny has this same passion—except he never has to leave home.

Ronny has avidly been exploring and documenting through photography the nuances of Cincinnati since 2007. His worldwide-popular queencitydiscovery.com has been a staple for Cincinnatians for the past eight years. *The Future Is One of Mighty Ducks T-Shirts and Discmen* was published in 2013. *Fading Ads of Cincinnati* is only the current chapter in his documentation of our fair city, and we are eagerly awaiting the next.

LAURA METZ

ACKNOWLEDGEMENTS

There are several people who made this book possible. When I started this project, so many lent their advice, insight and kind words of encouragement. Many offered up tips on where I could find several of these signs, and many others took time out of their days to talk with me and share their stories. I'd especially like to thank Bill Rinehart, Cameron Knight, John Kiesewetter, Carl Solway, Sue Sena, Adam Dean, Andrew Gould, David Maley, Kevin Holthaus, Bob Carpenter, Tod Swormstedt, Fred Jump, Bill Haas, Ed Gelke, Fred Lemon, Dave Greene, Don Helbig, James Engle, Amy Hartman, Chantel Oliver, Mayor Mark Mallory, Janet Reid, Chris Stegner, Barbara Houghton, Dave Rolfes, Maya Drozdz, Jake Mecklenborg, Laura Metz, Mike Taylor, Andrea Ward, the Evers family, Jeremy Martin, Andrea Brofft, John Vachon, Esther Bubley, Christian Glass, Kylie Seward and Doug Apple—all of whom provided help and inspiration. Also, Gus Holthaus, who painted iconic signs and left his signature behind.

Additionally, I'm especially thankful to my family—Dad, Mom, Nana, Papa, Grandma and Grandpa—for helping shape who I am and providing me with the resources to pursue photography and writing. And thank you to Laura, who encouraged me to take on this project and has always been so supportive and understanding of the stories I want to share.

Finally, thank you to Krista Slavicek, whose confidence and leadership gave me the opportunity to create this book and guide its development.

To everyone: I am eternally grateful.

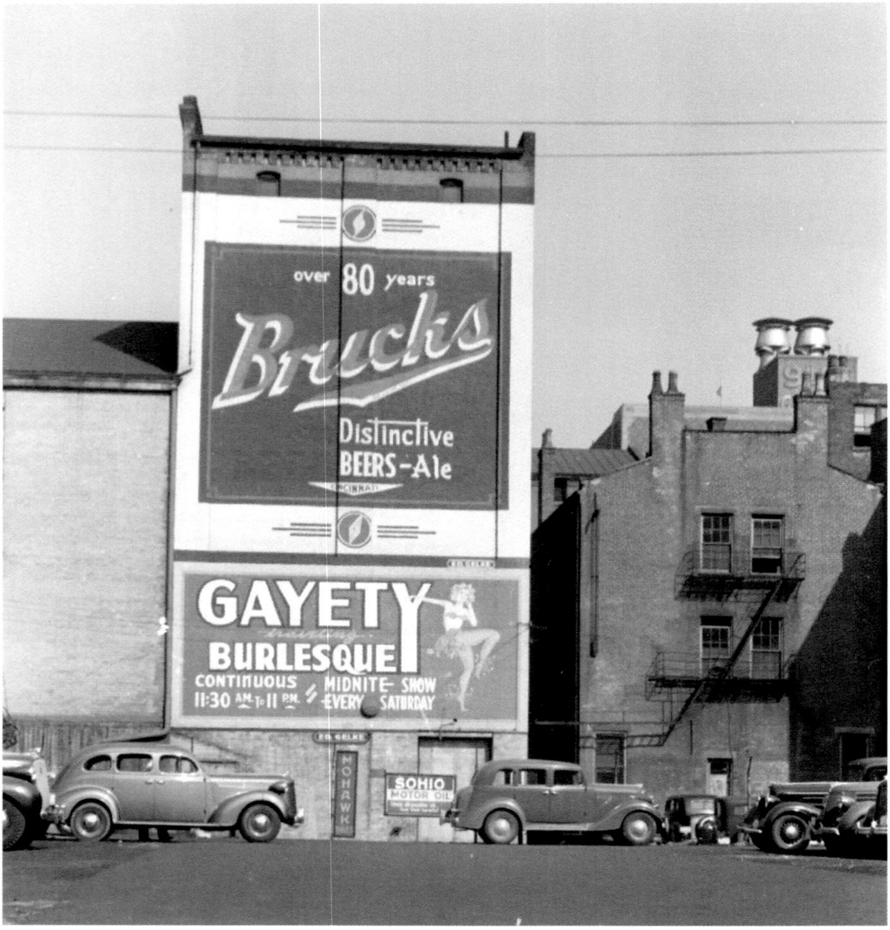

A parking lot scene in October 1938 features vintage automobiles along with painted advertisements for beer and a burlesque show in Cincinnati. When enhanced to its highest resolution, the image reveals the signature of Ed Gelke, whose name can still be found under the Major Savings and Loan sign seen later in this book. *Image by John Vachon, courtesy of the Library of Congress.*

INTRODUCTION

I think everyone wants to be remembered in some way, to have something to show for their lives. I'm also sure everyone has a different opinion on how to go about that. Our time on earth is finite, a small span in the grand scheme of things. We're burdened by our own mortality, and after we're gone, there's only the fading physical remnants of our past to remember us by. In a way, what we leave behind is similar to the fading advertisements, or "ghost signs," seen in the photographs throughout this text. In their infancy, they are attention-grabbing and meant to catch the view of those around them. Then they age, taking on new forms. Eventually, the companies they advertised go under or evolve into new identities. Sometimes the products they tout are no longer available. Often, the signs just stop being maintained, victims of indifference. They're left to live out their lives as lead-based paint clinging to the bricks. In that sense, are they truly dead? Are they truly "ghosts" of the past? Or are they like our own personal legacies, similar to the memories of ourselves we leave behind? For inanimate objects designed to take advantage of open space and generate interest, they possess surprisingly human qualities.

When people would ask me what kind of book I was working on, I had to be careful using the term "ghost sign." They'd immediately ask me if I had investigated some local urban legend or taken a tour of a supposedly haunted building, offering their suggestions of where I could seek out tales from beyond the grave. I'd correct them and show some photographic examples of these signs. They'd be intrigued, but there was always some disappointment that I wasn't writing about apparitions or curses. I don't believe in ghosts. As such, I've always struggled with the term "ghost signs." I feel the term "fading advertisement"—as coined by author Fred Jump in this series' first book—is much more appropriate. Fading is a verb; it implies that there's action. "Ghost" implies that something is dead, gone. These signs are still alive in a way, even if the products or the people who created them have passed. They're in action, physically warring against the distressed nature of the elements. They power on until external forces finally prevent them from doing so, until the last chip of paint has fallen. Essentially, that's the end of their life cycle. In a way, they're not really "ghost signs" until they're gone, remembered only in a book made during the summer of 2015.

I get it, though. Often they're viewed as snapshots from the past. They tout products that don't exist anymore or shout slogans no longer used. They're seen as "vintage" and "retro." They don't grab attention like they used to. They're not nearly as noticeable anymore and, as such, become the ghosts of our civilization's past, a city's past and a culture's past.

What's true is this: both terms make strong cases and are correct in certain regards. Deciding which to use just underscores that there's more to these signs than can be seen at first glance. They're the work of craftsmen, examples of a bygone era, physical manifestations of nostalgia. Behind each one, there's some sort of story. Sometimes there are just a few sentences needed to explain, while other signs could have entire separate books explaining the histories they represent. They're all around us, now part of the urban fabric, and they often go unnoticed. Even when you find them, some don't have enough clues left to point you in the right direction. Often, they've faded merely into abstract pieces rather than into the hieroglyphics of early advertising.

I've been interested in history since I was a kid, an interest brought on by watching World War II films like *Battle of the Bulge* with my father. As I grew up, he was the one taking me to baseball games. We'd leave our suburban home twenty miles north of downtown, catch the interstate and snake through the region on I-75. He'd point out things along the way, pieces of a history he adopted when transplanted here from Long Island via Holland and Texas.

I always had an interest in cameras, trying to coax him and my grandfather into letting me meddle with theirs. By high school, I was learning film and digital before setting off to Ohio University to study photojournalism in the fall of 2007. In a dorm room in late September, I took up the advice of some friends: to put together a website pairing photography with Cincinnati history. That's how Queen City Discovery (QC/D) was started. Later that school year, I studied legendary FSA photographer Gordon Parks. An interview he did before his passing struck me. He spoke about why photographers choose to shoot the things they do, how it can often be interpreted as a reflection of themselves. After I had transferred to Northern Kentucky University, I found that photographer Joel Meyerowitz had similar feelings to Parks. I chose to document the things that interested me, the stories I thought were worth sharing and bringing to light history and subjects that I felt deserved more attention. QC/D is a reflection of myself, not just in the words I've typed, subjects I've chosen or photographs I've made, but also in what I feel is worth knowing. In the years since founding QC/D, I've been casually trespassing into abandoned buildings, seeking out people I find interesting and telling the stories of things often overlooked.

The subject of "fading ads" and "ghost signs" had been on my mind for a while. It always seemed like an interesting thing to pursue but never jumped from the list in my notebook to an actual story on my website. I'm not the first to document this subject, not even the first person to do so in Cincinnati. When first approached about the idea, I wondered if there were even enough signs left to write an article about, let alone a book. I couldn't have been more wrong. The first time I went out to make the photographs for this book, I spent an entire hour on one block. People passed by, construction crews went on their way as the city was pulsing with its usual noise and activity. I came in search of one sign only to find that the 800 block of Main Street affords views of several. I started becoming aware of the signs everywhere I went in the city. Research sessions morphed into all-night trips down metaphorical rabbit holes in search of historical evidence. In the midst of a city with so many things to see, so much history to cherish and a future to be excited about, these fading ads are everywhere, dotting the landscape yet not demanding the kind of attention they once did.

They're snapshots, clues to the past, and these photographs preserve the state the signs were in during the summer of 2015. Even as I type this, they continue to erode. Two of the signs featured in this book have already been covered up by new construction. For a moment, though, they've been recognized, given a venue in which they can be remembered. One day, if they're all gone, at least someone will be able to look back

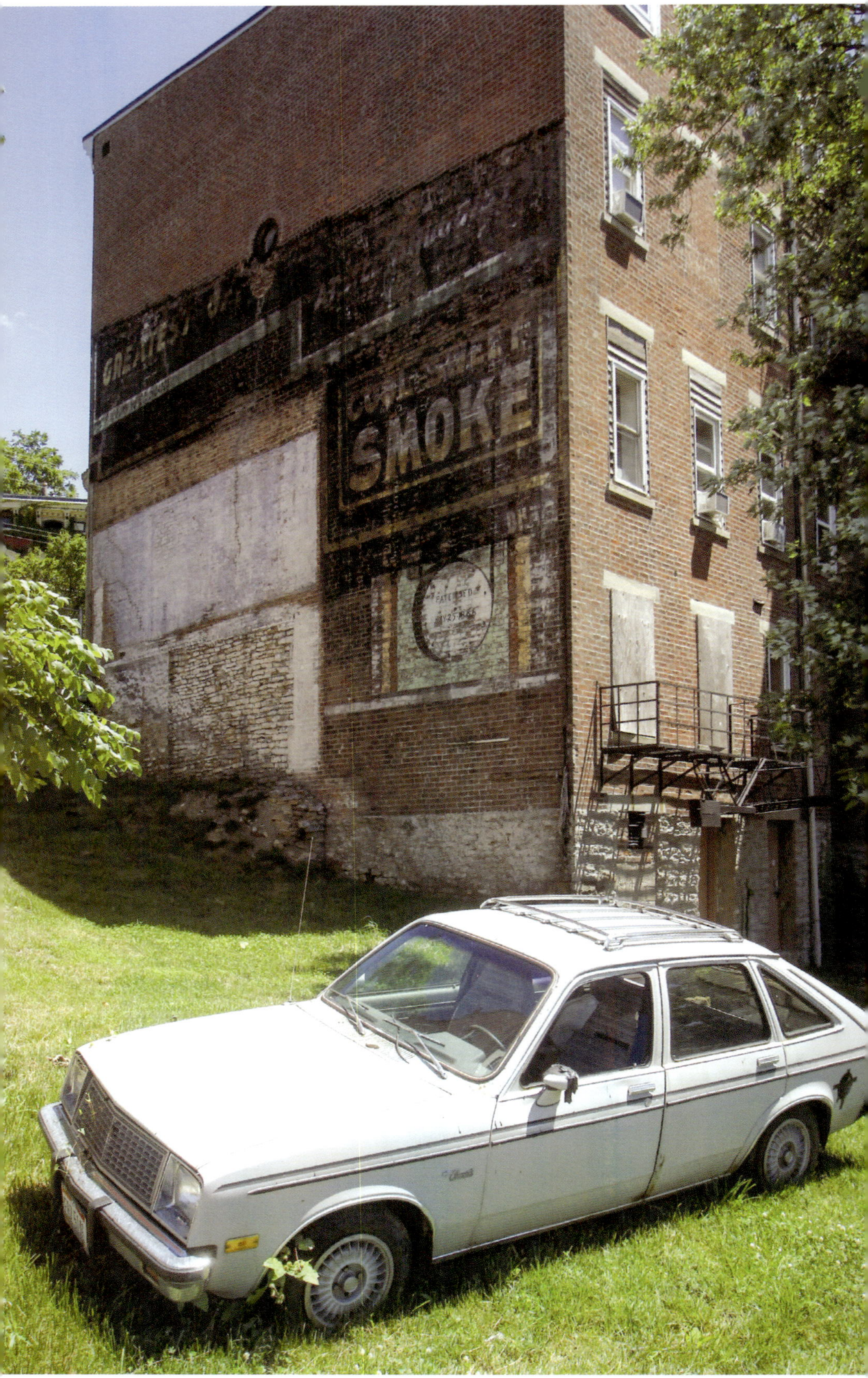
SMOKE

at this book and know they were there. One day, too, though, the pages of this book will yellow and it will be out of print. Maybe the images will be preserved in digital archives for some other author to stumble upon. Maybe this work will live on like some of these ghost signs have: faded but still around, preserving the memory, allowing something to be remembered, telling a story for as long as fading signs, or those who study them, can.

Opposite: With flat tires and weeds growing up through the grill, this old Chevy sits before a fading tobacco ad in Cincinnati's Brighton neighborhood, both subjects appearing as stark contrasts to the historical image at this book's beginning. *Photo by Ronny Salerno.*

1
QUEEN CITY OF THE WEST

It may be hard for people to believe, but at one time Cincinnati was bigger than Chicago, and well before St. Louis built the arch, the Queen City was America's gateway to westward expansion. As the Revolutionary War ended and a new nation began to form its identity, early settlers began laying claim to the sweeping hills and basin on the banks of the Ohio River.

According to U.S. census records, Cincinnati had a population of 9,642 residents by 1820, one year after it was officially incorporated as a city. Thirty years later, the population had increased nearly twelve-fold. Cincinnati was America's sixth-largest city, ahead of its contemporary counterparts like St. Louis, Chicago and New Orleans. Railroads expanded westward, and canals linked the city with its interstate neighbors, but the steamboat trade fueled the city's commerce like no other. Along the banks, industry rose and began to press outward. Businesses proudly displayed their names alongside their factories, painted by hand and reflecting a new industrial era.

The city weathered the Civil War as an important stop on the Underground Railroad, where crossing the industrious river often meant freedom. The Roebling Suspension Bridge (precursor to the iconic span in Brooklyn) linked the city with its satellite neighbors of Newport and Covington, Kentucky, in the years following the nation's bloodiest conflict. The centuries turned again, the steamboat trade died out and Cincinnati's population began to lag behind other major metropolitan centers, yet the river city's economic engine kept churning.

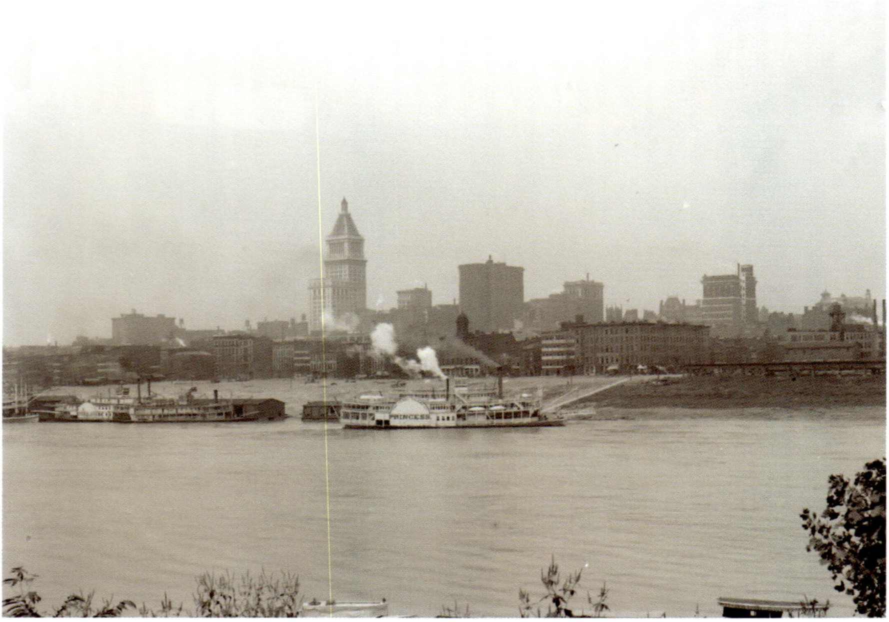

The skyline of Cincinnati, Ohio, with multiple riverboats docked at its banks in a photograph taken between 1910 and 1920. *Photograph by the Detroit Publishing Co., courtesy of the Library of Congress.*

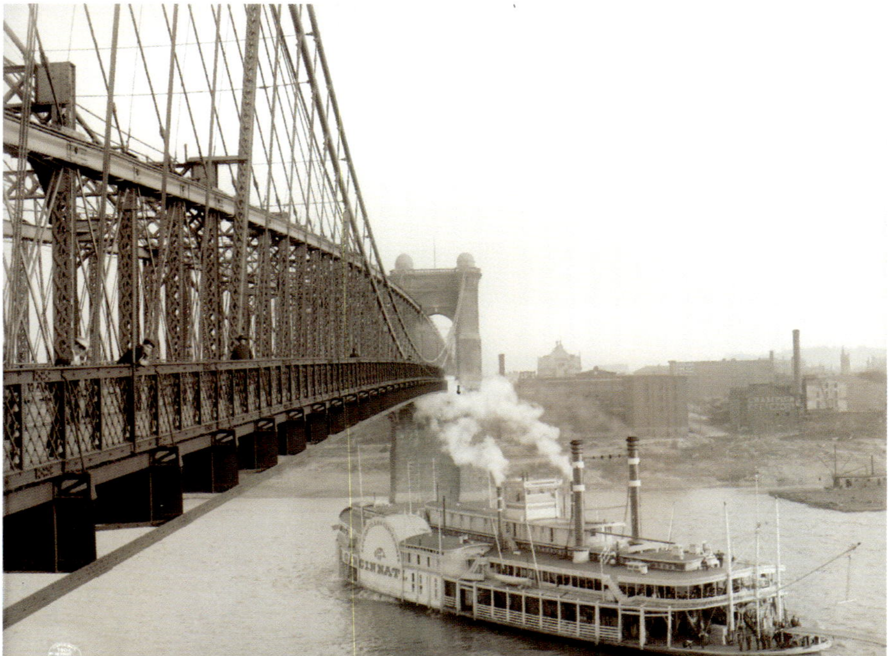

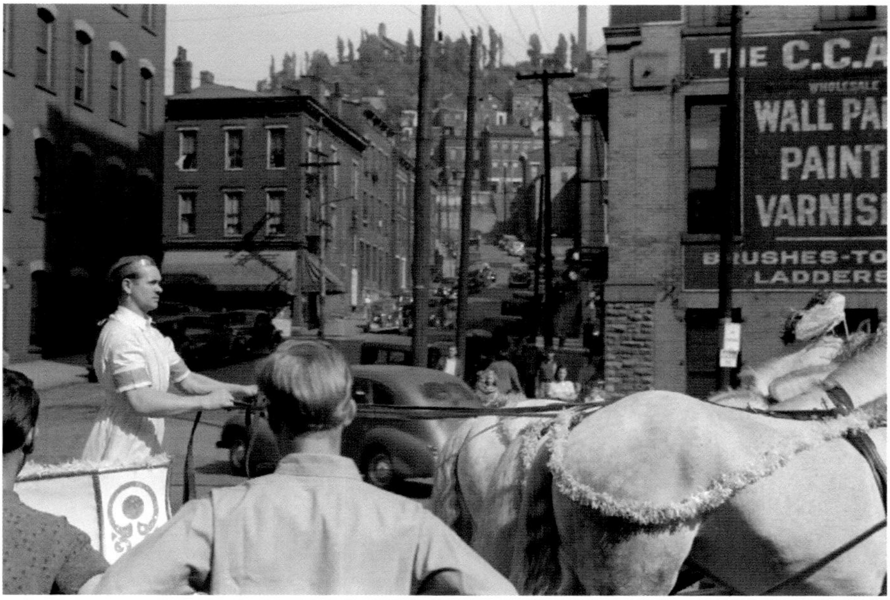

A chariot coming down the street at the end of the city's sesquicentennial parade passes in front of a hand-painted advertisement seen in the background. Coincidentally, the sign features "paint" as one of the products it touts in a prime attention spot along the parade route in October 1938. *Image by John Vachon, courtesy of the Library of Congress.*

Opposite, bottom: A 1906 photograph shows the iconic Roebling Suspension Bridge that connects the cities of Cincinnati, Ohio, and Covington, Kentucky, while the side-wheeler *Cincinnati* passes beneath. *Photograph by the Detroit Publishing Co., courtesy of the Library of Congress.*

The city bustled with business and commerce. Pork, beer, soap, radio and other industries boomed. Upward construction scraped the sky, while in an age before billboards, businesses emblazoned their names and advertised their products with hand-painted artwork on brick and stone.

Cincinnati weathered Prohibition, flooding and the Great Depression and sent its sons to two world wars. Like so many other midwestern cities, a postwar suburban expansion began. An ambitious subway system was cancelled, highways were built through swaths of once-dense urbanity and the economic landscape changed. Businesses ebbed and flowed between city and suburban realms. Hand-painted advertising began competing with roadside billboards.

Urban renewal projects of the 1970s and '80s replaced much of downtown Cincinnati's historic building stock with "modern" office buildings. The '90s ushered in a few new skyscrapers. New stadiums were built, neighborhoods

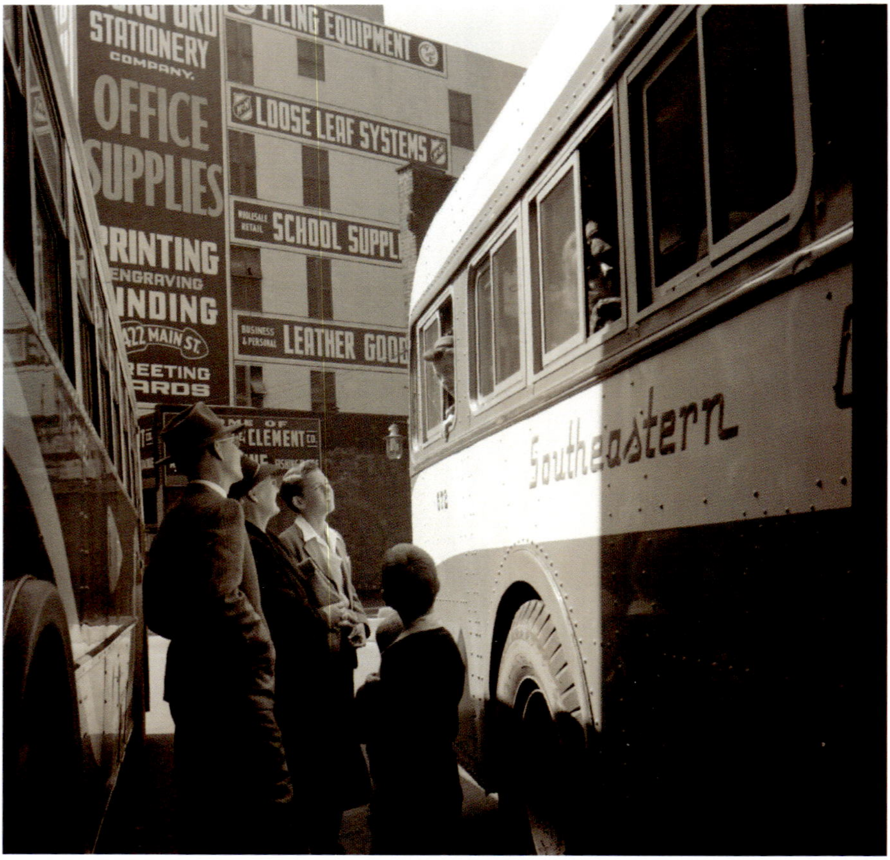

In this photograph from the Farm Security Administration's renowned "Saying goodbye at the bus terminal" collection, several hand-painted advertisements can be seen in the background. The image is archived as Cincinnati in 1943. *Photograph by Esther Bubley, courtesy of the Library of Congress.*

revitalized and by the twenty-first century a renewed sense of civic pride and identity was born in the wake of the 2001 riots.

Today, downtown Cincinnati has regained its prestige as the region's cultural and economic center. A new riverfront park spans the city blocks between two major-league sports venues. Downtown is anchored by several Fortune 500 companies, Proctor & Gamble at their forefront. The Central Business District is now measured in square footage of office space rather than in manufacturing capacity. Corporate monikers adorn the skyline atop skyscrapers housing cubicles. Yet much of old Cincinnati

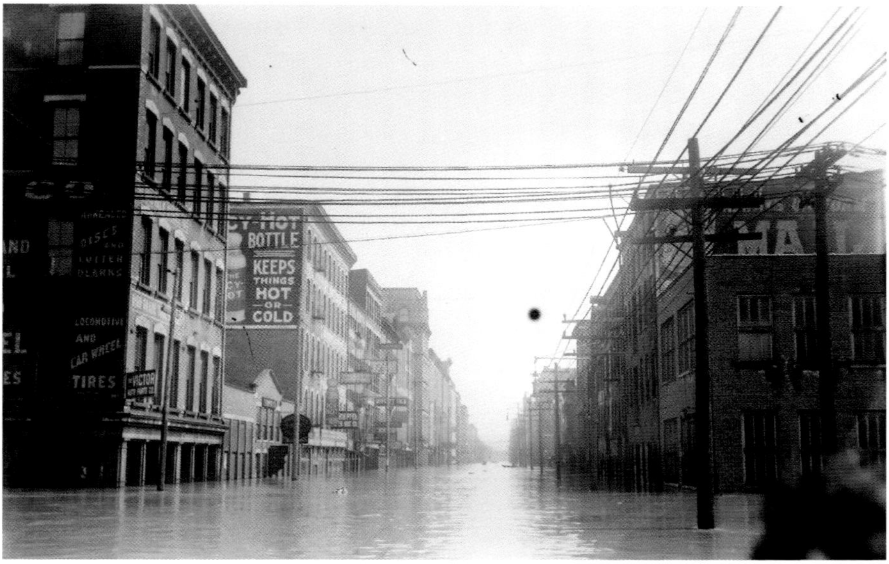

Most likely from the Flood of 1918, this photograph shows downtown's Elm Street covered in water while the hand-painted advertisements on the buildings persevere. Ads for locomotive and automobile tires can be seen, as can a multi-story ad for Icy-Hot. *Photograph by Bain News Service, courtesy of the Library of Congress.*

has managed to survive throughout, in the outlying neighborhoods and across the river.

They endure the sun, the rain and the erosion of time. They'd be nostalgic folk art for sale at antique shops if they weren't affixed to buildings that served as their canvas. They're works of art, reflections of a creative process hindered by zoning laws today. They provide clues, present a glimpse into time periods—into a city's economic and cultural history. And each day, they fade just a little bit more.

These are the Fading Advertisements of Cincinnati.

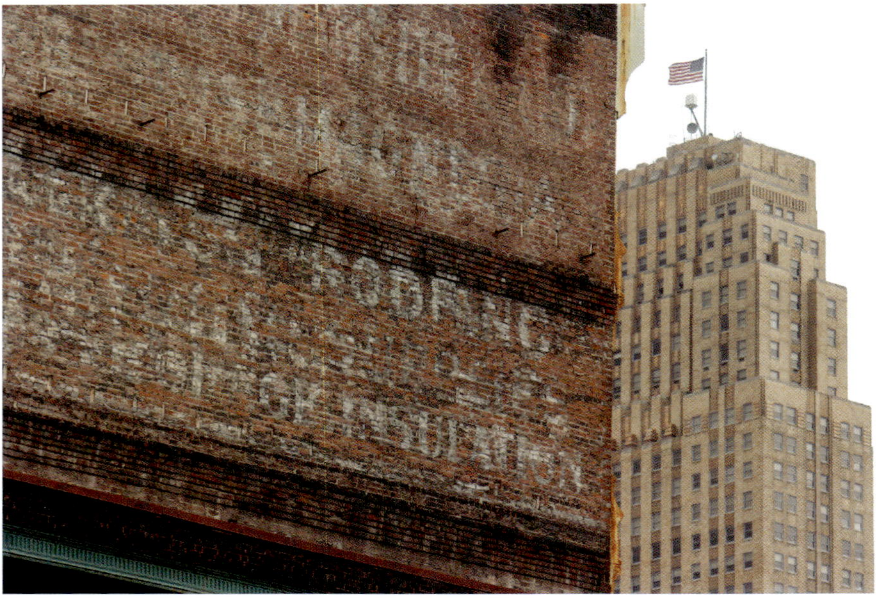

A fading advertisement just off Main Street sits in the shadow of the city's Fifth Third and Carew Towers. Like many of the city's ghost signs, several words and letters can be seen holding on to the bricks, but the overall message has disappeared. *Photo by Ronny Salerno.*

2
DOWNTOWN

Main isn't the most common street name in the United States; it's ranked as the seventh, just below Fifth Street. Perhaps it's fitting that as you stand at the corner of Fifth and Main Streets in Cincinnati, you can look down the canyons of office buildings and sense the energy of the Central Business District. As the city rose from the nearby river, downtown became the center of industry and holds the highest concentration of fading advertisements. These ghost signs tell several stories. There's elbow grease and true handiwork behind them. There's art, design and composition. Nestled on the sides of older buildings dwarfed by high-rises, they run the gamut of various industries and time periods.

In a way, downtown is like an urban art gallery. You have to block out the noise, ignore the distractions and level out the details. All the streetlights, windows, sidewalks and quirks have to blend; they need to become the pure white walls of an exhibition. Their pieces—parts of the collection—are everywhere. Some are in plain sight and some hidden down alleyways or partially obscured. You have to put in the effort, though. Whether you're lugging a camera around or just exploring, your attention has to be on the walls. Once you start seeing the fading signs, you'll notice them everywhere. You'll develop an eye for them. In some ways, it's like a scavenger hunt, going off tips sent to you by readers and those who have been documenting them before. Sometimes you'll discover them on your own, previously unaware of their existence despite how many times you've made that walk, stopped at that bar or eaten at that restaurant. You have to slow down, focus, and they'll appear to you. Once you've seen them, you can appreciate their detail, their remains and anything else that's been left behind. When the city becomes the gallery walls, the fading advertisements are its showcase.

Distributors of Champion Papers

The composition spans the entire side of the building, ceasing just above the neighboring structure. These days, the company name has faded into a collection of vaguely discernable letters, yet its business claim is still clear. It was "distributors of ...ion Papers." Though the sign is partially obscured by a modern billboard advertising a local gambling institution, it's safe to assume that the company distributed products of "Champion Papers." Champion originated and was a staple just to the north, in nearby Hamilton, Ohio.

Champion opened operations in Hamilton in 1894. Over the years, its products included not just office paper but also maps for Allied troops in World War II. Production and employment at the plant peaked in

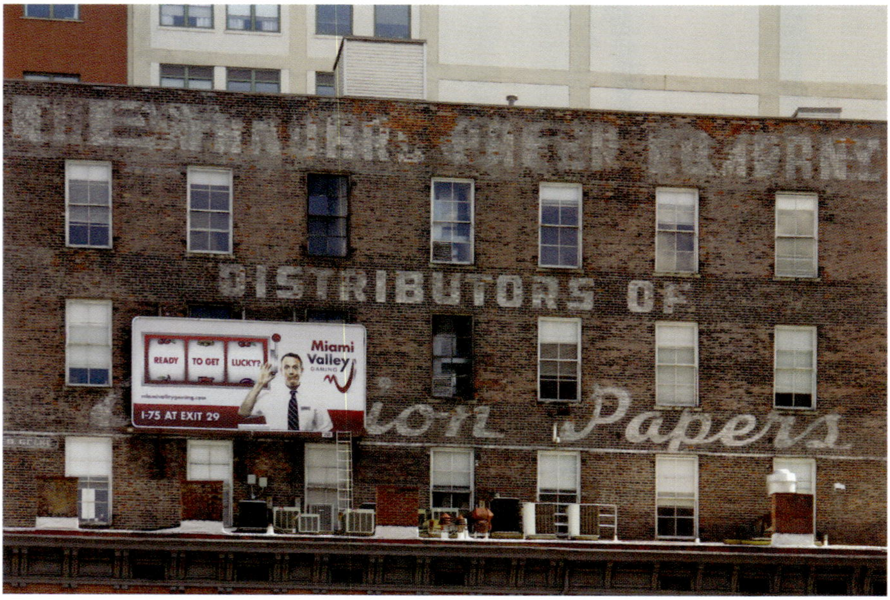

While the company's name has eroded, the product it distributed still shines through. Even with the obstruction of a modern advertisement, the product is likely Champion Papers. *Photo by Ronny Salerno.*

1961 with about 1,500 employees in 1994. The Champion name was well known and historically regarded as high quality, evident in the fact that a company in Cincinnati commissioned an ad over an entire building to tout the product. Environmental regulations started taking shape, pressuring the nation's paper mills on their waste and disposal of byproducts. Digital technology advanced, costs rose and companies began to cut back on how much paper they needed. Champion's stock price became stagnant. By 2000, a corporate merger had taken away the Champion name. By 2012, the Champion mill in Hamilton was gone. The company is remembered in the town; its former location is now the site of a proposed renovation project. While the Champion name may be more significant in Hamilton, it's still heralded as a quality product about thirty miles south.

Gibson and Perin

Gibson and Perin had been a local office furniture, equipment and services supplier since 1893. According to one of its print advertisements in a November 1985 issue of *Cincinnati* magazine, Gibson and Perin delivered "great values on the newest, most modern office furniture and supplies." At one point, it boasted three downtown locations: a furniture showroom and two stores. One store was located on Sixth Street and the other, which featured the painted advertisement pictured on the following page, could be found on Fourth Street. Today, the company survives in nearby suburbs on both sides of the river as the Office Furniture Connection. The new title is a little blander, lacking the personal touch of a family name. The sign marking the former Fourth Street location is full of echoed personal details. It's relatively well preserved, shielded by a nearby building. The owners' names are featured prominently in bolder letters of drop shadow and complementary colors. They were more than just a "connection" to office furniture; they provided so much more and listed those services for everyone to see. At the bottom, grounded by a gold-colored ribbon, the business was proud to proclaim how long it had been around: "Since 1893." It wanted you to know it had been here for a while. The company may exist in a different form outside downtown, but Gibson and Perin's pride still lives on—on the side of a building on Fourth Street.

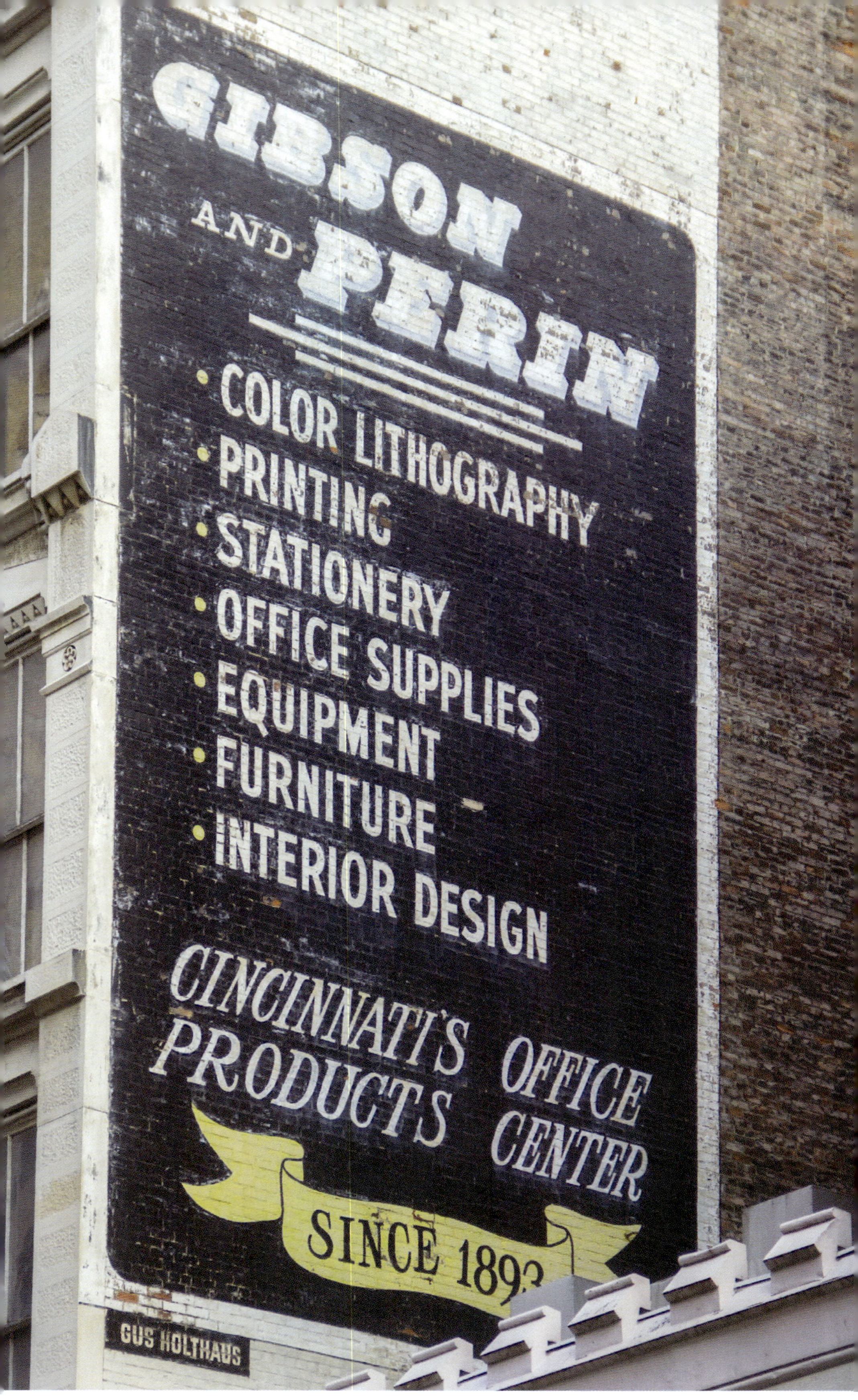
GIBSON
AND PERIN
COLOR LITHOGRAPHY
PRINTING
STATIONERY
OFFICE SUPPLIES
EQUIPMENT
FURNITURE
INTERIOR DESIGN
CINCINNATI'S OFFICE
PRODUCTS CENTER
GUS HOLTHAUS

The Polinsky Co.

Relatively well preserved, perhaps due to being in an alley, a sign for Polinsky Co. Office Furniture once provided direction to the business's assumed storefront on Ninth Street through an alleyway. While not accredited, the Better Business Bureau did have a file on the company as recently as 2006. Maybe at one point it had competed with Gibson and Perin for downtown office furniture customers. Like its thought-to-be competitors, though, the

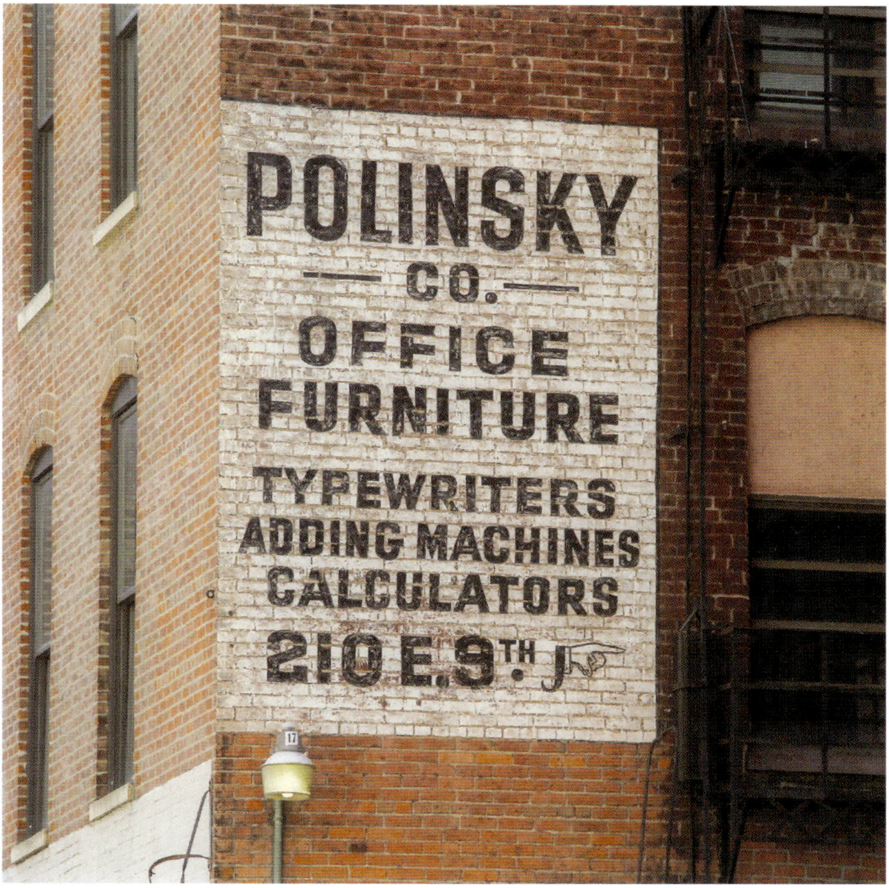

This sign for the Polinsky Co. has been relatively well preserved due to its location in an alley, shielded by a nearby building. Details such as the suit-cuffed hand and advertising of older technology, as well as the physical sign itself, all provide a hint of nostalgia. *Photo by Ronny Salerno.*

Opposite: The advertisement for Gibson and Perin not only touted the services and products that the company offered but also provided some insight into its history. Dating back to 1893, the company still exists under a new identity out in the suburbs. *Photo by Ronny Salerno.*

Polinsky name is gone from the business district today, remembered only in a fading advertisement.

Oftentimes, these fading ads reflect the needs of the people who were around them. As downtown Cincinnati transitioned from factory-backed industry to towers of offices, someone needed to supply the demands of office growth. It's no surprise that office supplies and furniture were in high demand. Having one's products close to potential clients offered huge advantages.

As I wrote this book, I utilized my desktop computer, an iPad when on the go and my iPhone when I needed to make quick notes or pinpoint one of these signs on a map. The devices I used to put together these words have all pretty much made Polinsky's offerings obsolete. Even as I write this, the phone in my pocket is capable of wrapping all three objects into one and connecting them with a vast communications network to the outside world. The devices that would eventually circumvent the advertised products are now the ones being used to preserve their memory.

Globe Furniture Rental

Once a chain with locations throughout the United States and headquartered in Cincinnati, Globe Furniture Rental was a well-known supplier of office furniture. Eventually, the company was acquired by international brand CORT Furniture. The acquisition of Globe Furniture Rental and five other companies helped turn CORT into the company it is today—with large retail showrooms throughout the United States and United Kingdom that cater to both home and office furnishings. For a time, it seemed that Globe operated under the name of CORT Global Furniture. However, the company as a whole is now branded simply as CORT, with one of its retail showroom locations in suburban Cincinnati.

The word "Globe" is incredibly popular among furniture stores. Enter "Globe Furniture" into a search engine and you'll get links to several businesses, most of them now closed, in several different cities across the

Opposite: The sign for Globe Furniture Rentals is quite a bit more modern, a stark contrast in design to another fading Globe advertisement found in another neighborhood. Like so many others, Globe catered to a city center full of office buildings that needed to be furnished. *Photo by Ronny Salerno.*

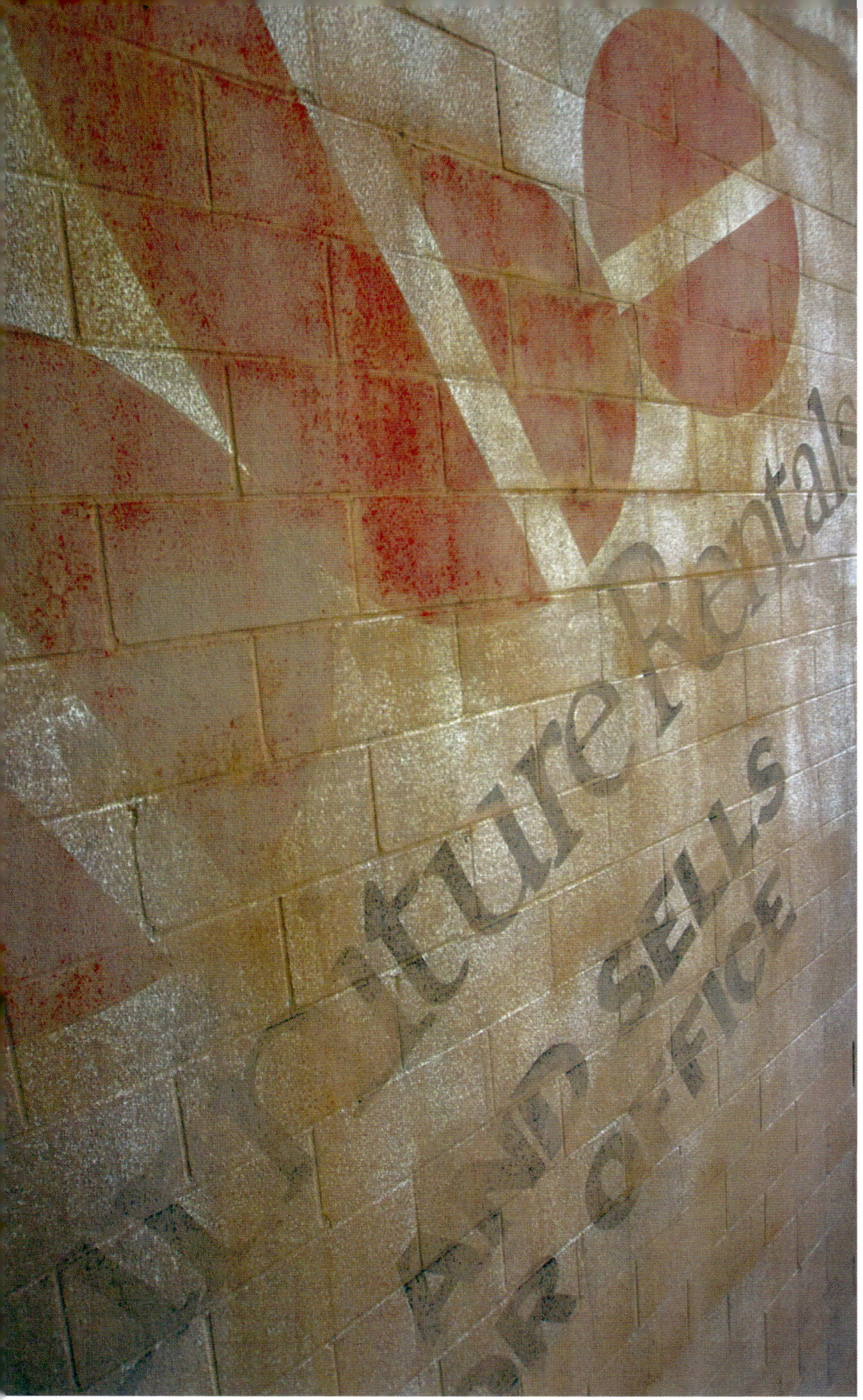
Rentals
SELLS
OFFICE

states. One of them is still active in Chillicothe, Ohio, about two hours away. Globe Furniture Rental wasn't alone in using the name even in the Cincinnati market. Another company was known as Globe, too, and like its colleague downtown, it also has a fading advertisement located within the city and highlighted in chapter six.

Twine Paper

Although downtown's Central Business District may be known for its vast amount of office space, the CBD is also filled with nightlife, entertainment, arts and culture. Within one block of this fading advertisement, you'll find the Aronoff Center for the Arts, the Contemporary Arts Center and some of the city's highest-rated restaurants. Advertising Twine Paper vertically down a black brick façade, this sign harkens back to a day before the modern balcony was affixed and a cocktail bar built within.

It's a glimpse of what used to be, a detail that would go unnoticed in the night by most hopping from bar to bar. Like many other signs throughout the city, this one has been allowed to continue living out its natural life despite the renovation of the building it adorns.

Harvard Rye

The building at 212 Eighth Street was renovated into office space in 1980. According to county property records, the building was constructed in 1892, while another source claims 1900. There's no telling how old the hand-painted name on the side is, but it gives us some clues. It's hard to discern, but the letters read, "Harvard Rye."

Harvard Rye whiskey is a long-dead brand. It was the creation of Samuel H. Klein, part of the Klein Brothers. Samuel's whiskey earned its Harvard name from the cap-and-gown-clad male featured on the bottles, referencing the renowned higher education establishment. The branding found on the

Opposite: The words "Twine Paper" have managed to continue their existence on the side of this building for several years. Most recently, they survived the building's renovation and the addition of new features: a balcony, an overhang, new wiring and a vent. *Photo by Ronny Salerno.*

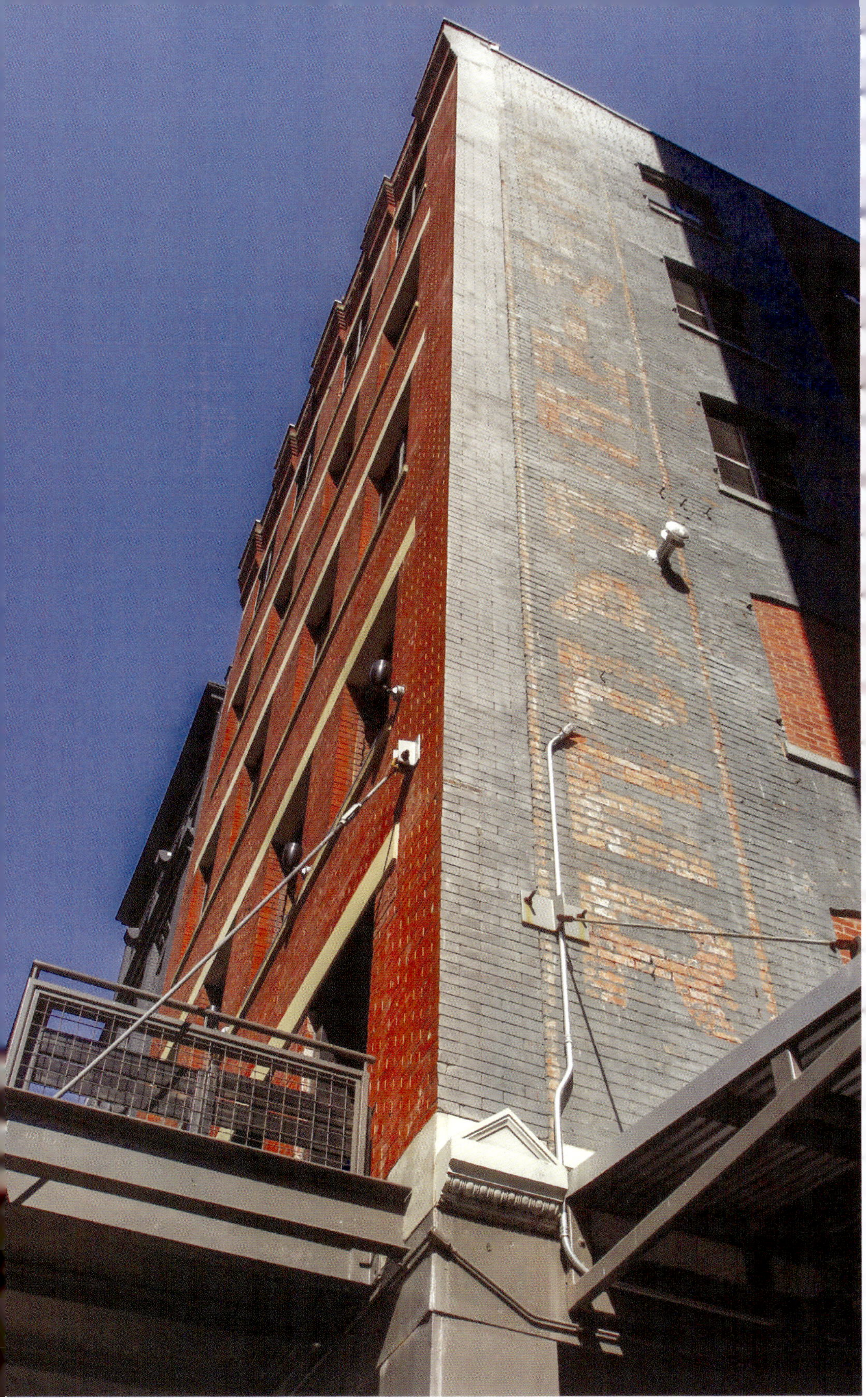

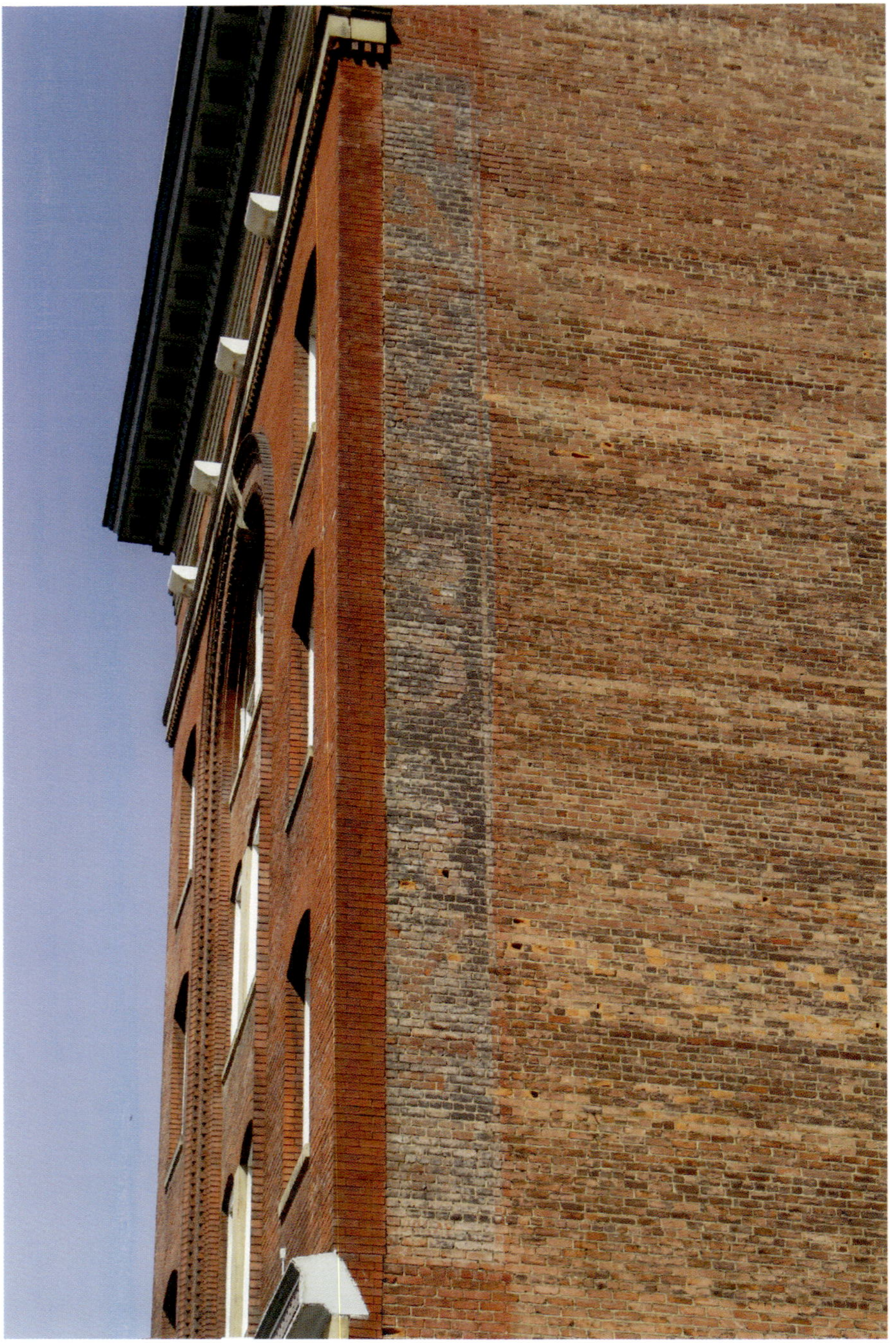

Making out the name of "Harvard Rye" takes a patient eye. The advertised whiskey is assumed to have fallen out of production with the onset of Prohibition in 1920. *Photo by Ronny Salerno.*

bottles echoed the advertisements the Klein Brothers set up in saloons and bars. Their Harvard Rye whiskey was often depicted in images that were viewed as somewhat scandalous for their time. Compared to today's Bud Light Super Bowl commercials featuring bikini-clad women partying to whatever music is popular in February, the Klein Brothers' paintings of graduation cap–wearing boys fraternizing with ankle-showing dames seem quite tame.

The brothers' whiskey advertisements pushed the edge of acceptable in the late 1800s, when their various brands flourished in Cincinnati. By 1914, Samuel had died and left the company to his family. The Klein brand ceased in 1920 with the onset of Prohibition and never returned after repeal in 1933. Given the company's age and demise in the early twentieth century, this hand-painted sign might just be the oldest one in the city.

The Dixie Terminal

The Dixie Terminal Building is one of downtown's architectural treasures. It has been an office building since its inception in 1921, but at one time it

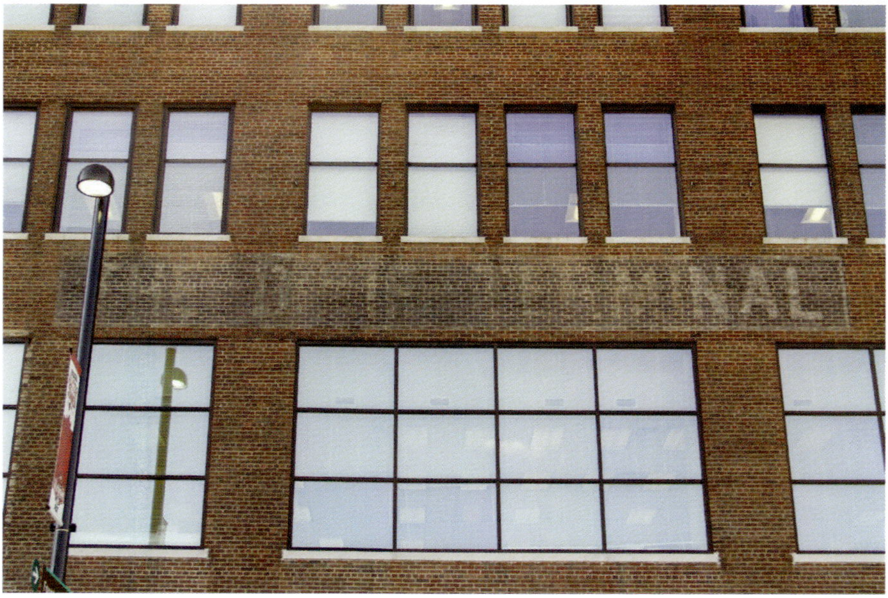

The Dixie Terminal building looks much different today, completely built out as an office, compared to its days as a transit depot. In the bricks above the windows, though, the Dixie Terminal name lives on. *Photo by Ronny Salerno.*

was also a transit depot. The terminal was one end of Northern Kentucky's Green Line streetcar service traveling from across the river. When streetcar service dried up in the area halfway through the twentieth century, the Dixie Terminal welcomed diesel buses. Dixie Terminal lent its beautiful interior to a scene in 1988's *Rain Man*, starring Tom Cruise and Dustin Hoffman. Just under a decade later, Dixie Terminal's status as a transit hub ended when the Transit Authority of Northern Kentucky ceased its operations there. Today, with all of its transit infrastructure removed, the building still houses office tenants, and the only exterior reminder of its commuter past are the faded words above Third Street.

Provident Camera

All the photographs made for this book have been shot with a Canon Digital SLR camera. I bought this camera, and all of my other supplies, online. The online route is cheaper, even more so than the suburban "big box" stores. I was trained to shoot and process film, but these days, digital photography has become more economical and requires less time to be processed. Even since the launch of the iPhone in 2007, digital cameras themselves are less likely to be used in comparison to smart phones. Cincinnati still has a few local camera shops around, but none was as iconic and revered as Provident Camera. Provident was the complete antithesis of a Best Buy or other chain retailers. It still provided film processing, emphasizing sales of film products right along with its digital offerings. The employees were photographers themselves, true to their craft and displaying their work on the walls. The place was like a New York neighborhood storefront but with the charm and friendliness of a small town. Professionals and hobbyists alike often made trips to Provident, a store that could be found six stories below the iconic blue and yellow hand-painted sign on Seventh Street.

I remember my first visit to Provident. I was still in high school, just starting a real foray into photography after meddling with my father's and grandfather's cameras off and on as a kid. My father and I went to Provident to see about getting an old Minolta 35mm repaired. We walked in and were immediately greeted by the two men behind the counter. After a quick inspection, it was evident that the Minolta dug up from my grandfather's collection was beyond economic repair. Nevertheless, the help was appreciated, and we continued to browse the shop. Vast collections of lenses filled the glass cases below the

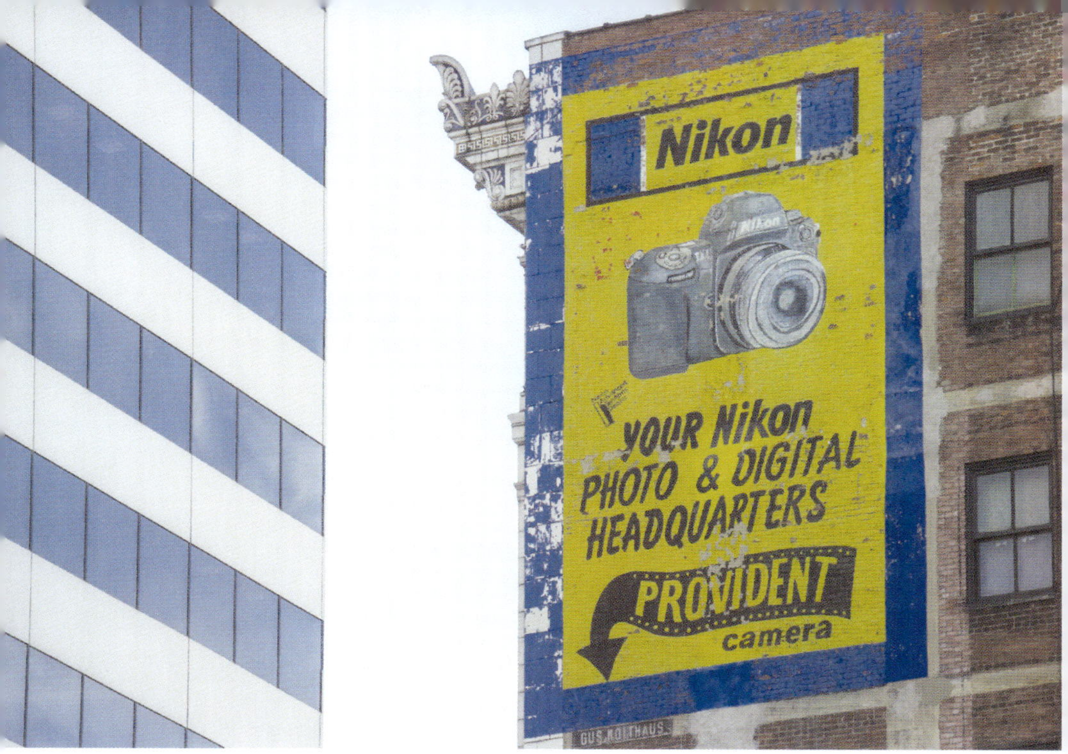

Weathered and worn alongside a historic building next to a modern one, the sign formerly marking Provident Camera's location prominently features a Nikon SLR camera. Provident was a favorite among local photographers, an oasis in a desert of big box retailers. *Photo by Ronny Salerno.*

counter, while camera bodies were displayed on the back wall. Near the door, a selection of photographer's vests hung on hangers—the kind of khaki garb you'd see shooters wearing on NFL sidelines. That visit must have been in 2006 or so. I never made it back there.

When Provident closed its doors, the local weekly arts publication *City Beat* ran a story by its chief photo editor, Cameron Knight. The article provides some insight into Knight's relationship with the store, but talking to him in person reveals even more. He had started going there his senior year of high school, loading up on camera gear before heading off to Western Kentucky University to study photojournalism. "I was the editor for my school's newspaper," he says. "Even back then, there wasn't a whole lot of options in the late '90s and early 2000s. Camera stores weren't exactly booming." Knight would ship off to college, returning to Provident as often as he could to get film processed, upgrade his gear or stock up on supplies. He would eventually intern with *City Beat* in the summer of 2004 before becoming a full-time staff member in 2008. He maintained his "regular" status at the store, often trekking to it from his office just a few blocks north. "It wasn't always the best place for new people to go. It was one of those places where they appreciated if you knew what you were talking about. They appreciated knowledge about photography and the craft." Nevertheless, Cameron remembers the staff being friendly even from his first visit there, although he had been sure to do his research before stepping foot in the door.

He graduated from college and began his professional career during a time of transition for the photography industry, especially in the vein of photojournalism. Digital cameras were finally boasting high enough quality to rival their film counterparts in some respects. On the consumer end, film was falling out of favor. As Cameron transitioned, so did Provident, but the challenges on their respective fronts were different: "Provident was always great because at one point you needed to have consumables. You needed darkroom paper, chemicals and film. When you buy a digital camera, all you really need is that camera and not much else." He believes that Provident faced the same challenges that so many other camera stores across the country were facing. Consumers simply didn't need to make as many return visits. There was also pricing. While Provident carried quality gear, online retailers could offer adequate imitations from "off brands." "I feel that places like Provident didn't really find a way to adapt to what people were buying," he says.

On April 7, 2009, Cameron stopped in for one final visit before publishing his article in *City Beat*. Provident closed for good that day. The article mentions how the business was reeling from the "Great Recession," changing consumer habits and increased competition from both online and big box retailers. Six years later, he still remembers the place fondly: "It had a really cool feel; it was like an old-school shop. Tons of stuff packed in there. They had film. They always carried film. Even on their last day, I bought film at their closeout sale."

In the fall of 2010, nearly a year and a half since Provident closed, I first met Cameron Knight. I stepped into his office at *City Beat*, interviewing for a photography internship while I was a student at Northern Kentucky University. I got the gig and soon was running all over the city covering local music, events, restaurants and stories for Cameron and the publication. Cameron taught me a lot. Even after my internship ended and graduation came, he and I are still friends. We trade stories, occasionally eat pizza and discuss music while working collaboratively on stories for my project Queen City Discovery. Nearly all the photographs Cameron makes for our work are done on film. He shoots with a body from his vast arsenal of cameras and develops the film at his own home. After all, there's no place like Provident anymore to take it to.

The Schuster Electric Co.

The Schuster Electric Co. was born in Cincinnati in 1904. Starting life as a general electrical contracting company, the business boomed in the 1920s and '30s as it began to distribute phonographs, radios and records. In World War II, the company's founder partnered his business with Wurlitzer to deliver music products to troops fighting overseas. By the 1950s, the company had begun focusing solely on distributing electrical components and today operates as a dominating presence in the Midwest. Although it left its downtown facility, its fading sign still remained when it relocated to the Cincinnati suburb of Blue Ash. These days, the fading sign represents an industrial past that contrasts sharply with the high-priced lofts and apartments now found in the building.

For years, the Schuster sign was partially obscured and somewhat protected by an adjacent parking garage that covered it up. Just as the Schuster building became apartments, many other new residences are popping up in the same area. The parking garage was demolished to make room for a Holiday Inn. As the structure came down and construction proceeded, the Schuster sign was given a more prominent presence than it ever had with the car park

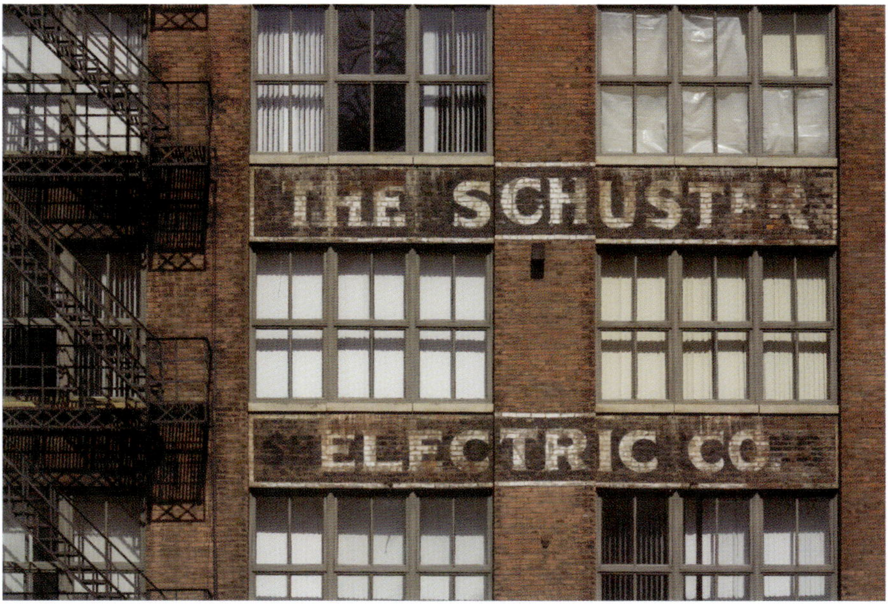

Apartments now grace the interior of a building that once housed the manufacturing of electrical components. Despite the building's reuse, its former tenant's name remains and adds an air of history to the structure. *Photo by Ronny Salerno.*

nearby. As the hotel rises, the name of Schuster Electric Co. might once again be tucked away. The construction also revealed another sign, one for the Aetna Finance Co.

Aetna Finance Co.

Aetna Finance Co. was a small financial services company specializing in consumer loans with operations in several states. In the mid-'60s, Aetna had come to find itself acquired by the corporate conglomerates known as the ITT Corporation. By 1995, ITT had completely killed off its financial services arm. Aetna still was mentioned in 1998, though for its time operating under the name of ITT Financial Services. It was taken to trial in the Ohio Supreme Court after a client took issues with his home equity loan. ITT/Aetna was "found liable for its part in an alleged civil conspiracy" against the plaintiff. Punitive damages were awarded.

The lot next to the building displaying its Aetna and Schuster signs is due to be replaced by a Holiday Inn, a result of development inspired by the casino that opened in 2012. In recent years, downtown has seen a string of

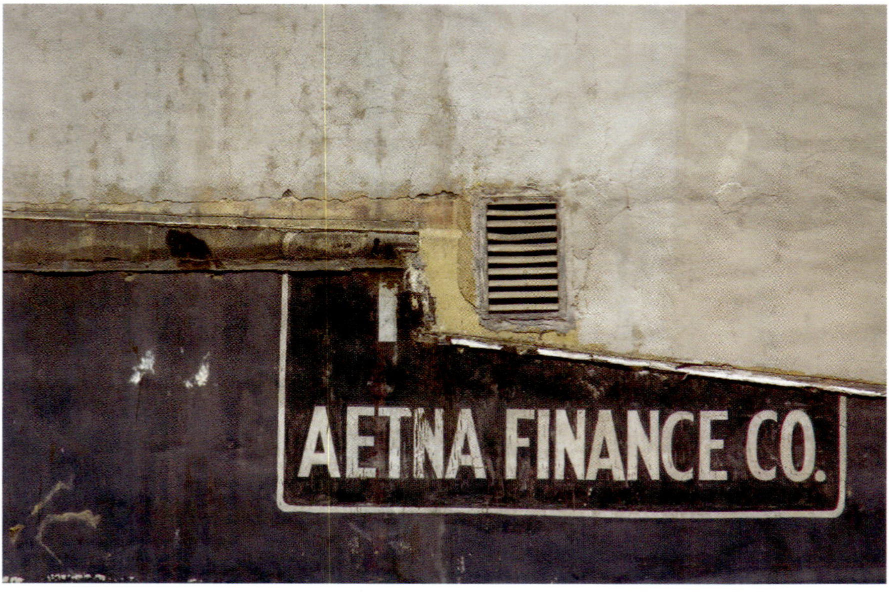

A sign for the Aetna Finance Co. was revealed, although remaining partially obscured, when the demolition of a nearby structure took place. *Photo by Ronny Salerno.*

hotels open up shop. Formerly home to only upscale options like Westin and Hilton, more wallet-friendly brands such as Best Western, Hampton and Holiday Inn are now opening. Downtown used to have plenty of hotels, but these were the days before corporate names, Wi-Fi and televisions—not to mention bathrooms—in every room.

The Fort Washington Hotel

In the early 1990s, the Cincinnati Reds were fresh off a World Series win. Fans would come down for games at the old Riverfront Stadium and then immediately head home. During the day, downtown was packed with business, but at night there wasn't much going on. Things started to change in 1995 with the opening of the Aronoff Center for the Arts, a then-new complex that seats more than three thousand and is capable of hosting numerous Broadway Acts. The Aronoff was the start of bringing people back downtown for more than just work, lunch and sports games.

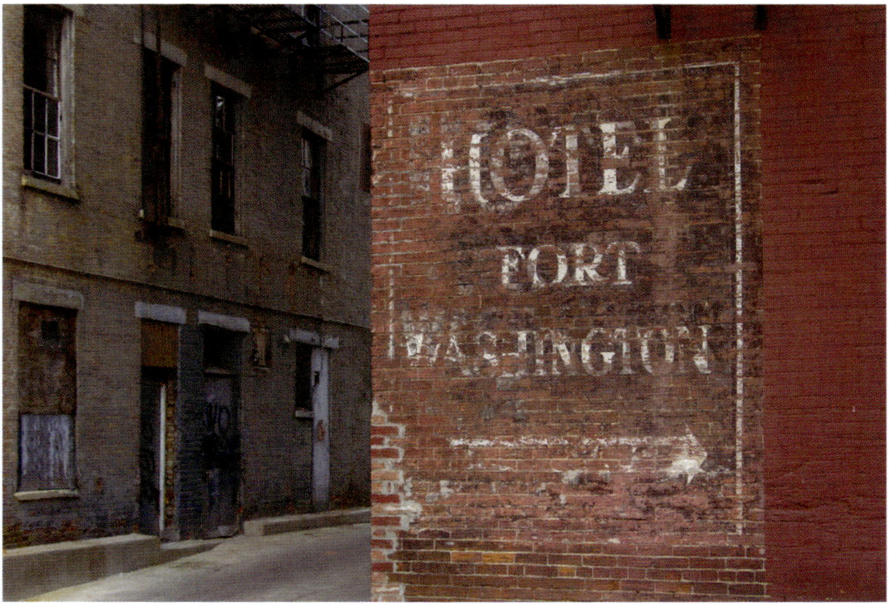

A directional sign points the way to where the Fort Washington Hotel's entrance used to be. The hotel itself is now filled with high-priced condos, a trend that started to gather steam downtown in 1995. *Photo by Ronny Salerno.*

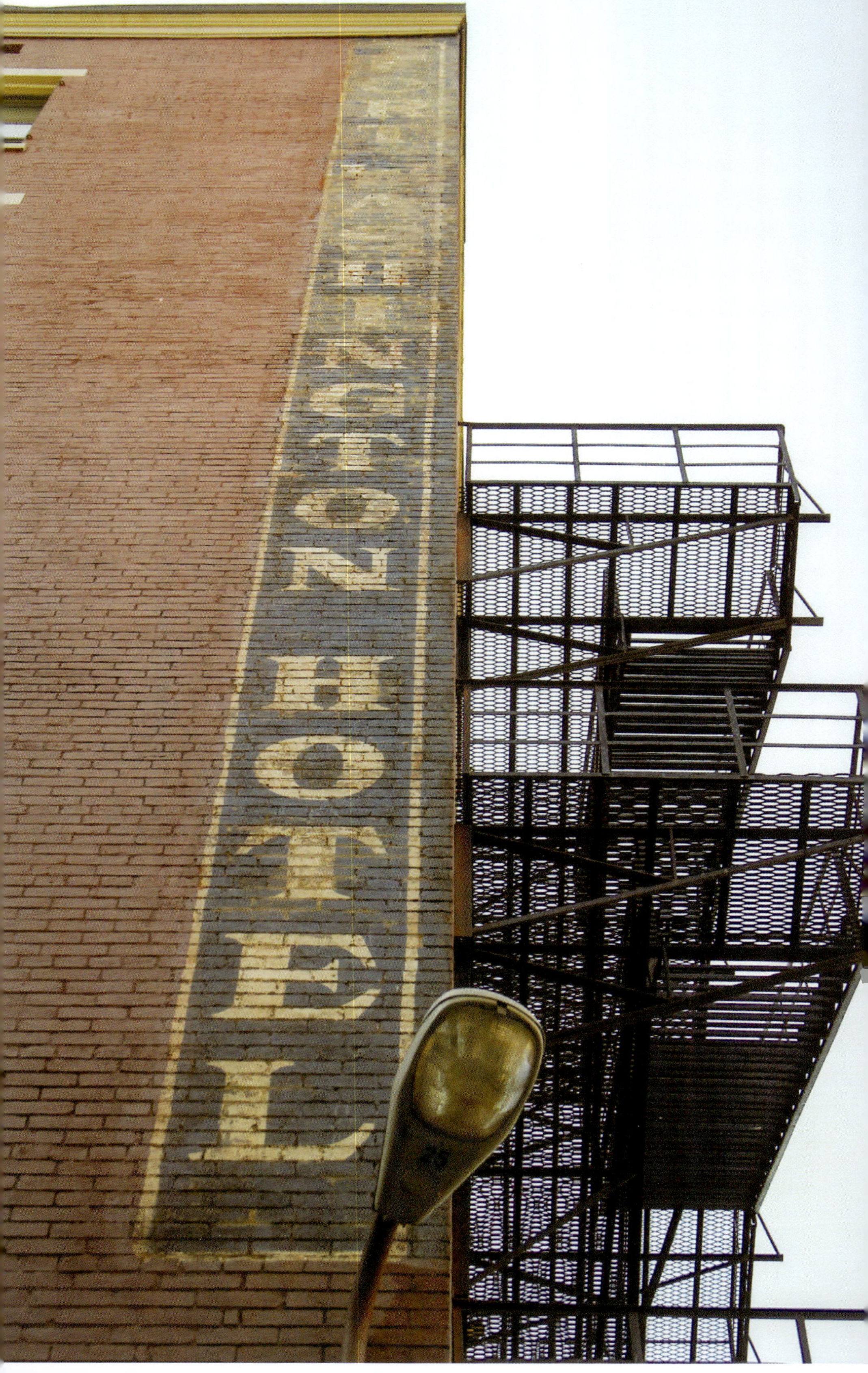
GTON
HOTEL

As nightlife picked up, so did a demand for living space. People wanted to live downtown again. The Fort Washington Hotel became a desirable place to start ushering in renovated new condos. The only problem: it was still occupied. The building would become the first battleground between boardinghouses and economic development.

Built in 1887, the building debuted as the Bodman Building. It housed the first offices for Cincinnati's iconic Western & Southern Financial Co. and catered to other tenants on a floor-by-floor monthly rent basis. Eventually, the building was converted into the Fort Washington Hotel and had a reputation as one of the premier lodging establishments in the city for a

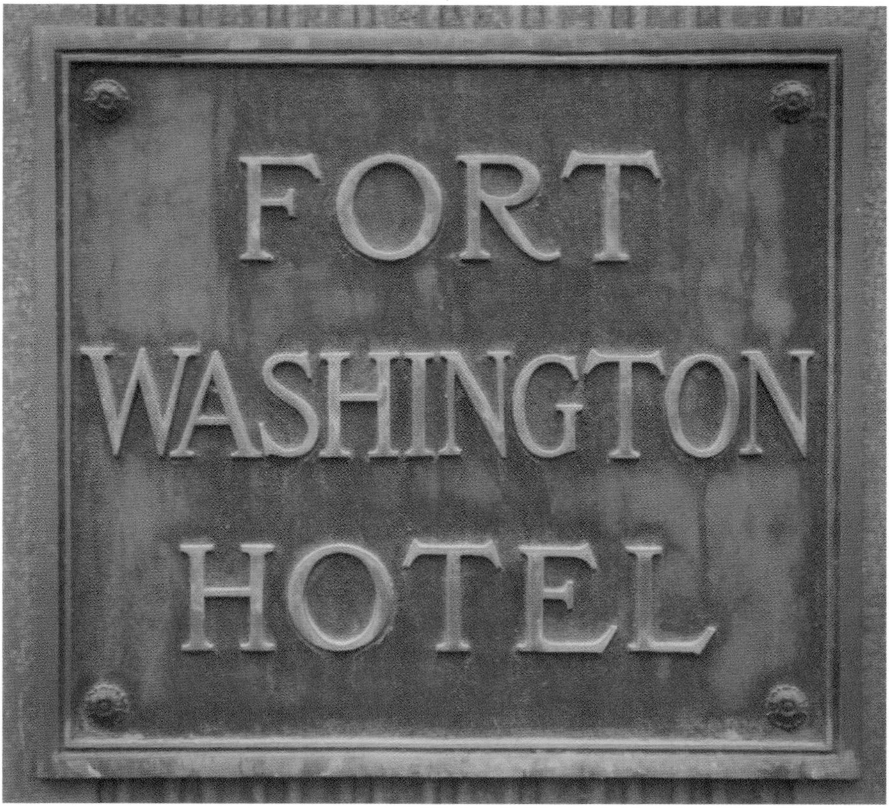

In addition to the two hand-painted works, the Fort Washington Hotel is also marked by a plaque—a relic of the building's history that has a bit more permanence. *Photo by Ronny Salerno.*

Opposite: This vertical sign for the Fort Washington Hotel may have once been very visible. These days, it is blocked by nearby buildings and seen only when stepping down an alleyway. The very thing obscuring it may also be shielding it from the elements. *Photo by Ronny Salerno.*

time. Hand-painted signs on the building provided directions through the alleyways to where guests could enter.

As time wore on and hotels became the business of chain corporations, places like the Fort Washington, with its aging building, floundered. Like many other locally owned hotels downtown, the building became a boardinghouse with rooms rented on a nightly, weekly or monthly basis, often to low-income tenants. Many guests paid for rooms with social security and veteran's benefits.

In May 1999, the *Cincinnati Enquirer* ran a story about the potential sale of the building. With a thriving theater directly behind it and a burgeoning arts scene, developers had been eying the property. A few years later, it was sold and its tenants upended, becoming the first modern condos in downtown Cincinnati. The building now houses one of the highest-rated living spaces, where rent ranges upward of $2,000 per month.

The Metropole

The Metropole shared a similar history with the Fort Washington. Born originally as office space, converted to a fancy hotel and then receding into a halfway boardinghouse, the property began catching developers' eyes as well. The building had become notorious. As the owners lived in the former penthouse upstairs, crime and drug use were rampant, and police were often called to the Metropole. The aforementioned Aronoff theater, the new Contemporary Arts Center and a renovated Fountain Square were all thriving places of human activity within walking distance of the crumbling lodging establishment. The owners held out, finally ceding ownership in 2012.

The Metropole reopened, becoming the 21C Museum/Hotel. The hotel is now a 156-room, upscale boutique and was named the "#1 hotel in the United States, #11 worldwide" by readers of *Condé Nast Traveler* in 2013. Its lobby features a contemporary art gallery that's open twenty-four hours a day, 365 days a week. The hotel restaurant was named the Metropole in honor of the building's past. Although the interior space was gutted and the front entrance redone, a ghost sign of the old Metropole Hotel still remains just under the building's peak, which houses a swanky, contemporary rooftop bar.

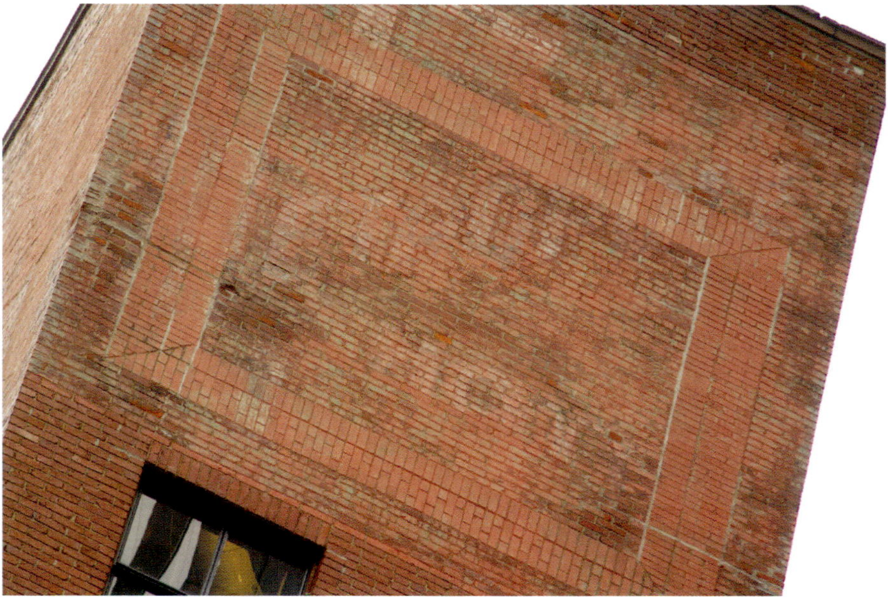

At the building's summit, the word "Metropole" can still be made out running diagonally upward. The Metropole Hotel is now the 21C Museum/Hotel. *Photo by Ronny Salerno.*

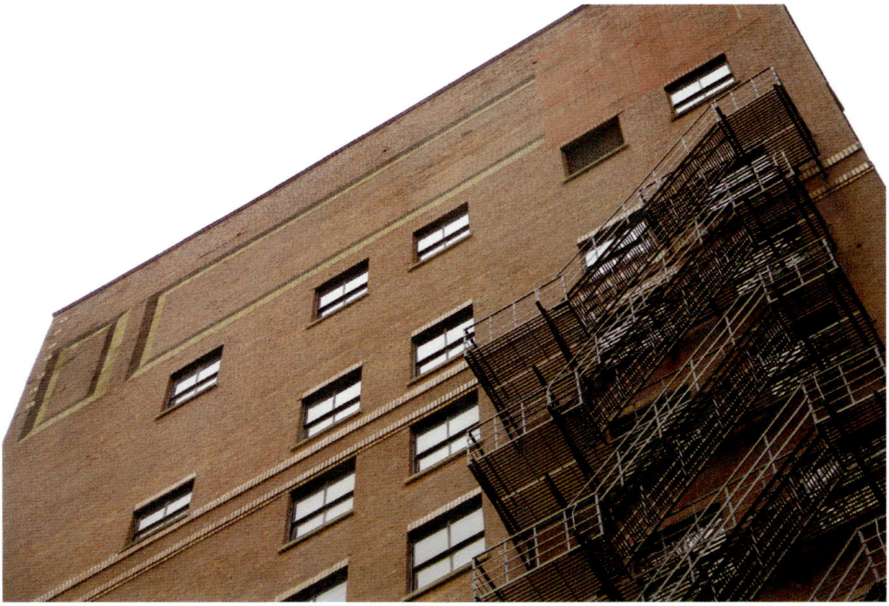

While no words can be seen, outlines and shapes painted on the side allow the viewer to guess how the composition might have played into an advertisement. The roof at the top now hosts an upscale bar at the former Metropole Hotel. *Photo by Ronny Salerno.*

The Dennison

The last of Main Street's halfway houses still stands. Its future, though, may not be as ripe as its Metropole and Fort Washington brethren down the street. The signs on the side of the Dennison Hotel are some of the most recognizable in downtown Cincinnati. They've weathered time and erosion pretty sturdily. It also certainly doesn't hurt that the bright red brick of the building stands out along with its towering nine stories. On the south side, an advertisement proclaims, "105 rooms, 60 baths"—reminiscent of the building's days as a low-income hotel with shared bathrooms. The hotel operation had ceased for some time before the building was purchased by private developers in 2011. The developers had plans to renovate the structure into high-quality studio apartments that would serve as housing for a social services organization helping people overcome addiction. In the lobby, plans for a café were drawn up that would be staffed by the organization's residents. The building's north side features a similar advertisement to its southern counterpart. Both are signed by Bill Haas. If you look closely enough, you can see the remains of other signage beneath the Dennison Hotel signs. With the building's height

In addition to hand-painted advertisements signifying the former Dennison Hotel, a metal sign still juts out of the front of the building. *Photo by Ronny Salerno.*

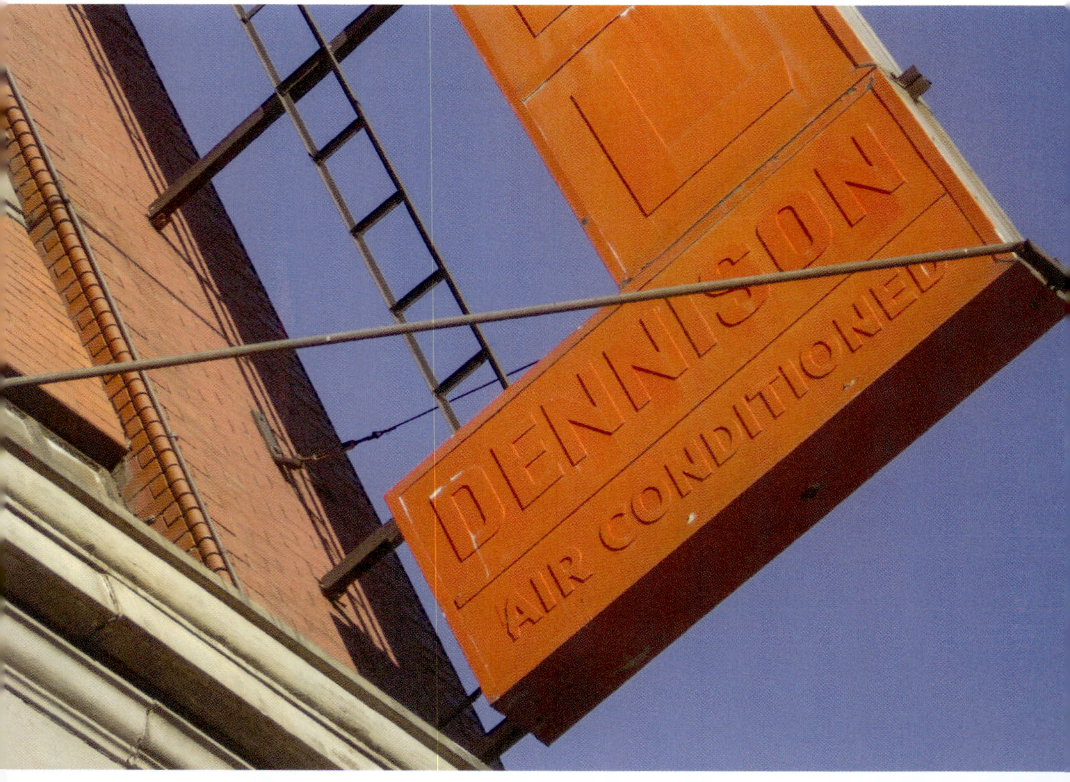

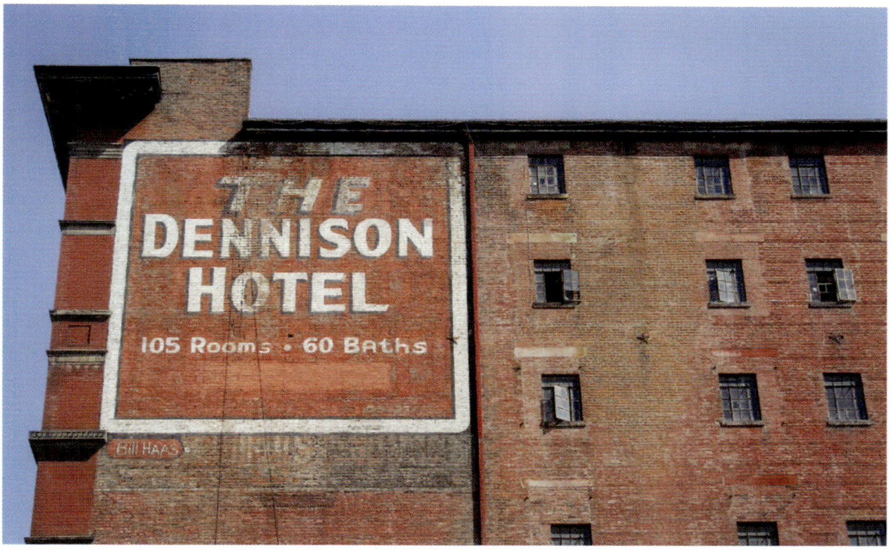

An ad for the Dennison Hotel touts 105 rooms but only sixty baths. Even in its heyday, the Dennison featured communal bathrooms that would be shared among the tenants. *Photo by Ronny Salerno.*

and position in downtown, it's no surprise that this structure would be lucrative real estate for advertising.

The building can trace its roots back to being an ironwork plant for horse-drawn carriage makers in 1892. It also played host to multiple office furniture companies, a recurring theme among Main Street's ghost signs. By 2013, plans for the renovated apartments and café had fallen through. The building went through multiple sales, eventually falling under the ownership of a local automobile dealership. As of May 2015, no plans have been announced for the Dennison Hotel, with many fearing it might become a parking lot to showcase this year's new models. Even if it avoids the wrecking ball, would the fading advertisements survive the fresh paint and handiwork of a restoration?

Quaker Oats

In 1901, Quaker Oats was born out of the merger of four separate oat mills. In the time since, the company has grown into a recognizable brand now under the conglomerate of PepsiCo. The Quaker Oats company was

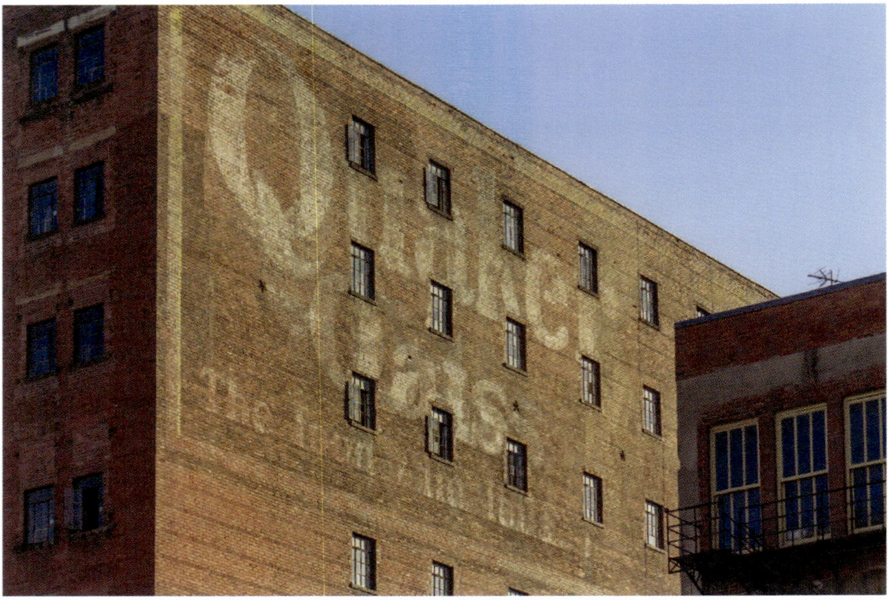

Like Coca-Cola and Mail Pouch Tobacco, fading Quaker Oats advertisements have been documented throughout the Midwest. *Photo by Ronny Salerno.*

known for its wall advertising. Like this fading sign seen in Cincinnati on the side of the aforementioned Dennison Hotel, Quaker Oats signs have been documented all over the Midwest.

The vast majority of wall advertising done today is created with adhesives or vinyl. There are advantages to the new materials: you can swap out content quickly and continually rent the space out to advertisers, and the production costs are probably far cheaper. Wall painting offers certain advantages, though; you pay for it once, and even if you agreed to a certain term, the end of your advertisement is really at the will of the building's owner. In the case of this Quaker Oats ad, the original terms are unknown. Either Quaker itself or a firm representing it got this put up. An artist or artists were hired, designs approved and plans set in motion. It was and still is in a prominent spot. In the heart of downtown, the Quaker Oats name could be seen from all over. Maybe Quaker had multiple contracts. Perhaps it had a mural updated or changed around over time. Either way, at one point, Quaker stopped being interested in not just its Cincinnati sign but also hand-painted wall advertisements all together. But today, the company name remains big and bold on the side of a tall building. Sure, it's not brightly colored or as noticeable as when it was first painted—and yes, maybe it's now more a part of the urban fabric than a marketing plan—but in a way, the sign is still carrying out its job. It's still advertising Quaker Oats. Long after the t's were crossed, the i's dotted and the paint dry, Quaker Oats are still being touted in downtown Cincinnati.

Rybolt Heating & Cooling

Rybolt Heating & Cooling began operations in 1910. As the name implies, the business specialized in ventilation services. According to the Better Business Bureau, Rybolt was purchased and absorbed into another local company, Apollo, sometime in the 1990s. With the acquisition, Rybolt left its location on Broadway Street. Despite still being displayed prominently, Rybolt is gone, and the more recent tenants sell bail bonds as opposed to air conditioners.

The name Rybolt Heating & Cooling still runs horizontally between rows of windows, despite the building hosting new tenants. *Photo by Ronny Salerno.*

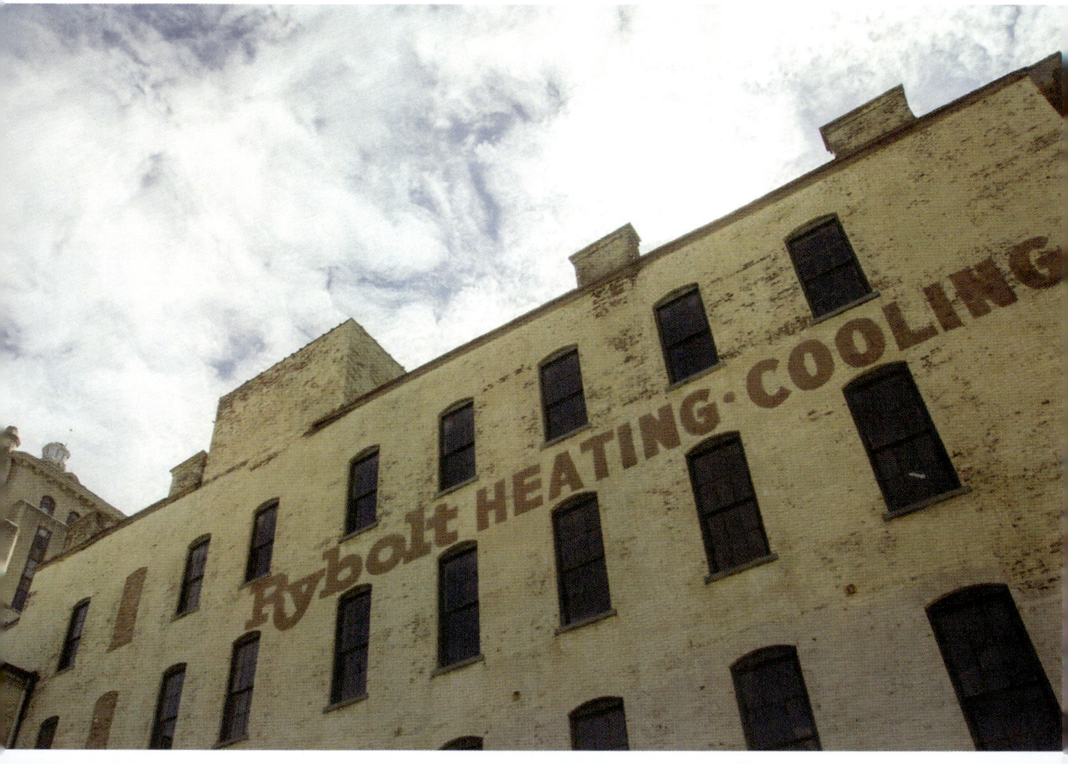

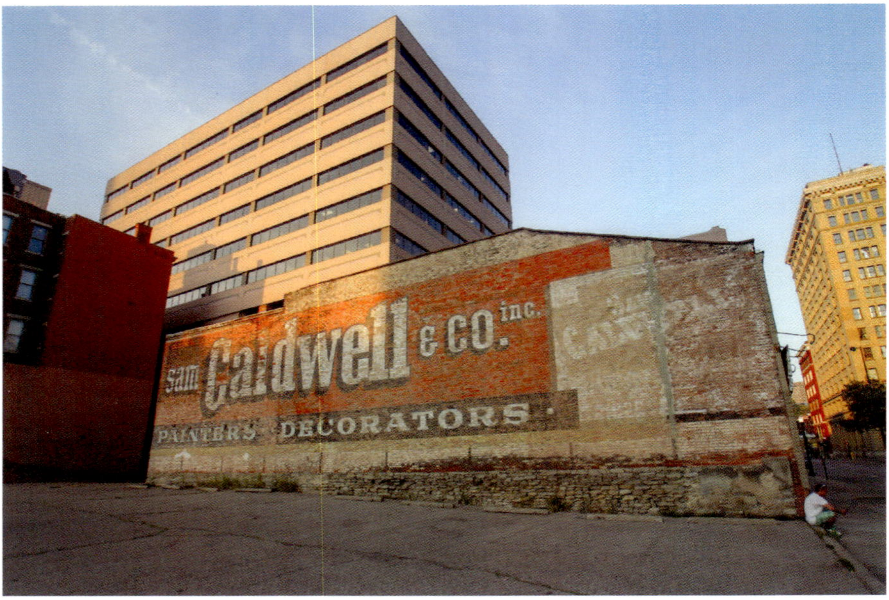

The name of Sam Caldwell, a painter whose name still exists in the fading remnants of the material he once worked with, can actually be seen twice in this image. While his company's name is preserved more prominently on the left, it, too, can be made out on the right-hand side. *Photo by Ronny Salerno.*

Sam Caldwell

It's fitting that Sam Caldwell would advertise his business with a hand-painted wall sign. Established in 1933, his self-named painting and decorating business may have been best known for painting advertisements on the outfield walls of Crosley Field, the former home of the Cincinnati Reds. Two stadiums and several decades later, this large ghost sign on the edge of the Central Business District is all that remains of the Caldwell Co. It is signed with "Keiger," the last name of one of Caldwell's employees. Sam Caldwell himself passed away in 1965.

Better Foods for Better Health

The fading paint holding on to the relics of a Spatz advertisement are accompanied by a dark storefront, locked doors, an old register and a dark

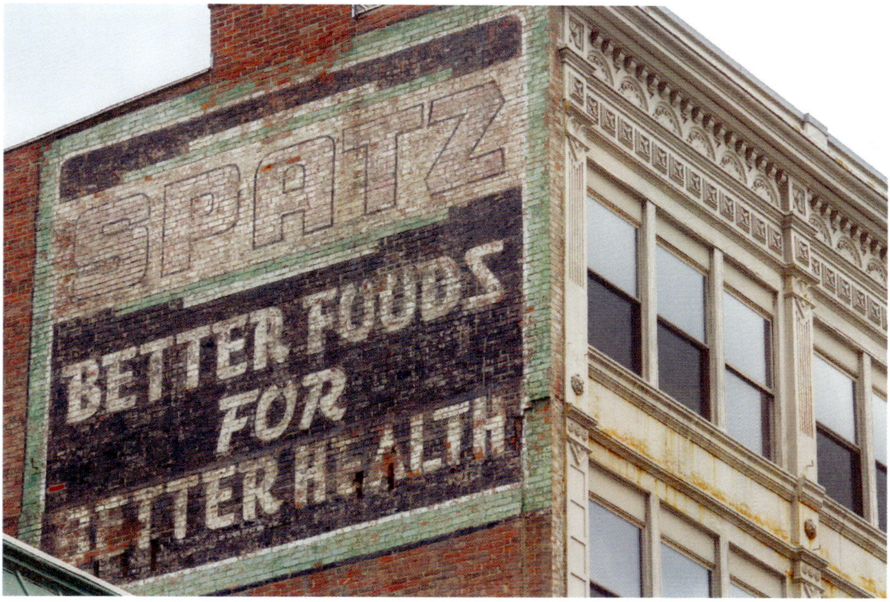

From 1931 to 2015, Spatz was one of the only grocery options downtown. Reviews of the store in its later years were mixed. *Photo by Ronny Salerno.*

neon sign advertising "Nature's Way." One of the few grocery options downtown, Spatz had been specializing in health foods since 1931. A November 1982 review of the business by *Cincinnati* magazine touted the juice bar, selection of health books, the company's own line of vitamins and the then-new concept of using aloe vera to treat sunburns. According to a July 2014 review posted on HappyCow.net (a self-proclaimed "healthy eating guide"), Spatz Natural Life Health Food was known for having a "vegan-friendly deli" but was now closed. Later in 2015, local publication *Soapbox Cincinnati* would remember Spatz less fondly, labeling it as a "health food store from the 1950s (i.e. unhealthy)."

The Other Place and Burger Chef

College Street runs south off Seventh Street and clumsily becomes Roots Alley, probably due to years of reconfiguration via a clash of modern office buildings and their proximity to historic ones. In the alley, you'll find several parking spaces crammed wherever they can fit, a few loading bays for trucks

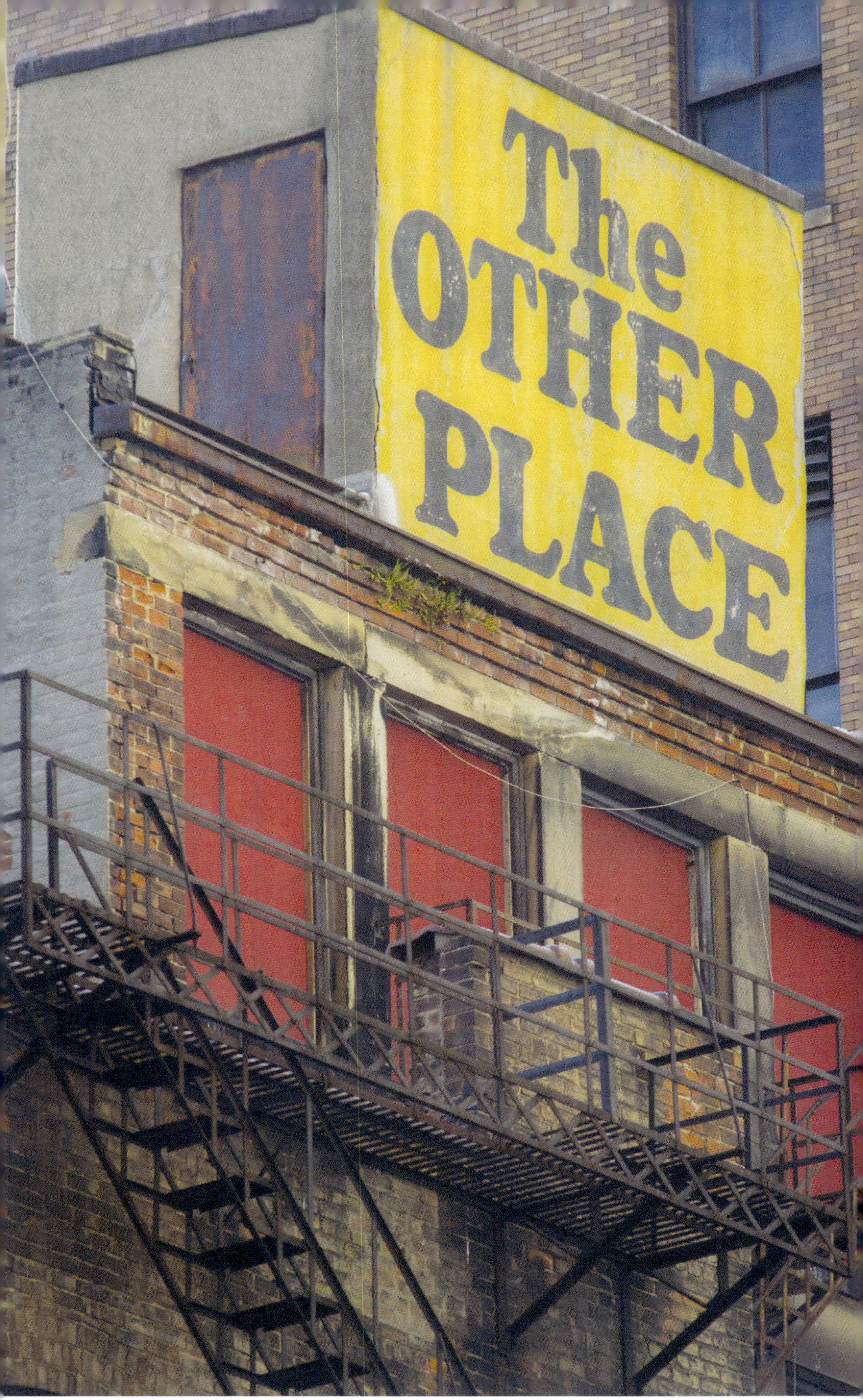
The
OTHER
PLACE

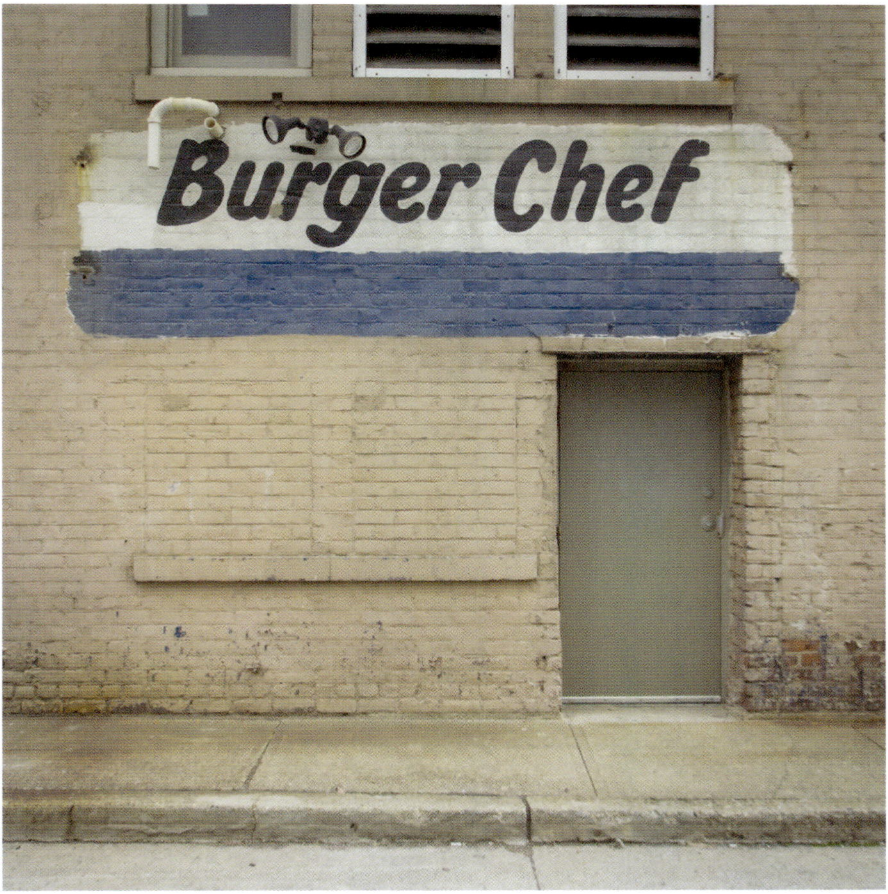

The Burger Chef chain disappeared from the Cincinnati market before eventually disappearing from the economic landscape altogether. *Photo by Ronny Salerno.*

Opposite: Atop a building and facing an alleyway, a mysterious sign advertises "The Other Place." *Photo by Ronny Salerno.*

and employees of nearby businesses taking their smoke breaks. If you look up, you'll see the black letters emblazoned on bright yellow paint that seem to have weathered time quite well: "The OTHER PLACE." It's at the top of a fire escape facing into the alley. If you didn't wander back here, you'd never see it—which makes you hope that it predates the nearby office towers or else it'd be a pretty poor advertisement. What it was advertising, though, no one seems to know. "The Other Place" seems to have faded from the memory of most Cincinnatians you talk to. Directly below the well-preserved yet mysterious sign is one that's a little more straightforward. As your eyes follow the fire escape down, you'll find "Burger Chef."

Like the mysterious "Other Place," the Burger Chef is gone, too. The clearly hand-painted letters loosely follow the motif of the former fast-food chain's corporate branding. The door is locked and the windows bricked over, and the pale beige colors surrounding the sign clearly came later at the hands of someone with enough consideration to not paint over the Burger Chef name.

Burger Chef was born in Indianapolis in 1958 and, by 1967, had used its flame-broiled hamburgers to become the second-largest fast-food chain in the United States, second only to McDonald's. However, as other fast-food chains rose, Burger Chef fell. By 1982, parent company General Foods (of JELL-O fame) sold off the entire company to rival Hardees. The last Burger Chef to still operate was in Tennessee in 1996.

Shillito's

Unlike so many other fading advertisements, the faint word "Shillito's" is found not on brick or stone but rather on an HVAC unit. It's faint, hard to discern from a distance and shows up best in the direct light of the setting sun. To older Cincinnatians, the name Shillito's will evoke memories, while the younger crowd and outsiders will be hard pressed to recall the old retailer and are probably much more familiar with its contemporary successor.

John Shillito was the dominant name in Queen City shopping when his new five-elevator store opened in 1878. The downtown landmark became the place for retail in the decades before shopping malls and was part of the local holiday pilgrimage from the suburbs, known for its elaborate Christmas displays. Despite the onset of the Great Depression, the Shillito's name lived on through the creation of Federated Department Stores, which saw it merge with Macy's, as well as F&R Lazarus Co. By 1986, the Shillito's name was dropped when the downtown store and its suburban locations were branded as Lazarus. In 1997, Federated built a new Lazarus store two blocks south, and the original Shillito's building was converted into luxury lofts—its fading namesake still on the HVAC unit overhead. By 2005, Federated had dropped the Lazarus branding and structured its stores under the Macy's name.

Today, Federated is based out of Cincinnati, tracing its roots back to the 1931 merger and now operating solely as Macy's. The company is

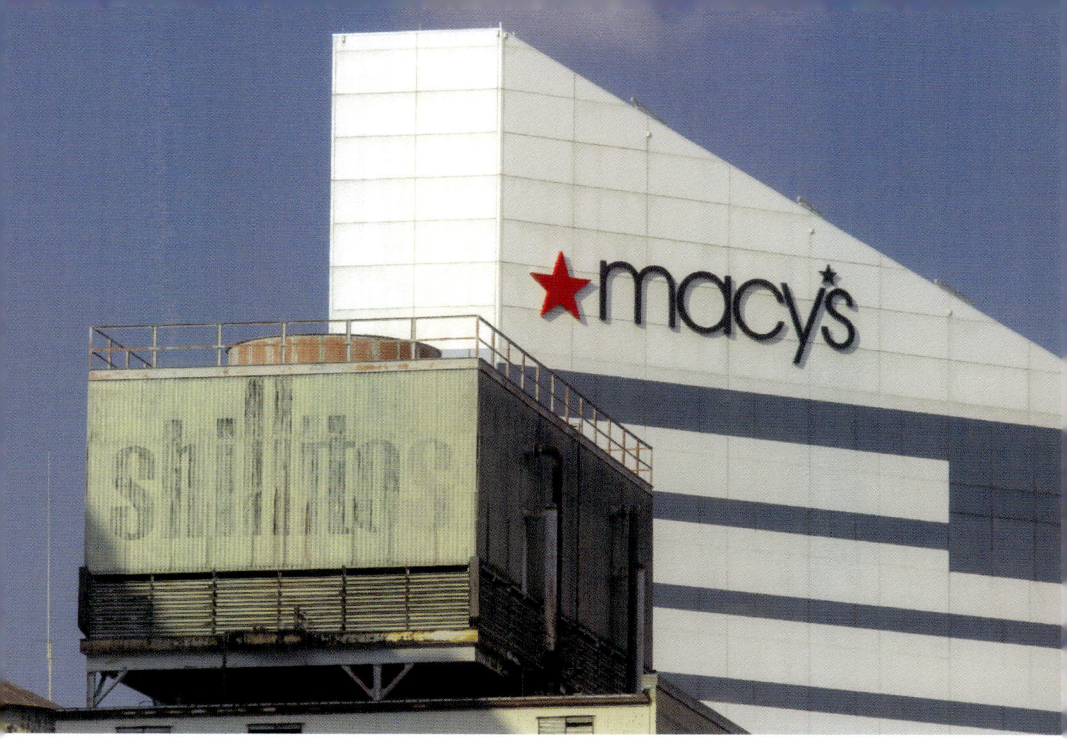

On an HVAC unit, the Shillito's name still stands atop a building named for the department store it once housed. In the background, the fading name is overshadowed by that of Macy's, the corporation that would eventually inherit the remnants of Shillito's. *Photo by Ronny Salerno.*

headquartered in a downtown office tower landmark with the Macy's logo at its peak. The logo is familiar to contemporary consumers, found at so many shopping malls bordering vast suburban off-ramps. It's a physical, molded representation mounted to the side of the building and large enough to spot with the naked eye from the streets or highways below. It pops out against the monochrome building structure, an example of modern construction featuring modern advertising. From its perch, it proclaims the Macy's name to the surrounding city from above, while below it, sharing the same setting sun, is a piece of history—a juxtaposed reminder of a corporation's roots.

The Beehive

The Beehive Club may be as nearly forgotten as the sports team it represented. Cincinnati's riverfront is anchored by two major-league sports stadiums. Paul Brown Stadium plays hosts to the Cincinnati Bengals of the National Football League, while Great American Ballpark hosts the Cincinnati Reds of Major

League Baseball. Since their inception, these teams have stood guard to the city's reputation as a "major-league" town—a reputation that was protected when taxpayers elected to finance new facilities for both teams. The stadia sit on the ends of the riverfront spanning Smale Park, often affectionately referred to as "Cincinnati's Front Lawn." The three publicly funded projects represent a massive investment in a downtown makeover and the sales tax hike that paid for them. Above them rises the skyline and Central Business District. Just off to the east, though, is a third sports venue, a remnant of the 1970s and riverfront revitalization ideas of years past. U.S. Bank Arena (formerly known as the Firstar Center, the Crown and the Riverfront Coliseum) is an indoor venue that was completed in 1975. It's the primary host for large touring events like the circus, pro wrestling and concerts. When it was built, however, a major-league tenant was the main goal. While Cincinnati currently enjoys franchises in two of America's major leagues, the NBA Cincinnati Royals skipped town in 1972 to eventually become the Sacramento Kings. With the arrival of a contemporary arena in 1975, the plan was to try and lure a third major-league franchise to the city.

As the arena's construction neared completion, there seems to have been no serious talks of luring the NBA back; rather, the focus was on pro hockey.

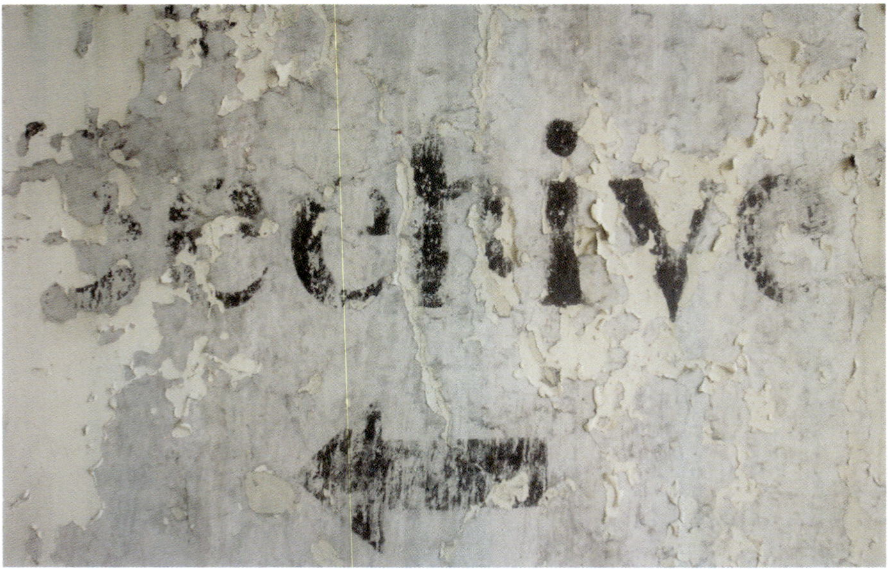

In the mid- to late 1970s, investors were embarking on the latest major-league sports endeavor for the city. The precursor to the suites and clubs found in modern-day stadia, the Beehive played off the name for the city's WHA hockey team: the Cincinnati Stingers. *Photo by Ronny Salerno.*

While Cincinnati had long been a successful host of minor-league franchises, two men envisioned the top-tier National Hockey League (NHL) expanding into the Queen City market. Brian Heekin and Bill DeWitt Jr. had both dabbled in sports team ownership before. They set forth to recruit the NHL, but North America's premier hockey league had little interest in expanding. The NHL snubbed not only Cincinnati but also several other cities. After years of not entering new markets, a renegade competitor sprang up. The World Hockey Association began play in 1972. The WHA sought to use lucrative contracts to lure NHL players and began placing teams in markets the NHL had previously ignored. By the league's third year of play, it had granted DeWitt and Heekin an expansion franchise: the Cincinnati Stingers.

The Stingers called the then brand-new arena home, and the upscale club/restaurant/bar at the top was dubbed "The Beehive," playing off the team's insect-themed name. The name was seemingly random, and according to local hockey aficionado Don Helbig, it absolutely was random. While the Reds and Bengals can trace their names back to local history, the Stingers received their title through a "name the team" contest advertised in the *Cincinnati Enquirer*. Helbig, a former executive with the Cincinnati Mighty Ducks (a later minor-league franchise in the city), recalls that the name was suggested by a local woman who saw the ad while drinking a stinger cocktail. When the name was chosen, she received season tickets for the first season but apparently moved to San Francisco and never saw the team take the ice in their bright yellow and black uniforms, which were adorned with a "C" stylized as a bumble bee.

The city's third major-league team had finally arrived. Kind of. While the WHA had managed to bring major-league hockey to cities toward which the NHL had previously been apathetic, the league's stability was often questioned. Franchises came and went, some not even lasting an entire season. Certain teams featured major-league-caliber rosters, while others were bolstered by young players, many of whom would have been career minor leaguers under the sole existence of the NHL. The league did its best to stay afloat, attempting to merge with the NHL on two occasions. After two years, DeWitt led the effort for his team and the rest of the WHA to be admitted into the rival NHL. The merger failed gaining approval by NHL owners by only one vote. Nevertheless, the Stingers and their renegade league trudged on. By the end of the 1978–79 season, the WHA was on its last legs, and the NHL was finally willing to admit the remaining six teams as expansion franchises. This plan, however, carried a hefty $6 million joining fee. Former *Cincinnati Enquirer* reporter and friend John Kiesewetter told me

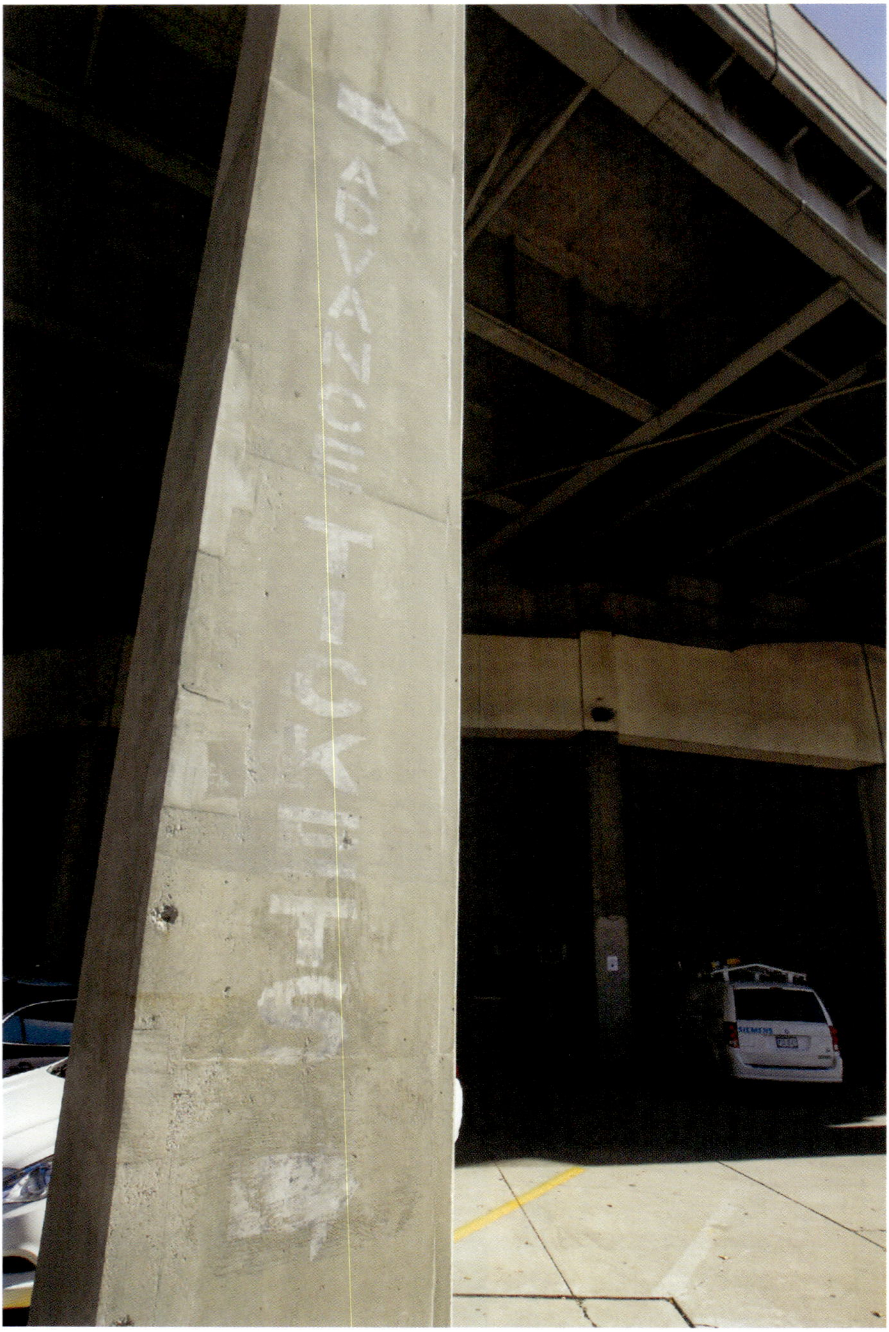

One of a few fading signs on the arena, this sign still points the way to the arena's box office. *Photo by Ronny Salerno.*

the story he heard while interviewing former Stingers radio broadcaster Andy MacWilliams. The day the merger was going to be announced, a Stinger employee was answering the arena phones with: "Riverfront Coliseum, home of the NHL Stingers." When the news officially broke, though, the Cincinnati team was surprisingly absent from the list of new NHL teams. Heekin and DeWitt had opted to forgo the $6 million expansion fee and instead received a $3.5 million cash payout from the league in order to dissolve. As for the cocktail-sipping woman who gave the team its name, she was contacted by the paper and told of the team's folding. According to Helbig, she had literally forgotten about the contest and the team. To her, the Stingers had faded like their signs beneath the arena soon would.

The city's third major-league sports franchise was gone, along with the renegade league that brought about its creation. The Stingers name lived on in the next year as a franchise in the lower-level Central Hockey League, but the minor-league Stingers folded midway through their first season. As the team disappeared, so did the Beehive. Several signs on the arena's lower street level can still be found on the concrete pillars. They once pointed to the elevator entrances that would whisk you up from the concrete underbelly of the arena into its upscale pro sports lounge. Now, they just point backward to when the Beehive was a thing, to when the Stingers still took the ice, to when the city came so close to being admitted into the fraternity of the National Hockey League.

The privately owned arena still operates today and announced a plan in 2015 to bring itself up to modern standards using a public-private partnership. In the meantime, the Cincinnati Cyclones, a "AA"-level professional hockey team of the ECHL, are the arena's primary tenant. The arena and pro hockey still live on, while the fading advertisements below point to a more ambitious history that never came to be fully realized.

Bolles and Brendamour's

Despite Cincinnati's lack of a top-tier hockey team, the Queen City is no doubt a sports-crazed city. On top of its two remaining major-league franchises, the region hosts three NCAA Division 1 college athletic programs at Northern Kentucky University, Xavier University and the University of Cincinnati. Additionally, youth leagues ranging in athletic competitions

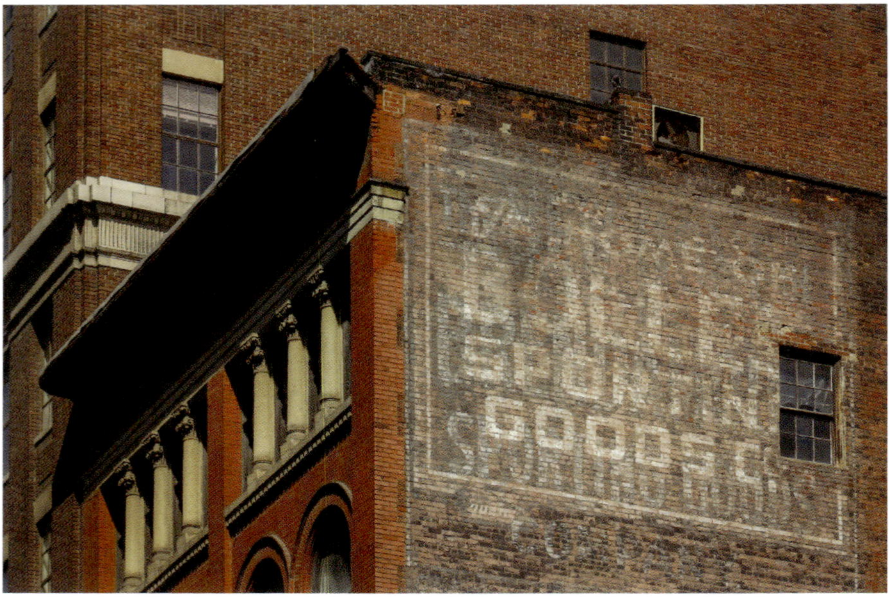

The overlay of two sporting goods companies' signs is a physical allegory for the two competitors. Even as it fades, names are still discernable, and the sign's condition reflects a story of competition and acquisition. *Photo by Ronny Salerno.*

Opposite: A vertical fading advertisement sits above Koch Sporting Goods, downtown's only remaining sporting goods store. *Photo by Ronny Salerno.*

from soccer to rugby to baseball and hockey can be found. While the big box giant of Dicks Sporting Goods may be the go-to for athletic supplies, downtown once hosted two local stores whose rivalry echoed the competition of the sports they supplied. The fading sign of Bolles Sporting Goods is interesting for the fact that, as it has aged, another sign can barely be made out underneath it—or on top of it, depending on when they were painted in the timeline of local sporting goods merchant history.

The first iteration of the Sixth Street sporting goods store came about sometime in the 1920s, when the Roll-Crawford and Brendamour motorcycle shop relocated to the location below this sign. The new store catered to a wider range of athletic goods and became known as Bolles, Brendamour and Co. By 1937, though, Brendamour had broken off to form Ed Brendamour Inc., while Bolles Sporting Goods Co. remained on Sixth Street. In 1956, Brendamour returned to buy out his original partners at Bolles, and the store property once again became known as Brendamour's. The fading advertisement on the building's side echoes the changing ownership, with

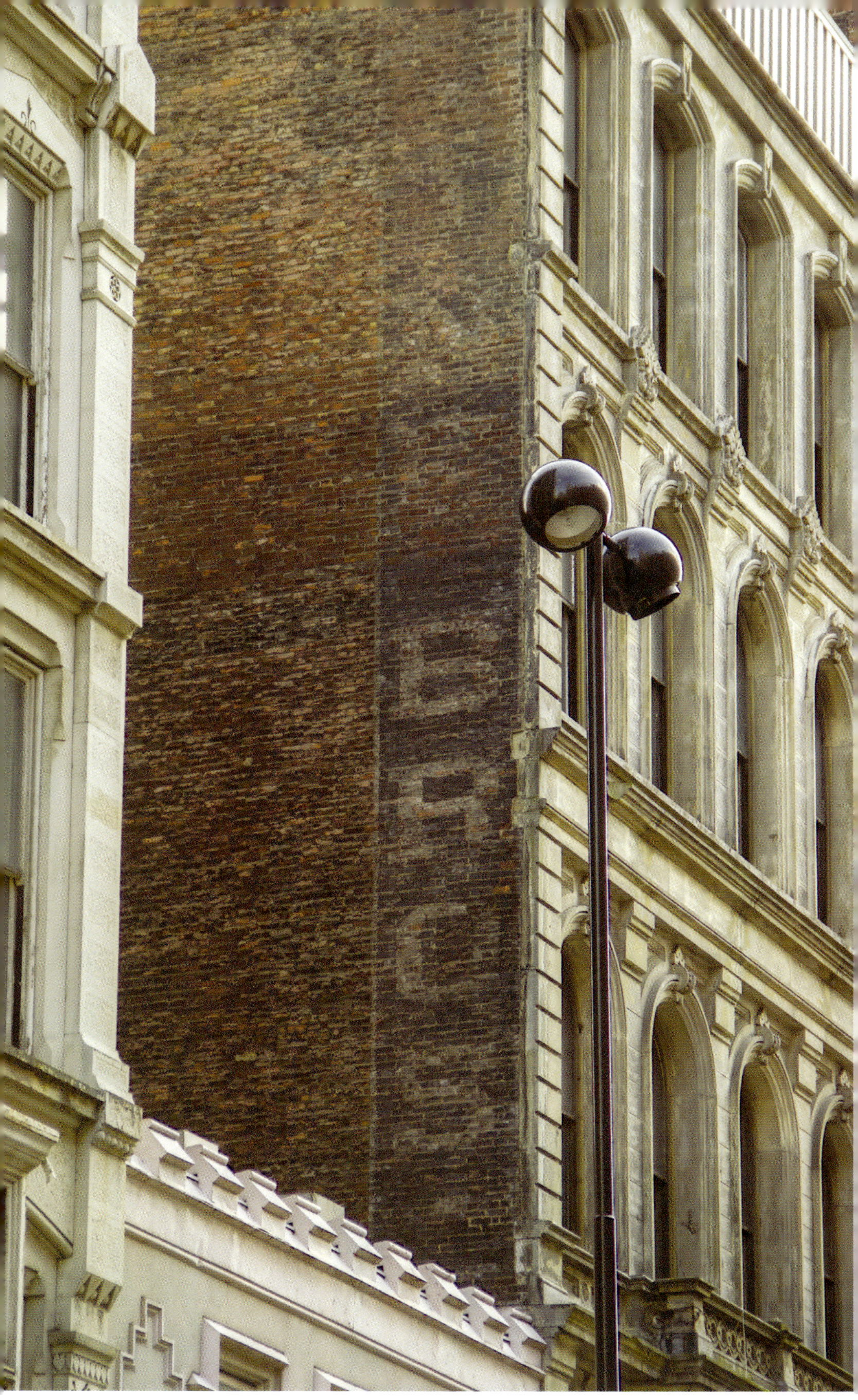

the Bolles Sporting Goods name slightly more legible than the Brendamour's Sporting Goods name.

Brendamour's eventually expanded with more stores in the suburban regions. The Brendamour family left the business in 1972, although the name was kept under new ownership. The new owners expanded the eight-store chain to twenty-eight and from 120 employees to 400 throughout the Midwest. By 1994, chain store giants had begun to take their toll, slowly eating away at the local market Brendamour's had cornered for years. In 1994, bankruptcy took hold; there was some reorganization, but by 1997, the creditors had come calling and Brendamour's was no more.

These days, downtown is still served by Koch Sporting Goods, a local retailer that not only carries traditional lines of athletic goods but also offers merchandise featuring the local major-league sports teams. Koch's is still going strong, and although a faded advertisement stands above it on Fourth Street, the sign is of the nondescript variety rather than a marker for the active store below.

Formosa Restaurant

Unlike most of the signs featured throughout this publication, this one isn't found on brick or concrete. It's down an alleyway beneath two lamps that have rusted sockets where lightbulbs would normally be. The paint was brushed on to a metal sign, which in turn was mounted to the wall. The word that has survived best is "ENTRANCE." Above it, and almost completely faded away, are the words: "FORMOSA RESTAURANT." Beneath this, legible only when the photograph had its colors inverted in Photoshop, was: "ON 12 W. COURT." While "entrance" has lasted the longest, it has deteriorated to a point where you can see the remains of the initial brushstrokes in some of the letters. Formosa now operates as a restaurant called Thai Taste on the other side of the building from where the sign can be found. Perhaps the addition of a modern parking garage directly in front of this sign is the reason it has never been updated. With no view from the nearby streets, it has been left to be forgotten.

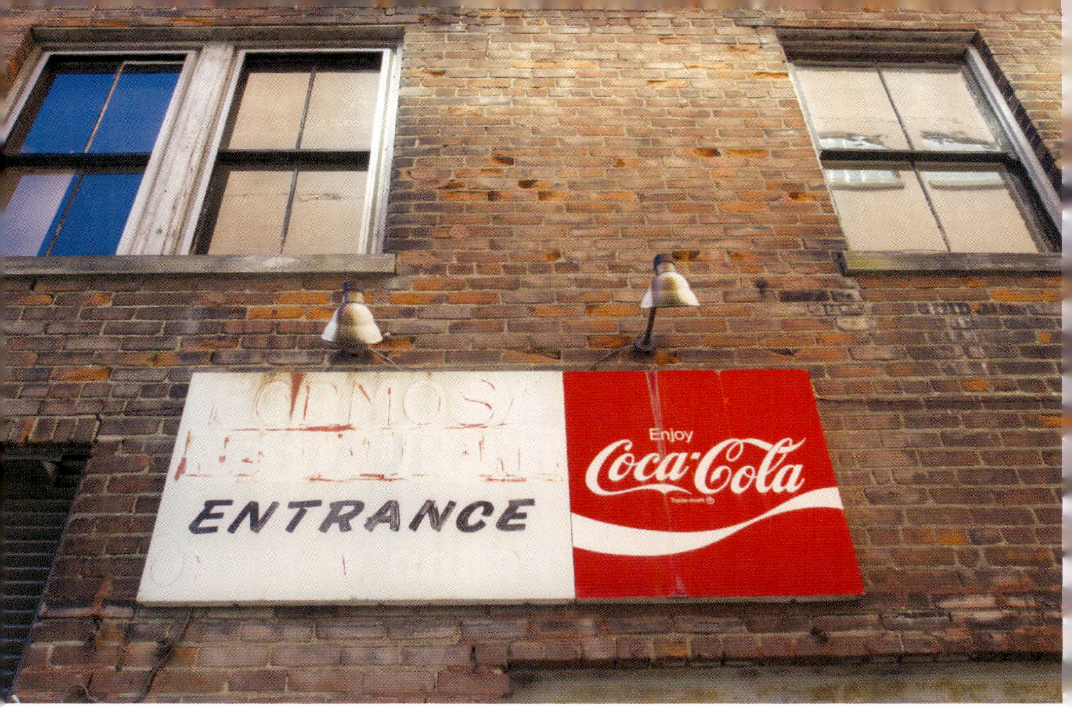

Above: "ENTRANCE" is the only word on this sign that has weathered time well, but even those words have deteriorated enough to show hints of the original brushstrokes. *Photo by Ronny Salerno.*

Below: The sign for Kay's Furniture is a battle of quality where spray paint has failed to conceal the original paint beneath it, eroding faster. *Photo by Ronny Salerno.*

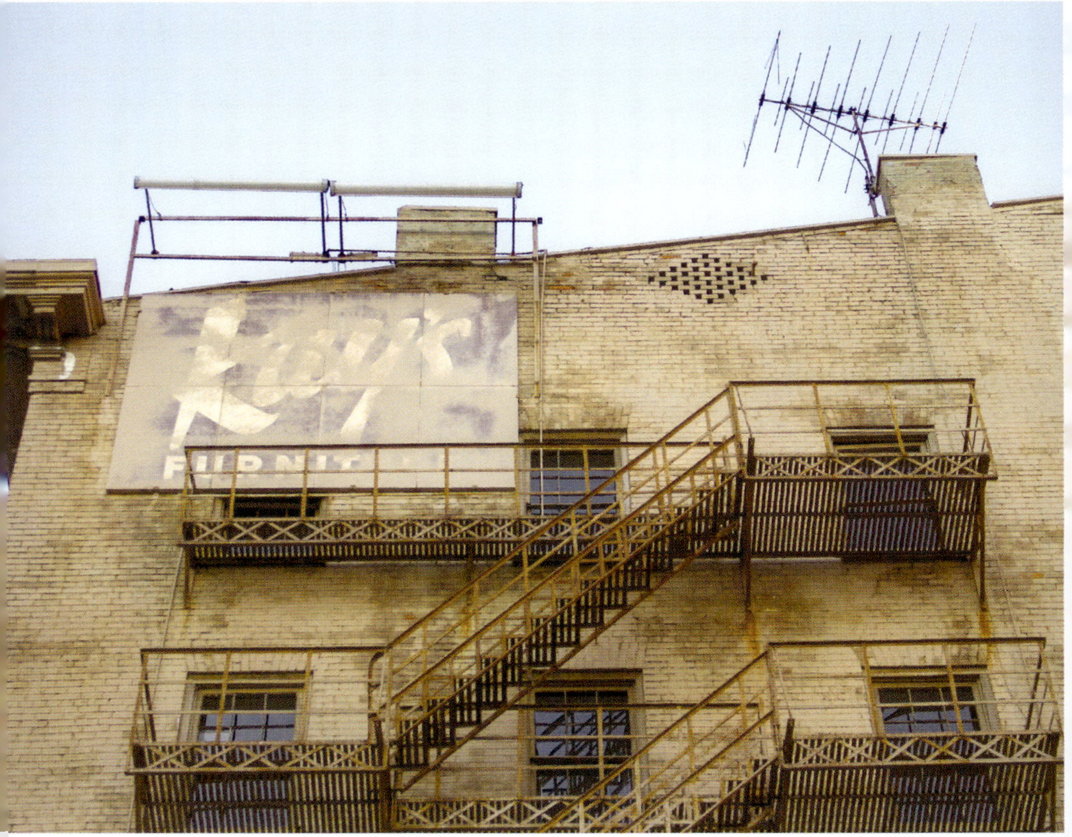

Kay's Furniture

Mounted at the top of a building above the fire escape, someone attempted to conceal this sign for Kay's Furniture. The quality of paint—probably from a spray can, judging by the way it has deteriorated—seems to be quite inferior to that of other signs that have toughed it out on walls for decades. The spray paint seen here didn't ever wear away at the original paint used to display the name of Kay's Furniture.

The Mystery of the Nondescript

The city's downtown collection of ghost signs is a reflection of the variety of businesses that have since moved on. The signs that are clearly legible have stood the test of time the best. Perhaps it's how they're shielded from the elements by nearby buildings or that they represent businesses that closed more recently. Some signs offer only a glimpse.

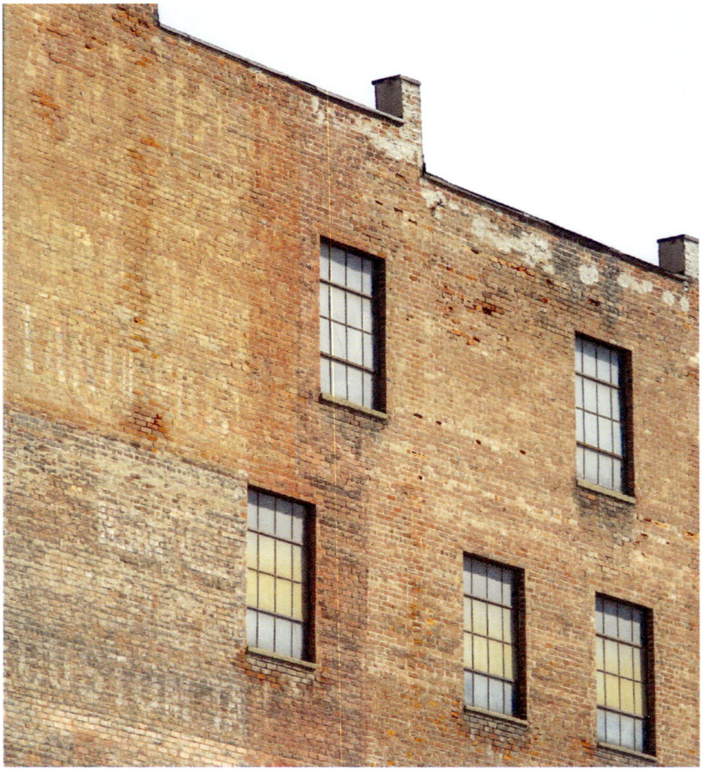

Left: "Custom Tailoring" can be made out in the bottom left of this sign. *Photo by Ronny Salerno.*

Opposite: An ad sporting only a few coherent words, with glimpses of other letters. *Photo by Ronny Salerno.*

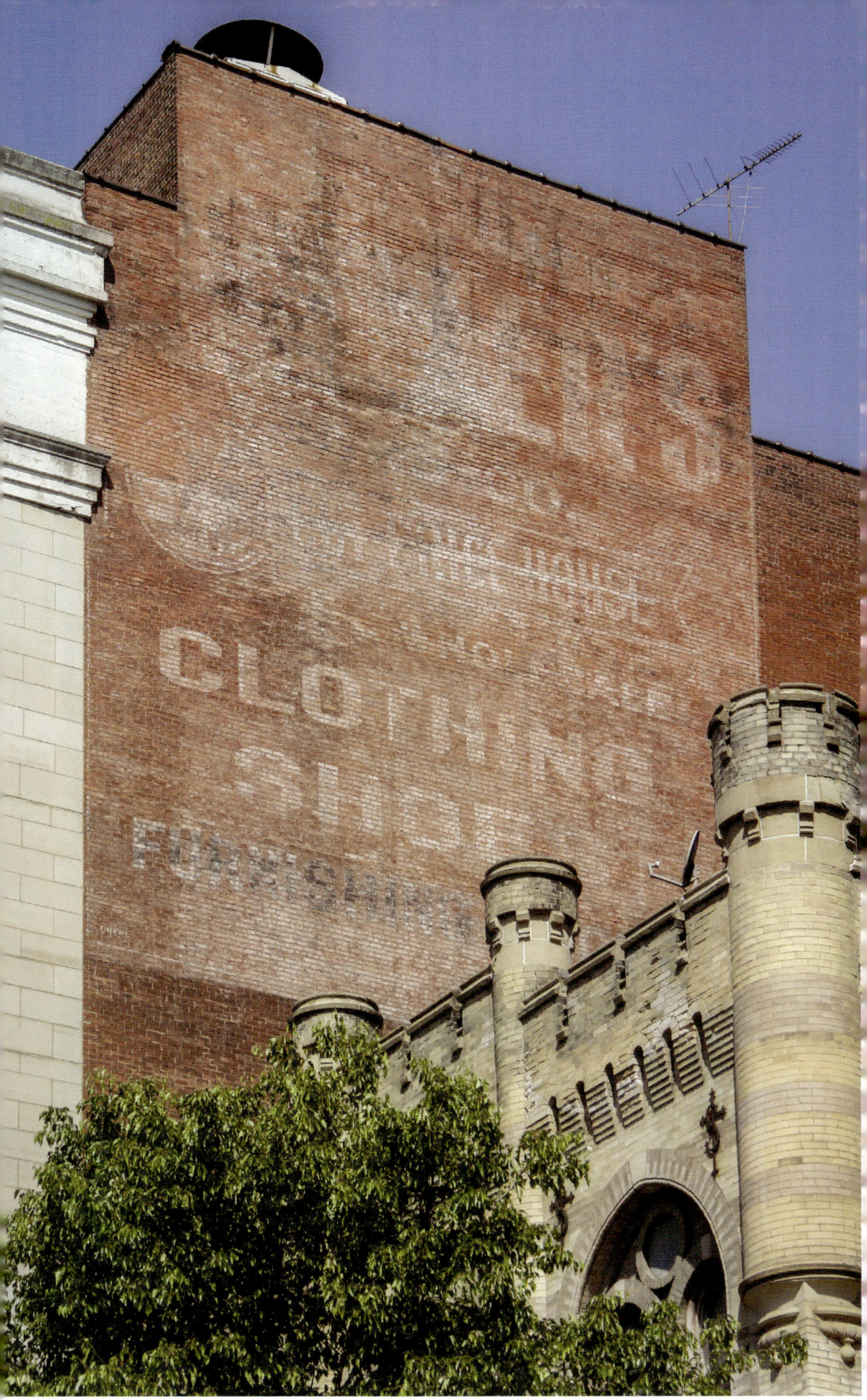
CLOTHING

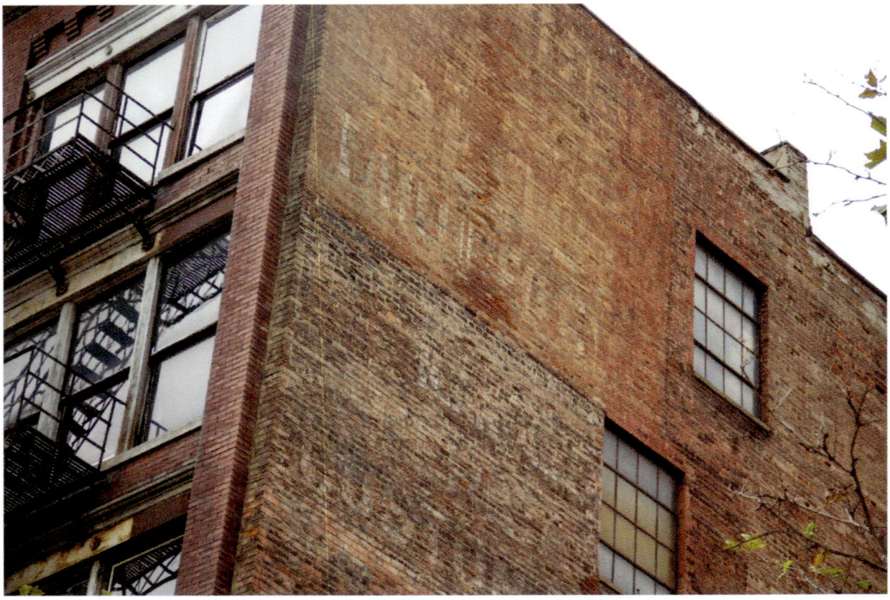

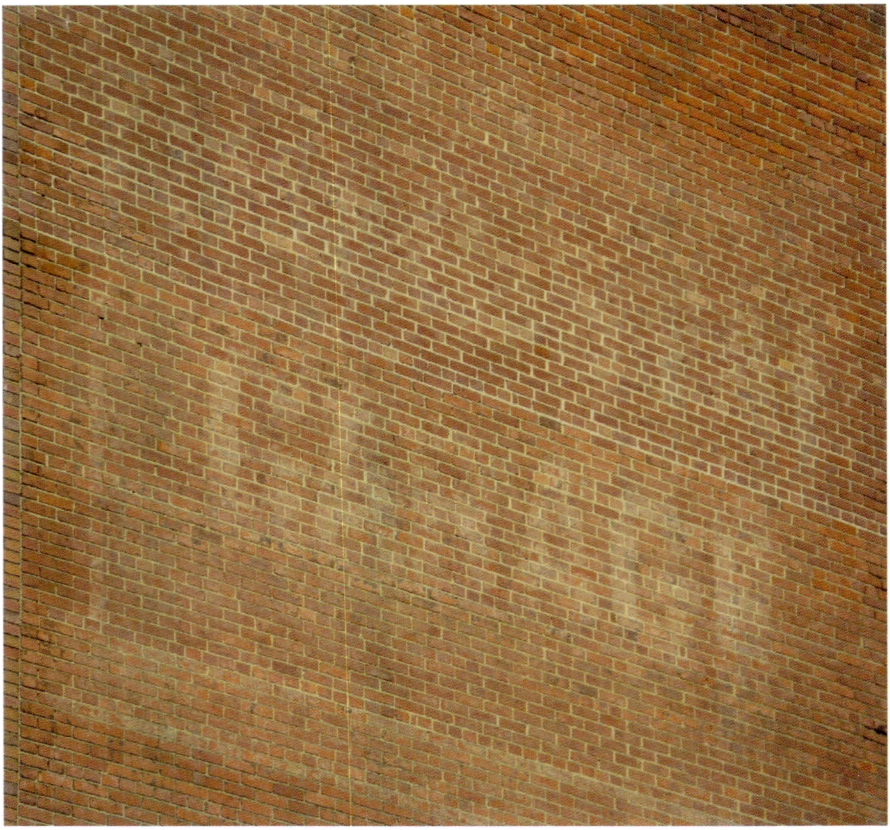

They hint at a service they offered: "Custom Tailoring"

They advertise a product: "Clothing, Shoes."

Some offer only a glimpse of a few discernable letters but not the entire shape of a familiar word.

The Baader-Meinhof phenomenon is described as stumbling upon a piece of obscure information and soon afterward encountering the same subject multiple times. An example commonly used is the way in which motorists often recognize other drivers operating the same vehicle they happen to own. Perhaps these fading advertisements are another example of said phenomenon. Once you start to find them, once you start to get an idea of where to look, when you bring your eyes up from street level and peer down the alleyways and onto the brick, the "ghost signs" start making their presence known. You get a feel for them, and in the patterns of weathered bricks you'll often find them still living. Often they seem like physical, urban manifestations of an optical illusion drawing.

They're remnants—an old form of advertising gone by the wayside. Yet still in downtown, among the brick canvases and fading advertisements, there are those surviving, both the former and the active. While they may have survived the businesses or products they touted, each day they fade a little more.

Opposite, top: Time and erosion can weather down the appearance of a fading advertisement. Oftentimes, the remnants of words begin to blend in with the regular wear and tear of a building's exterior. *Photo by Ronny Salerno.*

Opposite, bottom: Like the famous optical illusion books, making out the words of "Queensgate Garage" can be a challenge. *Photo by Ronny Salerno.*

3
"UNVISIBLE"

It's a warm, sunny Thursday evening as I walk down one of Newport, Kentucky's main drags, the skyline of Cincinnati in the distance across the Ohio River. Above the building, a hand-painted sign marks "The Pepper Pod," a twenty-four-hour diner.

The light from outside accentuates the haze of cigarette smoke and the yellow walls in the kind of establishment that's been replaced by fast-food drive-thrus along the highways. The Pepper Pod maintains its hand-painted sign, no obvious indications of weathering like with so many of the other bygone signs around here. In a way, it echoes how the business perseveres.

I shake hands and sit down with Bill Rinehart. We've met a few times before, but it's not his appearance I recognize so much as his voice. He's a former news anchor for the area's 700 WLW AM station and currently hosts *All Things Considered* on the local public radio station. He's also one of the area's foremost "experts" on ghost signs, if there is such a thing. Maybe he's best described as the guy who has taken the most time to care about or even notice them. We catch up with our respective lives and order greasy food. The conversation shifts, and soon I'm sharing photographs, the documentations I've made so far.

Bill's a transplant from Nebraska, having arrived in Ohio in 2003. In 2008, he began making downtown Cincinnati a home for himself. The ghost signs were something he'd see on the walks he took to get exercise. "They were something I always noticed, but once I moved downtown, I needed a hobby and started to notice them more and more," he says. He started wondering: "Is anyone paying attention to these? I kind of feel like they ought to be preserved or saved at least on film...digital film." Thus, the inspiration for his blog was born. In 2011, Bill launched "The Writing on the Walls." It started with the signs he found near his apartment and then branched out to the ones he'd locate in the farther reaches of downtown, other neighborhoods, the cities across the river and other places he's traveled. Bill developed an eye for spotting ghost signs, and he'd snap quick photos that he'd share via his online presence.

Bill and I had crossed paths both online and in the physical world. We'd met at a couple events downtown and occasionally see each other covering media events. On the Internet, we followed each other's work on our respective publications that covered facets of Cincinnati history. For a while, I didn't know that Bill was the man behind "The Writing on the Walls." He had kept his radio and amateur historian careers separate; that is, until he did a story for WVXU. Bill interviewed local organizations and people who, like him, had an opinion on the hand-painted signs adorning buildings throughout the area. His blog gained a little more traction after that story, and that's when I realized the eloquent voice on public radio was the same guy with whom I had been exchanging the occasional blog comment over the years. I reached out to Bill, and that's how we found ourselves sitting in the Pepper Pod, swapping stories of our pursuit of the past.

As Bill scrolls through the photographs I've made so far, he's able to recall the exact locations of the signs he's seeing, he points out their details and takes the time to digest the whole image, his eyes darting across the digital screen. "It's interesting what words stick around and what words disappear. It's like some words they gave an extra coat of paint to," he says.

Bill and I see things differently, and our methods vary a bit. While his work has relied on quick photographs often made from the window of his car, I've tried to photograph the signs with a nod to composition, light and framing. We both see the same signs, but we document them differently. We also interpret them differently.

Looking at an image of a faded Quaker Oats advertisement, I point out that I think I can see the remaining shape of the cereal's mascot. To Bill, it's not obvious, but he sees other words hidden in the painting, ones my eyes weren't picking up—possibly an indication of a sign that predated the one we're looking at. These ghost signs, often overlooked by the general public, can be so detailed and rich with information and at the same time so mysterious. Even once their existence becomes evident, the way they're seen and the way they're documented can differ greatly—two people staring at the same image and interpreting a piece of urban archaeology differently. Who knew a hand-painted advertisement for breakfast cereal would fade into such an interesting piece of history?

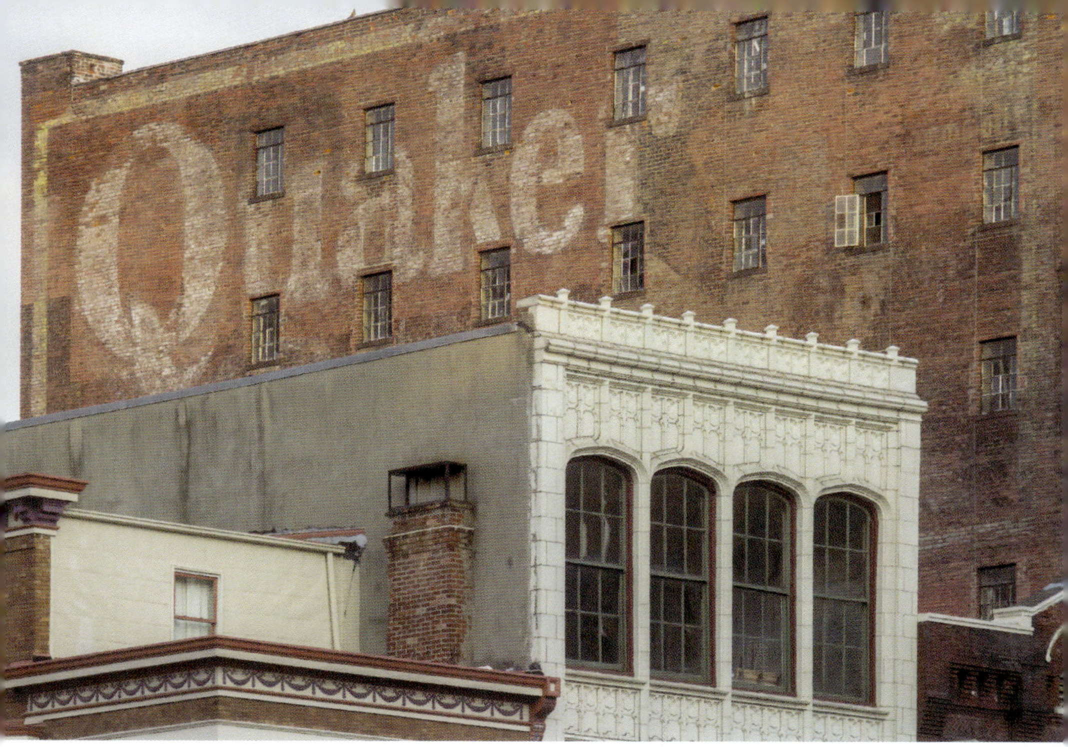

The Quaker Oats ad downtown is in a prominent location. Even with easy visibility, the ad's details have meshed with brick as they've faded, lending credence to Bill's term of "unvisible." *Photo by Ronny Salerno.*

We stand at the counter to pay up, and as we walk out into the setting sun, Bill points out several signs within eyeshot of the block we're standing on. We start moving up the street. There's one for a clothing outfitter on the right above a bank, a nondescript one another block up and then one for a long-closed department store back in an alley.

As we walk, Bill describes the fading advertisements as "unvisible" in the sense that they exist out in the open but aren't easily seen. Soon, we're spotting new ones that neither of us has caught before. Some of them are right in front of us. "If it was a bear, it would've jumped right out and attacked me," he says, marveling at how we missed one that in hindsight seemed so obvious.

A woman passes us on the sidewalk, noticing how we're craning our necks and pointing cameras at a building with a fading map of the United States on its side. She stops, looks up, smiles at us and then continues on. Would she have noticed the sign had we not been pointing it out?

Bill and I head back to our cars through a few alleyways and side streets, looking for evidence of fading paint and the sight of words on brick. As we part ways, we promise to keep in touch and share our findings. These signs mean something to each of us, and we're not the only ones out in the world pursuing the "unvisible."

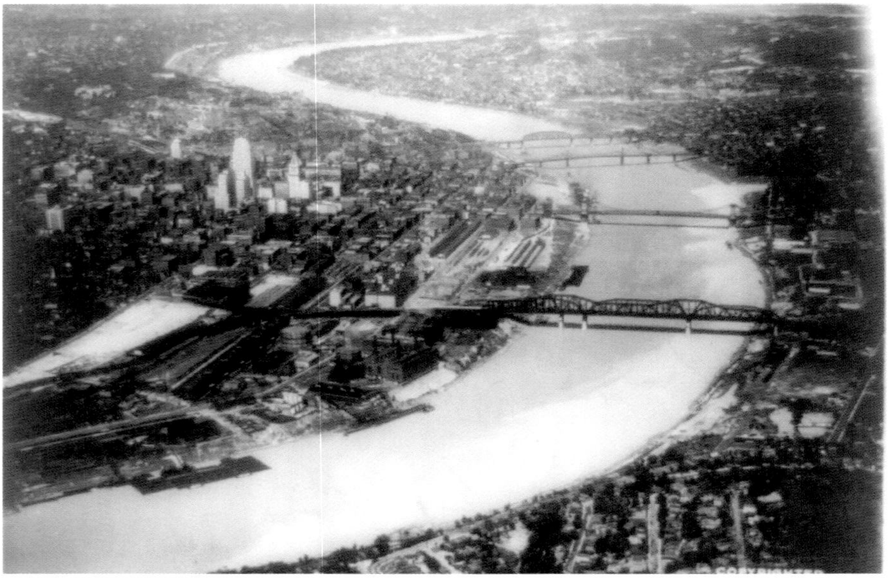

A 1934 photograph from the Aero-Graphic Corp. of Louisville, Kentucky, shows an aerial view of downtown Cincinnati and its Northern Kentucky neighbors across the river. *Courtesy of the Library of Congress.*

4

NORTHERN KENTUCKY

New York City is known for its five boroughs, former independent municipalities that consolidated to form one great city. Each of the boroughs has its own unique identity, neighborhoods and individual quirks. The Bronx varies greatly from Queens, Staten Island contrasts sharply to Brooklyn and Manhattan holds the center of attention. At the end of the day, though, they collectively form New York City and consolidate into the identity of the nation's largest population center. Then there are the suburbs and New Jersey across the river—all forming one massive metropolitan area. Cincinnati is different from New York, not just in population size or international scope, but also in regional identity. While New Yorkers and New Jerseyans can bicker all day long about their inherent differences, they tend to be viewed in a similar East Coast vein. Cincinnati and its neighbors across the river are connected, but their identities often don't span the bridges that link them.

I remember when I first moved to Northern Kentucky, relocating thirty-five minutes south out of the Cincinnati suburb I had grown up in. My roommate and I stopped into a local chili parlor and ended up explaining to the waitress how we had come from north of the river. She quipped about how much she disliked Ohio drivers while she plunked down cheese coneys and ashtrays (on this side of the river, you can still smoke inside). From where we hailed, Northern Kentucky was viewed more like a borough of the city rather than another state. From where she was standing, though, the river was a dividing line of culture and identity, not just government.

Northern Kentucky isn't like the rest of the the commonwealth either, though. It's essentially an extension of the Queen City's sphere of influence. It even holds the international airport. At first glance, and despite varying license plates, the NKY cities and suburbs seem identical to their Ohio counterparts. However, once you're immersed, it's clear that the smaller cities like Newport and Covington are comfortable developing their own plans and identities separate from, but with a degree of respect to, the major city across the bridges. At the same time, Northern Kentucky is linked with Cincinnati both physically and emotionally. Bridges hold together the riverbanks, businesses have locations on both sides and the love for local sports spans the gulf. Although the federal government considers Northern Kentucky to be part of Cincinnati's Metropolitan Statistical Area, Covington and Newport maintain their cultural independence. Nevertheless, these cities are linked historically and continue to evolve together. In places that may just seem like another Cincinnati neighborhood, these cities hold their own histories, and their buildings reveal their own collections of fading advertisements.

Covington

Covington lies at a point where the Ohio and Licking Rivers converge. Founded in 1815, the city is now the fifth largest in Kentucky. The city is linked to its Ohio brother via the iconic Roebling Suspension Bridge, the precursor and prototype to the well-known span in Brooklyn. The city is known for its picturesque views, boasting a riverfront lined with northern-looking apartments and condos. Turn around, away from the view, and you'll find a city with its own culture and identity—separate but complementary to the metropolis across the river. Behind the levee walls, the Interstate dumps into a cacophony of fast-food restaurants and gas stations, but beyond the cheap eateries are neighborhoods, nightlife, industry and history. The city is notable for Mainstrasse Village, a neighborhood known for unique eateries, bars, shopping and festivals. The name literally translates from German into "Main Road." Like its Ohio neighbor, Covington shares a strong German and brewing history.

Walking through Covington, fading advertisements are harder to come by as opposed to Cincinnati across the river. A local branch of Republic Bank and Trust Company still utilizes a hand-painted sign, albeit an updated one

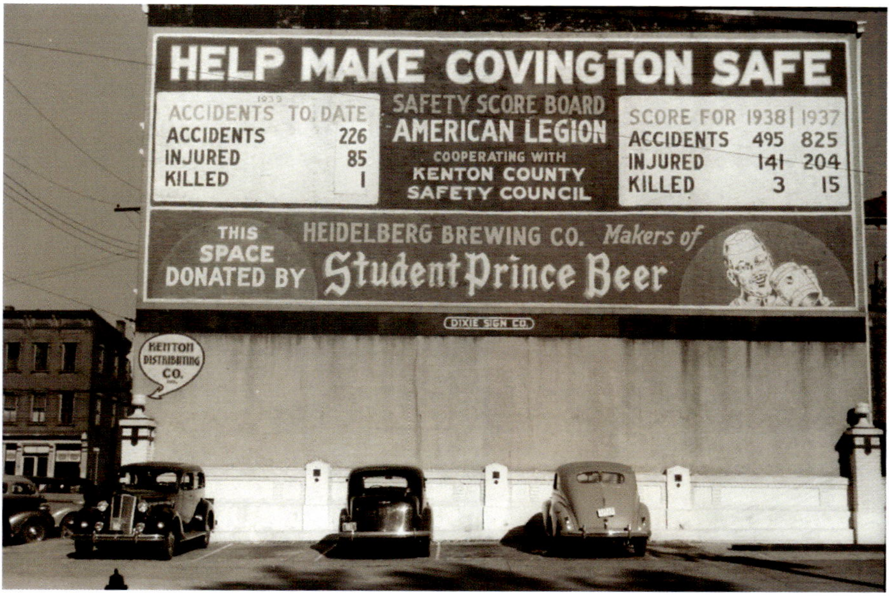

Seen in 1939, this advertisement in Covington was continually updated with fresh paint to reflect changing statistics in local driving safety. Maybe somewhat ironically, the ad notes that the space to create it was donated by a local brewing company. *Image by John Vachon, courtesy of the Library of Congress.*

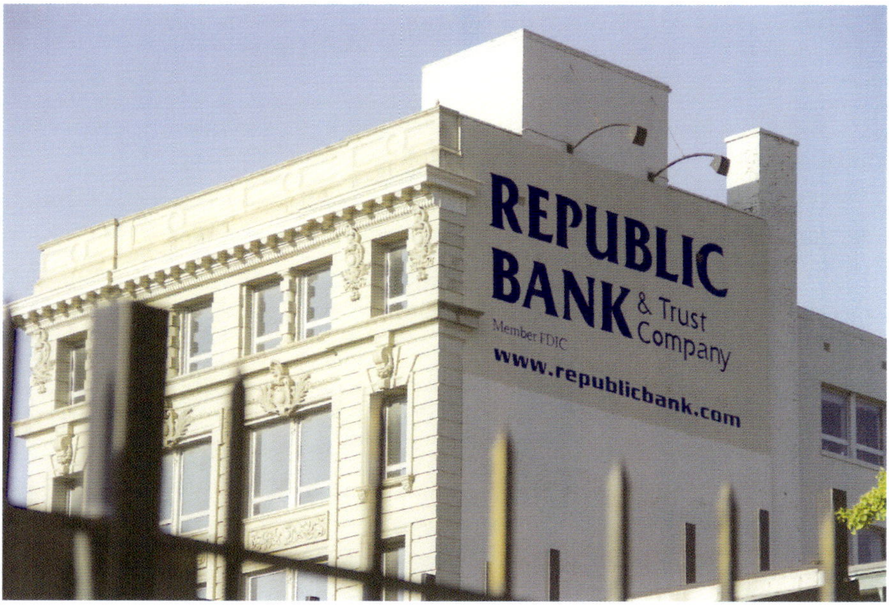

Republic Bank and Trust Company in Covington still uses a hand-painted sign to advertise its branch on the street below. This particular sign was created recently enough to sport the company's website. *Photo by Ronny Salerno.*

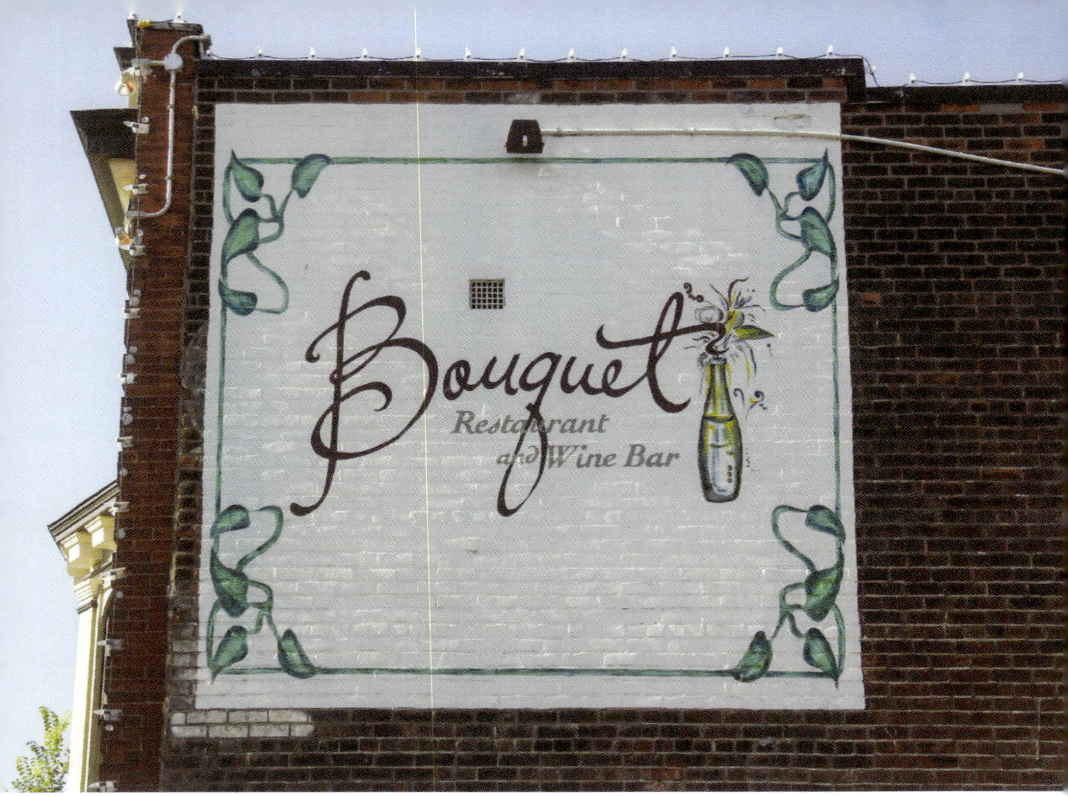

The Bouquet Restaurant and Wine Bar features a fresh, brightly colored hand-painted sign on the side of its location. At the bottom, a solid white oval can be seen, along with remains of a former sign around the edges. Perhaps the oval was once a sign painter's signature. *Photo by Ronny Salerno.*

that advertises its website. Meanwhile, the Bouquet Restaurant and Wine Bar features one prominently painted over an older sign.

The arts scene is prominent in Covington, with galleries popping up all over the city in recent years. Much of the available wall space Covington has alongside its buildings has been taken up by murals reflecting the thriving art culture. Every now and then, a ghost sign still shines through, a few words slightly discernible among the brick patterns. Even though I've come to develop an eye for finding these signs, spotting them still has a few challenges. While in my journey I've found some that prominently remain, others are more elusive. You start to develop a knack for where to find them—ducking down alleys and staring intently at brick walls. Of all the areas I searched, Covington is the toughest to wade through. Eventually, you start to wonder if the wall you're staring at is just dirty, or maybe it's showing the remains of another building that has since been demolished. Eventually, you have to make a decision: are you just seeing things, or is your mind actually identifying something? It's like urban archaeology, searching

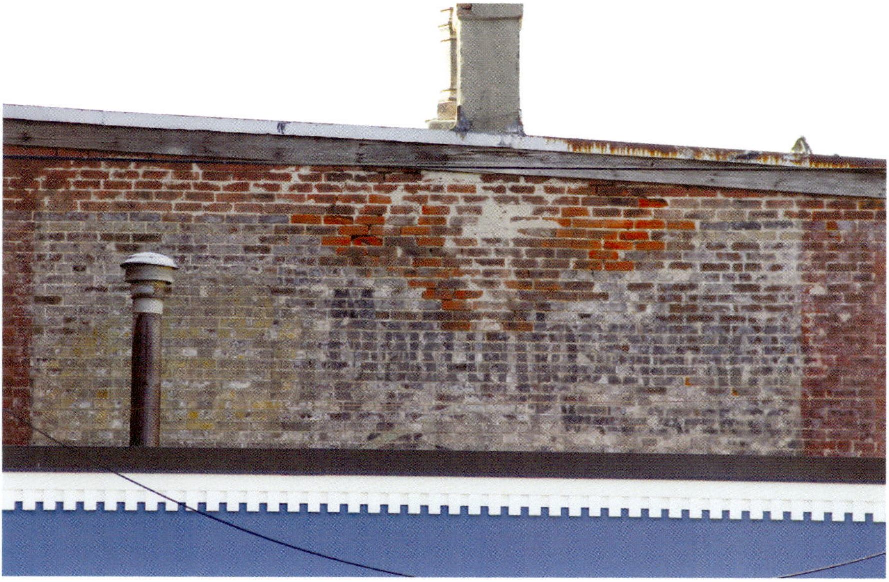

Above: A nondescript sign in Covington barely hangs on while several bricks shine through in their original colors. *Photo by Ronny Salerno.*

Right: Despite multiple ads blending together through erosion on the side of a Covington building, the words "Personal Loans" can still be seen. *Photo by Ronny Salerno.*

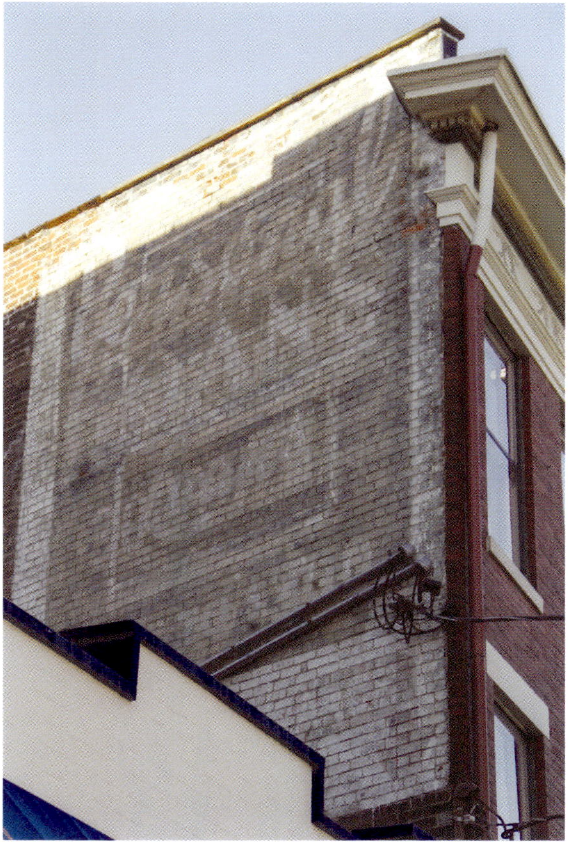

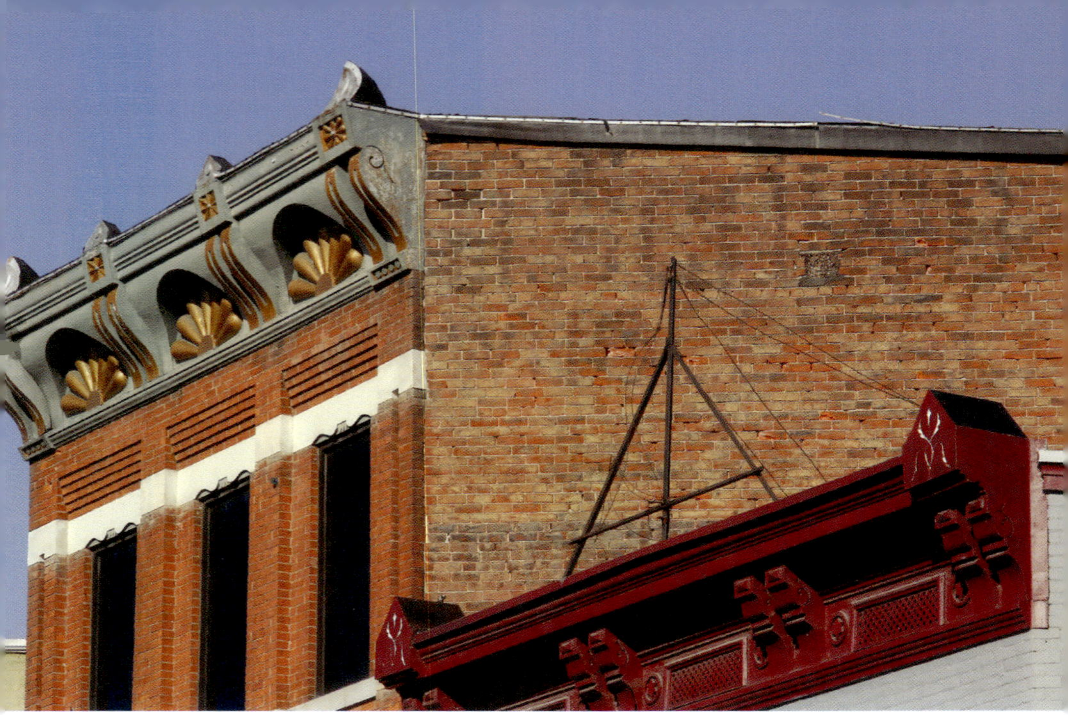

A fading ad in Covington might be mistaken for the normal wear and tear on the side of a building. If you look closely, though, you'll see the shapes of letters still forming from a sign that's gasping its last breath. *Photo by Ronny Salerno.*

for a sign representing a not-so-ancient civilization. Stare at a Covington wall long enough and you might just see the faded remains, shapes of letters and paint still barely clinging on after all this time.

But Covington still has a few easily seen signs, ones that have weathered and survived the test of time more intact. The John R. Green Co. is a nice example. It's not the advertisement hawking office/school supplies but the one beneath it. There's the beginnings of words: "BIND," "COR" and "MANUFA." While identification through a common language can lead one to surmise "manufacture," "manufacturing" or "manufacturers" as a likely candidate for the last word, the first two are a little more mysterious. A presentation on Covington history revealed that the building was originally constructed as a tobacco warehouse. Today, the John R. Green Co. calls the building its home, with a painted sign of its own. A school supply distributor, the Greene Co. was founded on Sixth Street in 1950. Today, the business is still very active, the latest tenant to use the building's walls for advertising.

In my time talking to Bill, he mentioned something he found particularly interesting: why certain words of a faded advertisement remain while others disappear. Maybe it's the environment around them, parts of a sign shielded by nearby structures. Or, as Bill noted, sometimes it seems like certain words

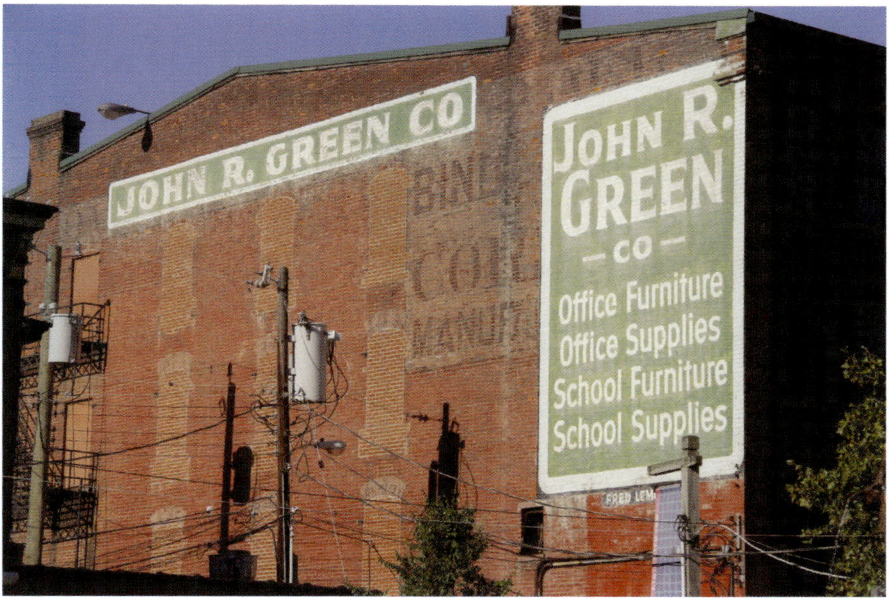

The painted signs of the John R. Green Co. reflect a business that is very much still alive. At the same time, they partially obscure the remains of another painted sign. *Photo by Ronny Salerno.*

got "an extra coat of paint," lending to their permanence. At the corner of Seventh Street and Washington Avenue there's a parking lot butting up to the side of a brick building. A few trees line the lot and the street, where public transit buses dart loudly toward a railroad underpass, echoing their haste. The wall has several coats of paint, some of it abruptly ending where building supports clearly once stood. One word remains: "delicious." I stopped into the building that features the sign, a location of the regional Steffen's Tool Rental Company. The clerk up front finished helping a man, nodding as he wheeled out his borrowed equipment. I stepped up with a question of history rather than construction. "Honestly, no idea what the business was," said the clerk. "I know they had a lean-to. I think it was a produce stand." If there was anything left to back up his theory, an indicator of the former neighbor remembered only in a deteriorated sign, it was the one word left: "delicious."

Cincinnati and Covington are linked not just by several bridges but also by a common ancestry. The two river cities share a strong German heritage, each hosting its own annual Oktoberfest and taking pride in its brewing history. At their peak in the mid-1800s, Cincinnati and its Northern

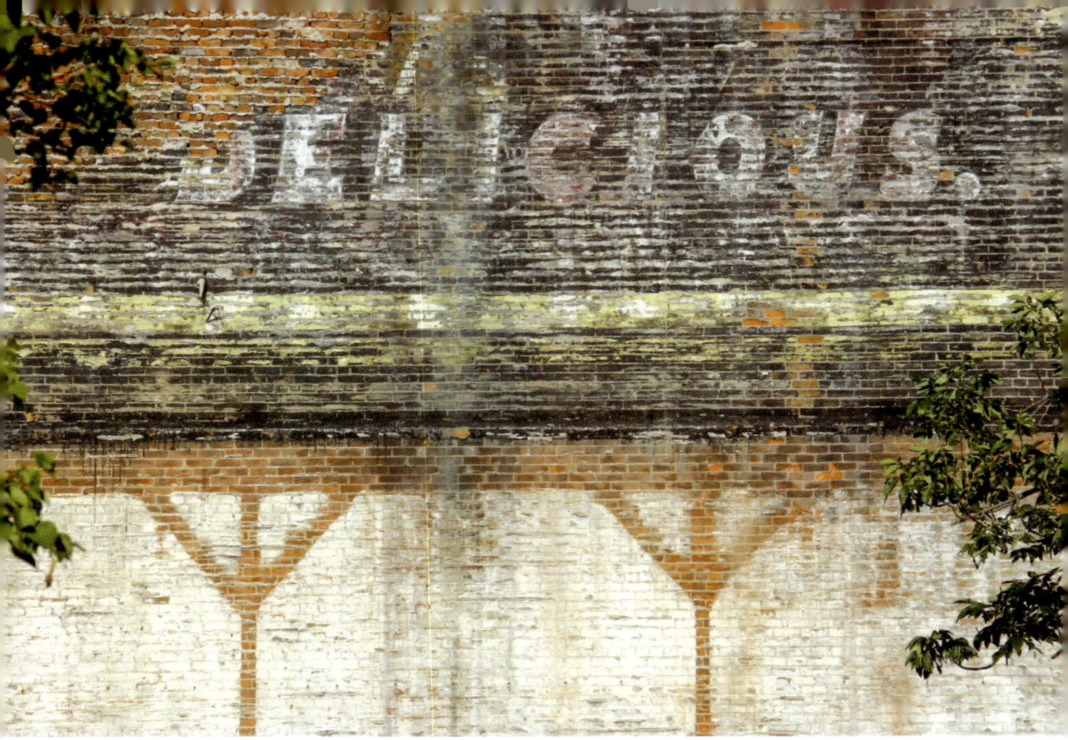

A former structure prevented this building from being painted entirely; along with the word "delicious," these clues give credence to the thought that a fruit and produce stand may have once called this parking lot home. *Photo by Ronny Salerno.*

Kentucky brethren were producing upward of thirty million gallons of beer. Covington at one time boasted one of the more prominent companies: Bavarian, named after the German state. The Bavarian Brewing Company traces its roots back to 1866. The name managed to survive ownership changes and Prohibition, temporarily producing soft drinks like so many other breweries during America's dry years. With alcohol legalized again in 1933, the Bavarian brewery once again fired up its bottling plant. Advances in manufacturing and marketing began to take their toll in the post-Prohibition years. Larger brewing companies such as Anheuser-Busch were starting to become household names in the national scope. All across America, and particularly in the Cincinnati area, local breweries struggled to compete. Bavarian was unique, though, in that it took a stand. As Busch began to be more prevalent in the local market, Bavarian's owners weren't too happy about the St. Louis–based giant debuting "Busch Bavarian Beer" in 1955. They took their rivals to court, claiming infringement, and by 1957, the United States Sixth Circuit Court of Appeals had a ruling.

The court believed that the term "Bavarian" was associated with the local company, at least in the main distribution areas of "southern Ohio, northern Kentucky and southeastern Indiana." It mentioned how Bavarian's

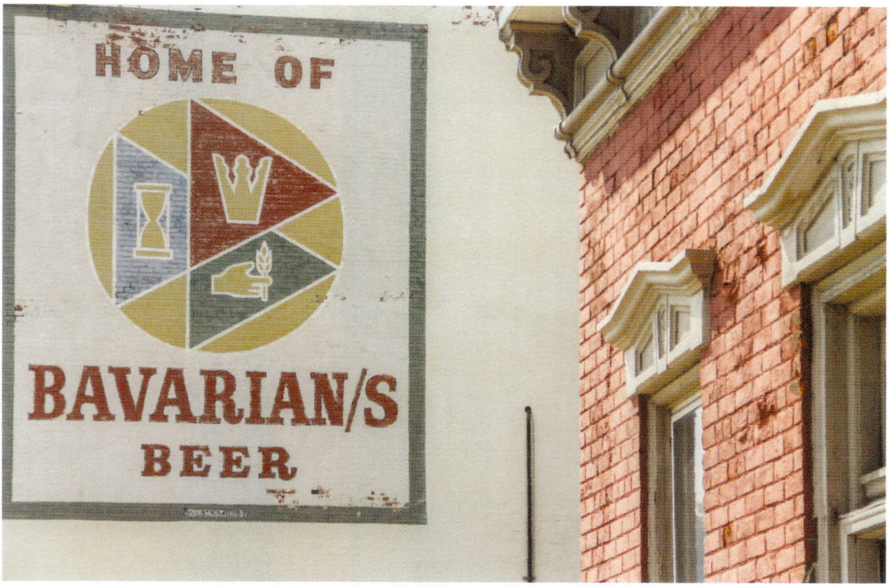

The company crest of Bavarian can still be seen on the outside of the former brewery. Once operating as a nightclub and concert venue, the building now faces an uncertain future. *Photo by Ronny Salerno.*

consumer marketing budget of "$500,000 per year since 1946" had made the term distinctive to the brewery itself. At the same time, though, it agreed with Anheuser-Bush's testimony that the word Bavarian meant "a type or style of beer." A compromise was reached. Anheuser was permitted to use the title of "Bavarian" while marketing its Busch brand but could not sell its product within the Covington brewer's defined territory. For Bavarian Brewing Company, this was a victory, a triumph of the little guy over the big guy. It might not have won the copyright infringement argument, but it was successful in at least keeping some of a major competitor's products away.

Despite the legal victory, Bavarian still faced challenges. Ever-declining sales led to a merger with a Detroit-based brewer in 1959. Although it kept the Bavarian name, the brewery continued to lose money and was closed in 1966, a century after it opened.

Like in many cities in the twenty-first century, brewing has made a comeback in Cincinnati and Covington. Both cities now host their fair share of micro and local breweries, their products offered on tap right next to those of national chains at pubs all across the region. While many historical brands have resurfaced, Bavarian currently isn't one of them. Nevertheless, historical pieces of the company still remain. The former brewery was placed

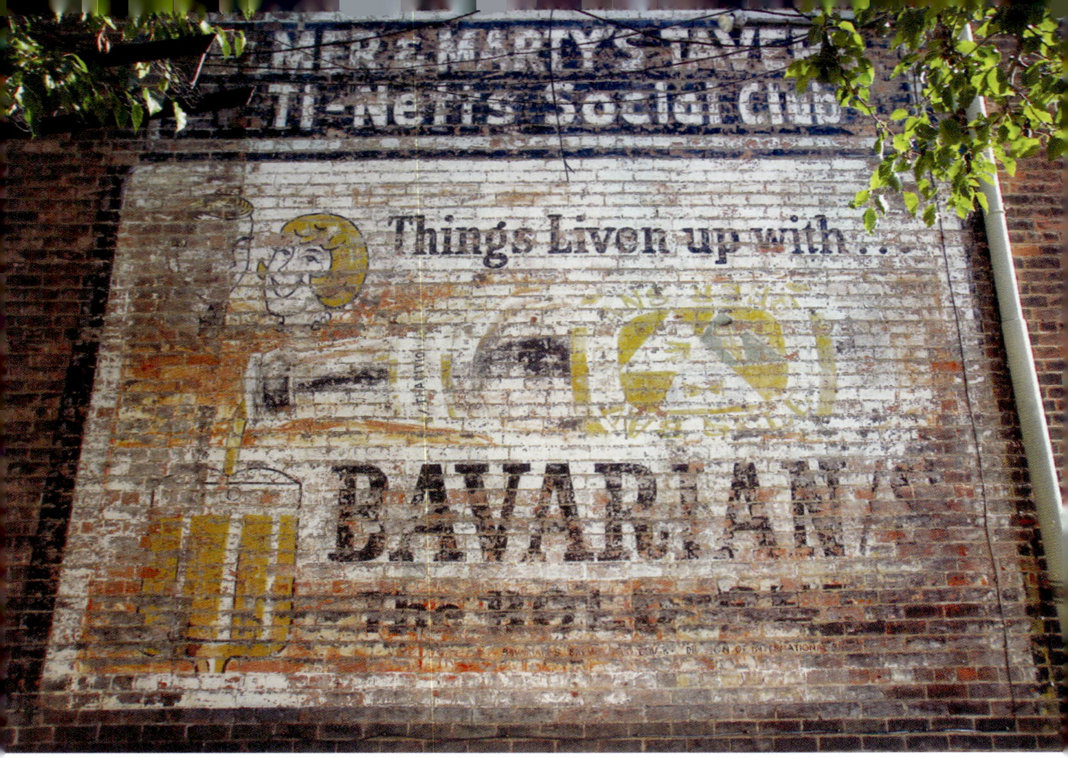

On a quiet street in Covington, an ad for the once local Bavarian Beer remains. Featuring a bottle pouring into a mug, the sign also touts the name of a former tavern. *Photo by Ronny Salerno.*

on the National Register of Historic Places and was temporarily renovated into a nightclub. Today, it sits empty, the brewer's name still proudly emblazoned on the structure's façade, awaiting either another revitalization project or the wrecking ball. Down at the corner of Seventh and Bakewell Streets and under the shade of trees, a hand-painted advertisement still remains—fittingly, on the side of a bar.

The sign depicts a smiling couple juxtaposed by a bottle of Bavarian being poured into a mug. The tag line reads: "Things liven up with BAVARIAN/S," trailing off into faded paint with "THE BOLD BEER." Above this is more painted writing—advertising for the establishment's former owners and a social club. Today, a local joint named Rosie's operates out of the building, serving a few varieties of local brew. Although Bavarian is no longer one of them, the brick walls still house the latest incarnations of the local beer scene while the history of it is affixed outside.

Covington is Covington. Covington is not Cincinnati, but there's no denying that the riverfront hotels and high-rise office buildings benefit from their proximity to the picturesque neighbor they overlook. Nevertheless, the city has always strived to preserve its own identity and pride, with "Love the

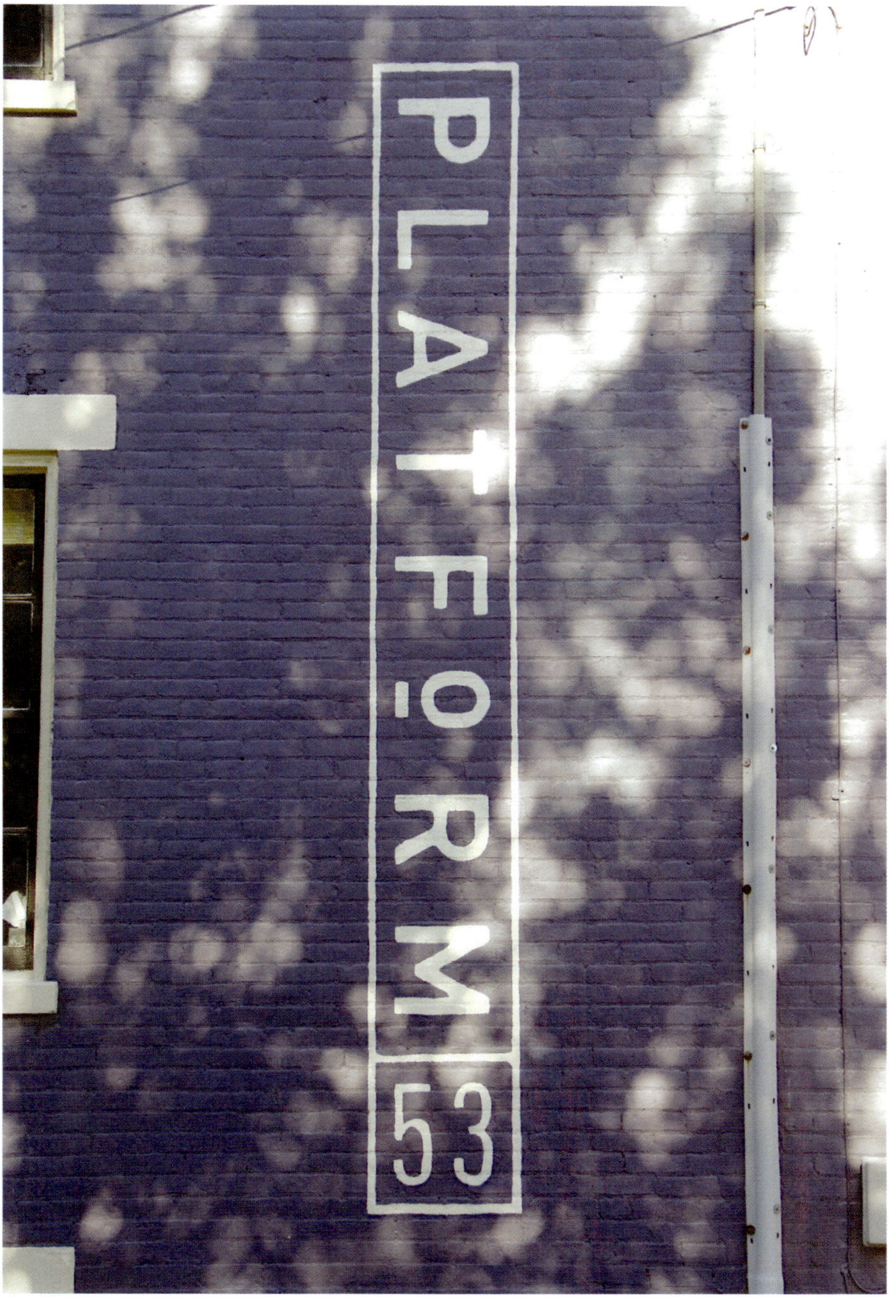

Platform 53 utilized a simple hand-painted stencil piece to reflect modern design trends while acknowledging a nostalgic form of advertising when it opened its business. *Photo by Ronny Salerno.*

Cov" slogans appearing throughout. For some, it's a place of inspiration, where you can come together and work collaboratively. That ideal is embodied at Platform 53, a co-working space and startup incubator housed in a multilevel brick building. You won't find a sign out front for the business that started in January 2012, but you will find its name brush-stroked on the wall—a call back to the advertising of old.

"In Covington and around Cincinnati it's something that's not done anymore," says Adam Dean, a local Covington businessman and one of Platform 53's founders, as he describes the sign painted on the outside. "People like to hang these big, ugly signs. We wanted to make a permanent statement. What better way to make a statement than painting the side of your building?" Platform 53's signage is simple: a single-color stencil that stands out against the purple backdrop. It's not elaborate or intricately detailed like its nostalgic brethren, but at the same time, it evokes the feel and spirit of the days before billboards. Adam says that he and the other founders were inspired not just by fading ads in the region but also by Covington's extensive collection of wall murals: "The side of your building is a huge façade; it's kind of indie." The simple sign is a tribute and declaration—a nod to both the history of Covington and its emerging art scene. It's an embracing of what Covington has been and hopes to become.

Newport

Newport was born out of military history. As Cincinnati grew, its Fort Washington military base was relocated across the river as the Newport barracks. Newport became incorporated as a city in 1834. Throughout the years, it gained a reputation as one of America's sin cities. Casinos and gambling parlors operated throughout, along with the more typical businesses found on midwestern Main Streets. Even as the gambling dens and rumors of mobsters faded away, Newport was the place for vice, a quick jaunt for cigarettes and booze that were cheaper there than in Ohio. By the 1990s, Newport was pushing for a more family-friendly identity and wanted to capitalize on tourism. The Newport-on-the-Levee entertainment complex opened alongside the Newport Aquarium and was linked to Ohio via a rusting railroad bridge that had been rehabbed into a pedestrian-only path. Condos rose up and chain restaurants came in, but Newport has

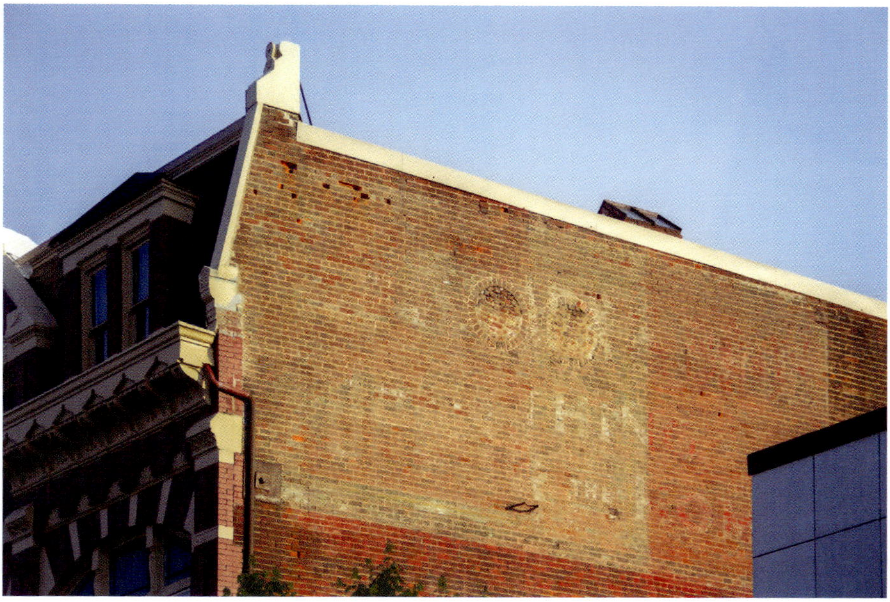

Many of the signs on Newport's Monmouth Avenue have faded into a state of obscurity. A few letters shine through, but the entire composition can be hard to make out. In the setting sun, the signs get a few minutes of more pronounced attention. *Photo by Ronny Salerno.*

always retained its charm. Even as you walk it today, old Newport still shines through despite the decades of change.

There's a road labeled Main Street, but it's short and tucked away in a hillside neighborhood. The actual primary thoroughfare is the eclectic Monmouth Street. It has its fair share of dive bars, one strip club, plenty of locally owned businesses, a few all-night diners and a small handful of empty storefronts for sale. It's the main drag where Bill and I met at the Pepper Pod. It has never been the target of gentrification while at the same time never deteriorating enough to warrant subsidized efforts of revitalization. It's blue collar and unpretentious but still holds its own in regards to unique restaurants and a few higher than normally priced eateries. It's not surrounded by skyscrapers or office parks but rather neighborhoods and the occasional gas station. The street's collection of brick buildings outnumber the few examples of more modern construction. As you walk down Monmouth, you can glance up and see remnants of fading advertisements. Unlike the abundance of ghost signs in downtown Cincinnati, Newport's collection is smaller, with many of them barely discernable or legible.

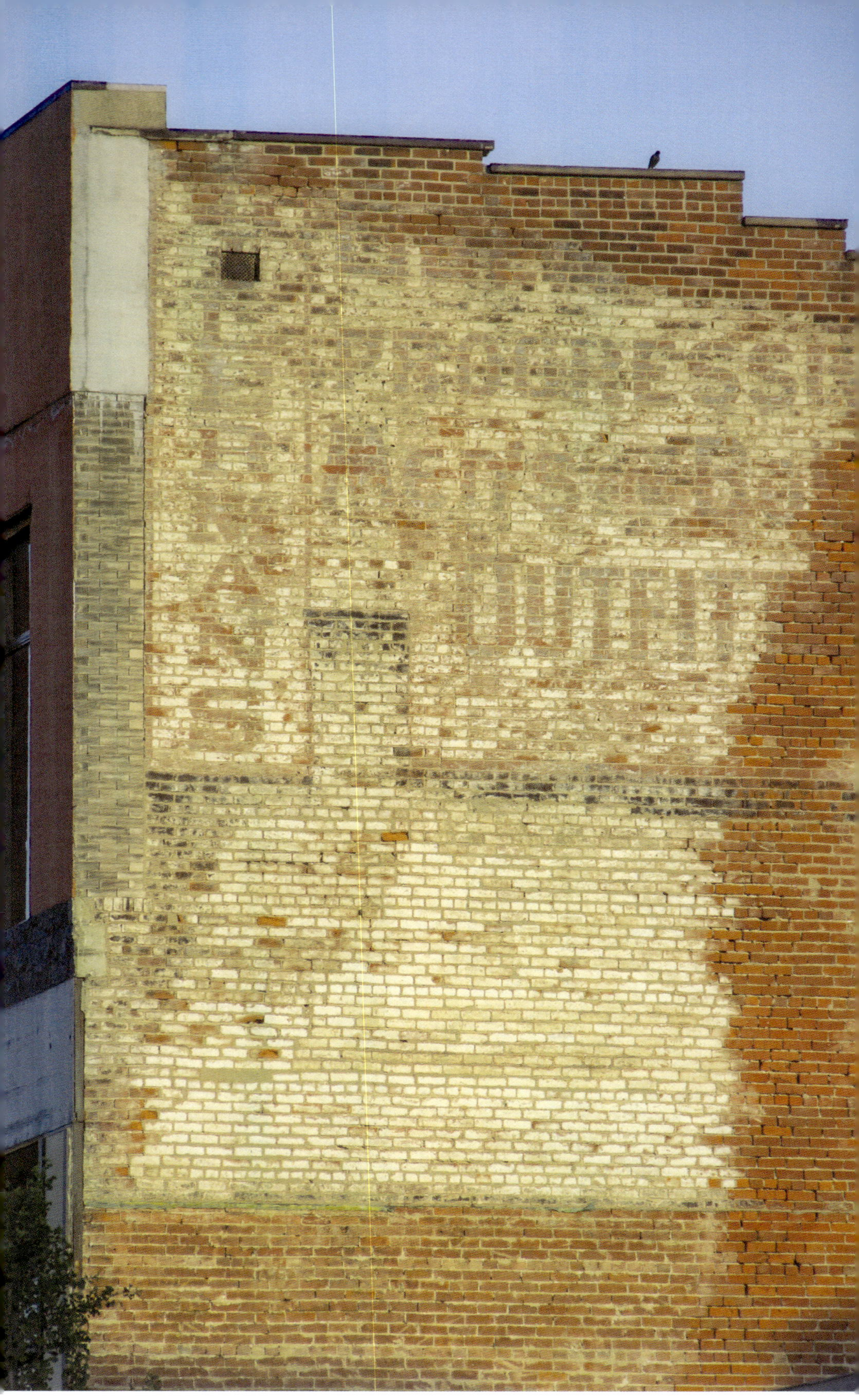

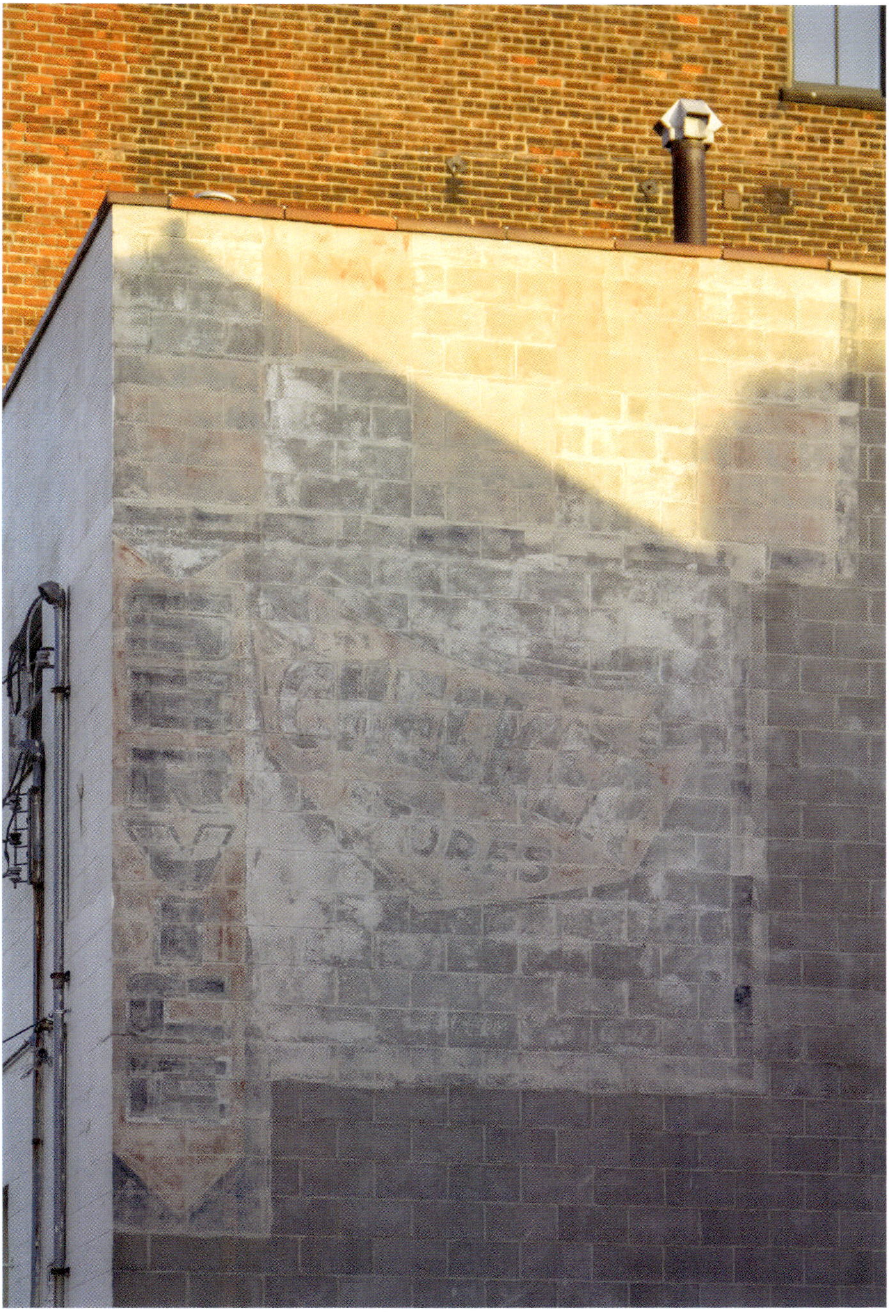

Long after a Checker store left the building, a sign marking its service entrance can still be seen in a Newport alleyway. *Photo by Ronny Salerno.*

Opposite: A nondescript sign in Newport still has a few words left to show, the most notable being "outfit." *Photo by Ronny Salerno.*

Hidden down an alley, painted on the side of cinder blocks and overlooking a residence's backyard swimming pool is an ad for a bygone regional retailer. At its top, the outlines of a checkered paintjob can still be seen, while a vertically running arrow points down displaying the word: "Service." In the center is: "Checker Stores."

Checker Stores at one time was a well-recognized regional name. It boasted five stores in the city of Cincinnati, with locations also in neighboring Newport and Covington and as far away as Portsmouth, Ohio, and Lexington, Kentucky. The company often utilized advertisements through the mail, sending out postcards offering "free gifts" of hand towels, coffee makers, clocks and table lamps (if you brought the card to a store and made a purchase of "$19.95 or more"). The fading advertisement found in the alleyway is the only remaining physical indication of the Newport location. The building's façade doesn't seem to reflect any of the former retailer's branding.

Often, these fading advertisements tend to represent businesses or products that can be viewed nostalgically, remnants of eras typically held in high value. While some current businesses still utilize the practice of hand-

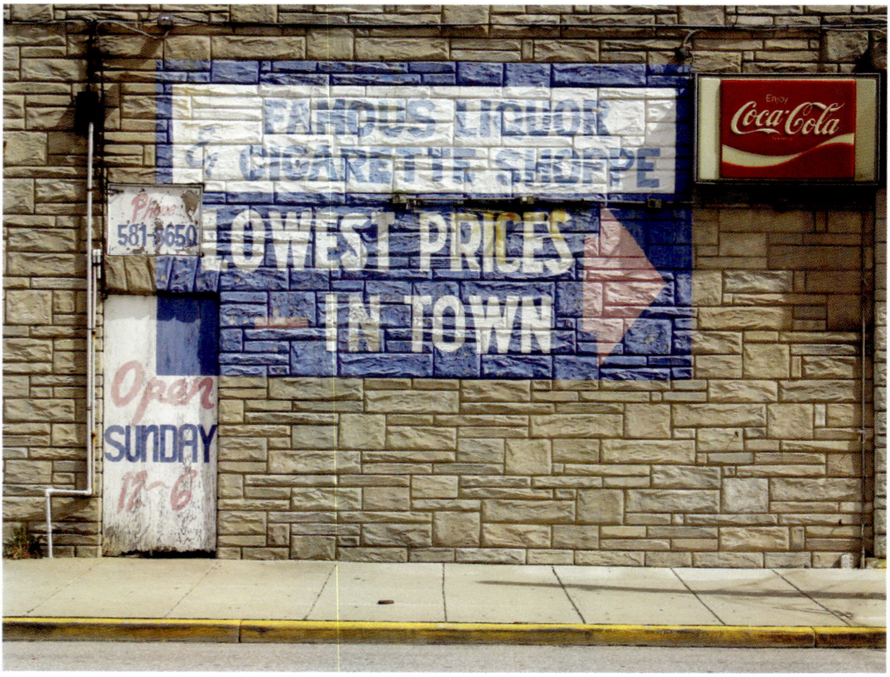

A more modern take on wall advertising, the Famous Liquor & Cigarette Shoppe in Newport is no more. *Photo by Ronny Salerno.*

painted advertising today, most of the ghost signs show some age, not just in their faded appearance, but also in their content. One particular piece in Newport, though, is a little more recent, despite the implication of the extra "p" and "e" in the word "shoppe."

Famous Liquor & Cigarettes seems to have been your standard convenience store and carryout place. It is unique in that it utilized a hand-painted sign but not unique in the products advertised. Kentucky generally has lower prices on alcohol and tobacco, leading to a thriving business in the northern cities that attracts consumers making trips from Ohio. The Famous Liquor & Cigarette Shoppe seems to have been just one of the many others that called, or continue to call, Newport home. The painted sign extends off the brick onto the wooden board covering a door. Accompanied by a plastic Coca-Cola sign, it proudly proclaims the "LOWEST PRICES IN TOWN." This must not have been enough to keep the doors open. Famous wasn't open long enough to see the age of Internet reviews; while listed, it seems to have been ignored. Its hand-painted ad is well preserved, though, placed prominently on a main road. There's very little chipping of the paint, with most of the damage coming from the rust of an electrical conduit. Unlike its historical predecessors, the sign representing Famous Liquor & Cigarette

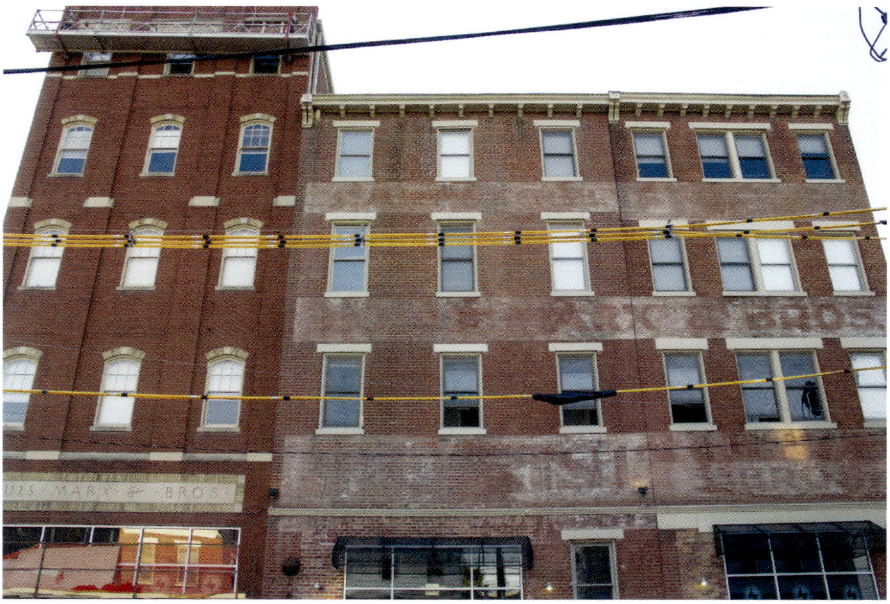

As the building underwent exterior renovations such as new windows, the remnants of the Louis Marx & Bros. name remained. The fading letters add a touch of history to the building while showcasing its longevity. *Photo by Ronny Salerno.*

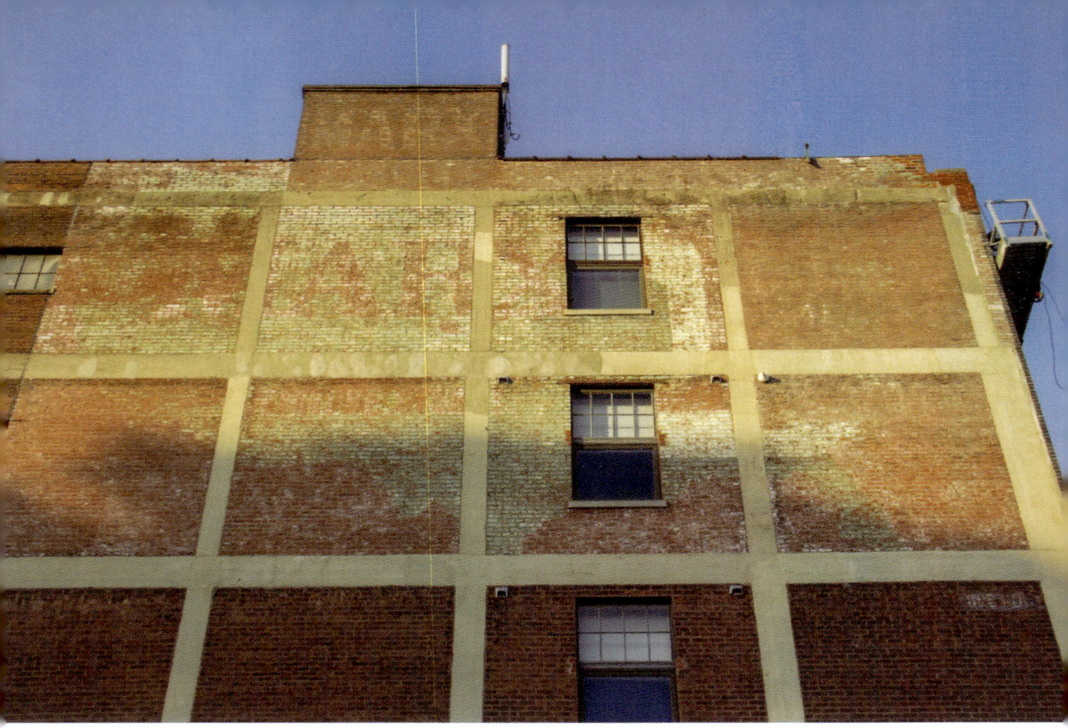

Above: The side of the building features an abstract collection of colors meshing with brick. The shades of green resemble the outline of the contiguous United States, while the name Marx can still be seen at the top. *Photo by Ronny Salerno.*

Below: The signature of Gus Holthaus, a common name found beneath hand-painted signs in the area, is seen beneath the outline of the United States on the side of the Louis Marx and Bros. building. *Photo by Ronny Salerno.*

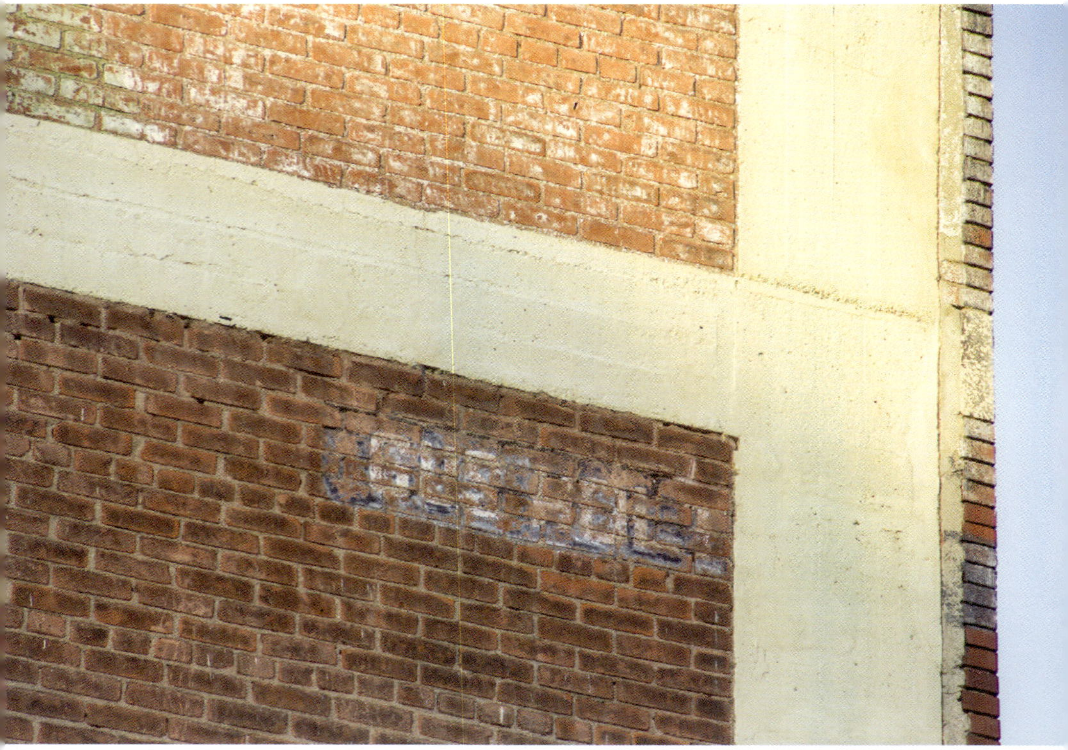

is absent of a worn and distressed look. It's a more modern take on classical advertising, now joining the ranks and left to fade in the same way as the signs that inspired it.

The true gems of Newport's collection are the ones found on the Louis Marx and Bros. building. Louis, along with his brothers Milton and Simon, was once a fixture of Newport's economic activity. Their company traces its roots back to 1888. Not to be confused with classic toy manufacturer Louis Marx and Co. (developers of nostalgic creations such as the Big Wheel and Rock 'Em, Sock 'Em Robots), the Newport Marxes were furniture proprietors. The *Kentucky Times-Star* heralded the company as "one of the leading furniture and home furnishing houses in the state" in 1923.

The Marx storefront and warehouse on Ninth Street was a combination of several neighboring buildings, two combined four-story structures and a five-story warehouse that was commissioned in 1926. One side of the complex still maintains the faded words "Furniture, Carpets, Stoves." The other side is a little less subtle. Like a complex painting in a fine art gallery, a viewer has to really look at the westward-facing brick wall from the details to the larger picture. The hidden message is due to erosion rather than technique, but the concept of finding detail is the same. At the top, "MARX" is emblazoned in capital letters. Farther down, an "A," "R" and "X" shine through. Faded green paint blends into white and then to brick. If you step back and look at the image as a whole, you can see the outline of the contiguous United States. From right to left are the Florida panhandle, the bottom of Texas and the upward-sweeping lines of California and the western coast. At the bottom right is a signature: Gus Holthaus. Holthaus's name can be found on several signs in the region. Here, it's as faded as the United States outline.

Today, the Louis Marx and Bros. company is long gone. Some of its pieces can be found listed on the Internet, the pursued items of antique hunters. The building has been renovated into luxury lofts, and despite the changes, the faded advertisements have remained—tying the urban living space to its historic past.

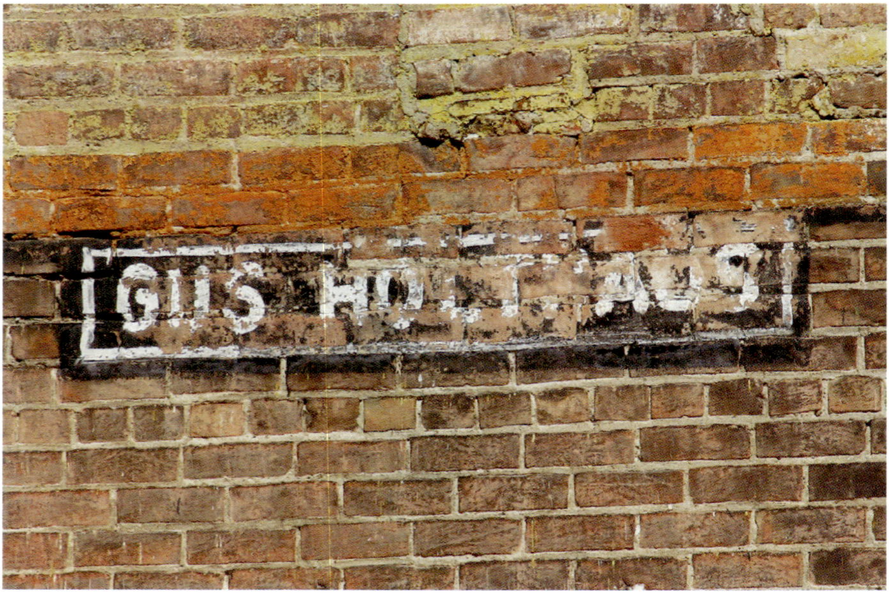

The signature of Gus Holthaus in its customary fashion. *Photo by Ronny Salerno.*

5

SIGNATURE LEGACY

Even before we can read, we are inundated with advertising. As soon as our eyes develop enough to see past the car window, we're aware—another human being glancing up at the billboards and signs promoting the economic engine. Advertising exists everywhere, not just on the roadside, but also on the television, on the radio waves and through the digital signals sent to the smart phones in our pockets. Advertising adapts; it's always innovating and trying to reach us wherever we go. Universities churn out thousands of students armed with degrees, looking to join an ever-growing marketing workforce. Even in a rapidly evolving digital age, physicality is important. A sign is sometimes more than just promotional material; it's a notification, directions to where you're going or a symbol of where you are. Kevin Holthaus understands this better than most people. He's the grandson of one of Cincinnati's most prominent painters, and although the world—and city—has changed, he carries on the family tradition today.

Holthaus Lackner Signs is located in Cincinnati's Avondale neighborhood, a quick climb up the hill from downtown. The business is headed by Kevin Holthaus, with his nephew, niece and son among those he employs. Holthaus is one of the premier names in signage not just in Cincinnati but also throughout the region. The company's work can be found throughout a one-hundred-mile radius of the Queen City in places like Dayton, Lexington, Louisville and Columbus. Its work runs the gamut: interior work, illuminated posts, vehicle graphics, digital messaging boards, scoreboards and much more. It seems to create everything from local restaurant signage to more iconic pieces like the name of the Horseshoe Casino, illuminated and shining alongside the highway-facing building. Everywhere you go around here, you're likely to find work from the portfolio of the Holthaus Lackner company. The local sign empire comes from humble roots, tying the company back to the fading advertisements on the walls.

"It used to be you could paint as big a sign as you wanted on the side of a building," says Kevin. "When all the signs in Cincinnati were hand painted, you could drive around and tell who painted what. Everyone had their own style." One of the most prominent styles of hand-painted signs in Cincinnati belonged to Kevin's grandfather the late Gus Holthaus.

Gus's name appears everywhere, including on several signs documented in this publication. His signature is simple: small, maybe a few bricks wide, all caps and white letters on a black backdrop. Occasionally, the colors are reversed, but it can always be found at the bottom right, dwarfed by a client-commissioned creation. Even before I talked with Kevin, there was a connection to Gus. I'd notice his name—sometimes in person and other times while reviewing the photographs on my computer screen. There's a certain flair to his work, and even on signs where there was no signature, I'd often pause and wonder: "Was that Gus?" It's odd to call him by his first name as if we knew each other well enough to sidestep formality. Our paths couldn't have crossed, as Gus passed away in 1969, twenty years before I was born. Artistic creations always have a personal touch, though. You can look at a painting and see the way an artist grazed the canvas. You can look at images and glean what the photographer must have felt while shooting. Gus's work was commercially driven rather than fueled by artistic inspiration, but nevertheless, a piece of him still exists on the brick walls in the works he created. He takes on complex shapes—like the outline of the contiguous United States. There are imperfections, but you only notice them up close. There's particular attention to detail with script writing, and the lettering is always shadowed just right, allowing words to pop even after all these years. Looking at his work, you try to sense what Gus might have been thinking while painting. How close did he consult with a client before painting? How many ideas came up in the moment as he sat on a scaffold in the summer heat? How often did he need to step back and look at his work fully? Did he ever drive around town, checking up on how his pieces were holding up in the days, months or years following their creation?

Before Gus's name was imprinted beneath signs across the region, he was a house painter. After losing his job at the onset of the Great Depression in 1929, he went into business for himself. For Gus, the work was fitting. He was a third-generation painter. His own grandfather Gustav was an emigrant from Germany, a fresco artist by trade. He passed his talents down to his son Arnold, who adapted landscape works of rural country scenes into wall advertisements for the H.H. Meyer Meat Packing Co. "There used to be one on the side of a butcher shop in Northside," says Kevin, recalling one of his great-grandfather's meatpacking murals. "But I haven't looked in fifteen years."

Kirby Avenue is a quiet street not far from the main drag of the Northside neighborhood. Virginia Avenue connects right where a row of houses meet. The house on the end features a northern-facing wall aimed at the street—the perfect place for an advertisement. The doors are locked, the windows dusty and rubbish is strewn about inside. An old sign hangs above, advertising a deli and carryout that has been closed for some time. The entire structure is wrapped in peeling white paint that flakes off and falls to the ground with even the slightest touch. Something can be seen, though—a few letters here and there that imply the word "beer." If this was, in fact, the building that once featured Arnold's mural, it is now buried underneath the work of another painter and the crumbling white flakes on top of that. While Arnold's fresco is gone, his son Gus's work remains elsewhere, helping to preserve his family's legacy.

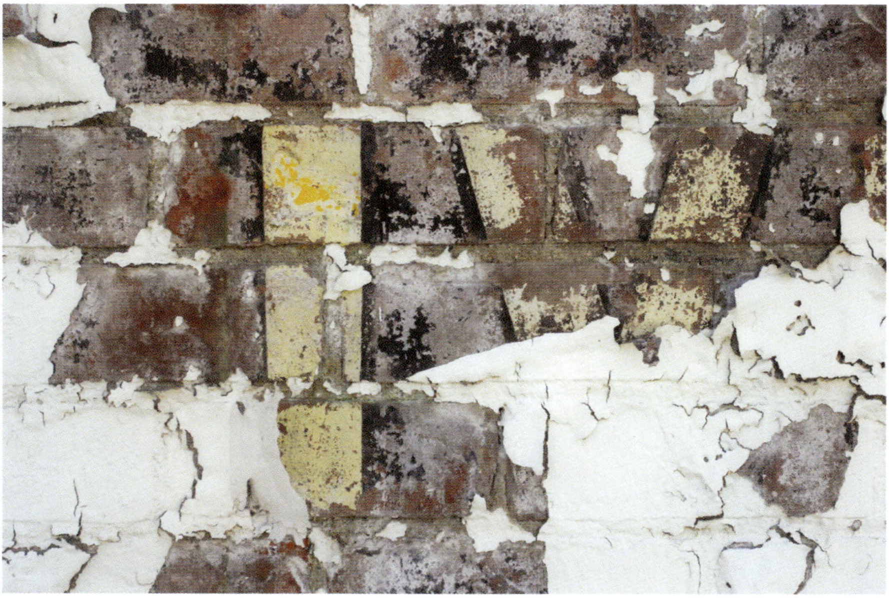

At the building thought to once feature a fresco-style advertisement by Arnold Holthaus, only another sign's few letters remain beneath layers of chipping white paint. *Photo by Ronny Salerno.*

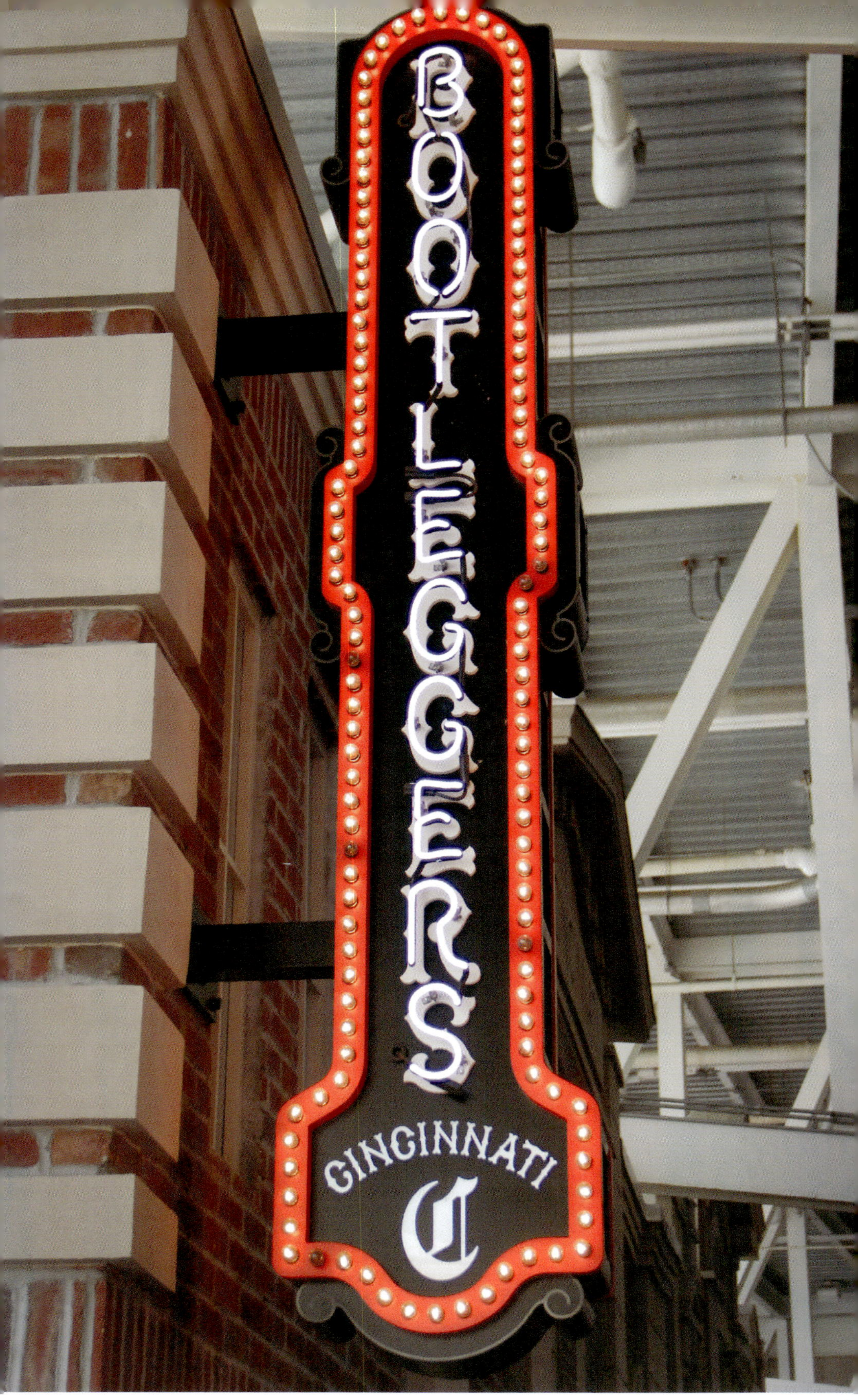
BOOTLEGGERS
CINCINNATI
C

Kevin began working in his grandfather's shop when he was in the seventh grade. He started spending his weekends and summers there in 1965, sweeping up the place. Twenty years later, Kevin became president of the company, adapting new technology as it became available. Zoning laws have changed and so have economics. Businesses want more advertising per square footage, and Holthaus Lackner signs has been offering just that. You won't find a signature in the corner anymore, like on Gus's work, but you'll find hundreds of examples in the company's portfolio and across the region. Nevertheless, Kevin certainly has an appreciation for his grandfather's work and style.

Great American Ballpark is the seventh incarnation of a home for the Cincinnati Reds, professional baseball's oldest team. Having opened in 2003, Kevin says that approximately 97 percent of the ballpark's signage was done by his company. There's team branding, directions to concessions, glowing marquees for the gift shop and a quote—"Rounding Third and Heading for Home," the sign-off phrase of legendary Reds player and broadcaster Joe Nuxhall—illuminated in glowing red letters on the ballpark's façade facing the city. The Reds organization was awarded hosting duties for an All-Star game set to take place in 2015. When the event's logo was unveiled, the team sought out Holthaus before it pulled back the curtain to reveal a massive sign mounted on the lights in right field. As other improvements came to the park, Kevin's company sought to use a nostalgic twist, a throwback to the days of wall paintings. Atop the smokehouse, one of the ballpark's concession stands, there's script lettering advertising Ole Smoky Tennessee Moonshine. The sign can be seen only when looking down from the ballpark's upper deck. It's a nice detail, an imitation of a bygone form of advertising, but the strongest nods to the hand-painted legacy are found deeper within the stadium. For the 2015 season and the approaching All-Star game, the team debuted a new attraction known as Bootleggers. The new beer stand was themed to look like an early twentieth-century gin joint, with several local brews on tap. Holthaus Lackner manufactured the glowing, vintage-style sign out front, but the best details can be found on the stand's brick walls. Flying pigs donning Reds baseball caps have been created here, done with the same detail and refined paint skills that Gus originally used to launch his company. They're more than just a "throwback" or "retro" design; they're

Opposite: Designed by Holthaus Lackner, the entrance sign to Great American Ballpark's Bootleggers bar features a retro flair. *Photo by Ronny Salerno.*

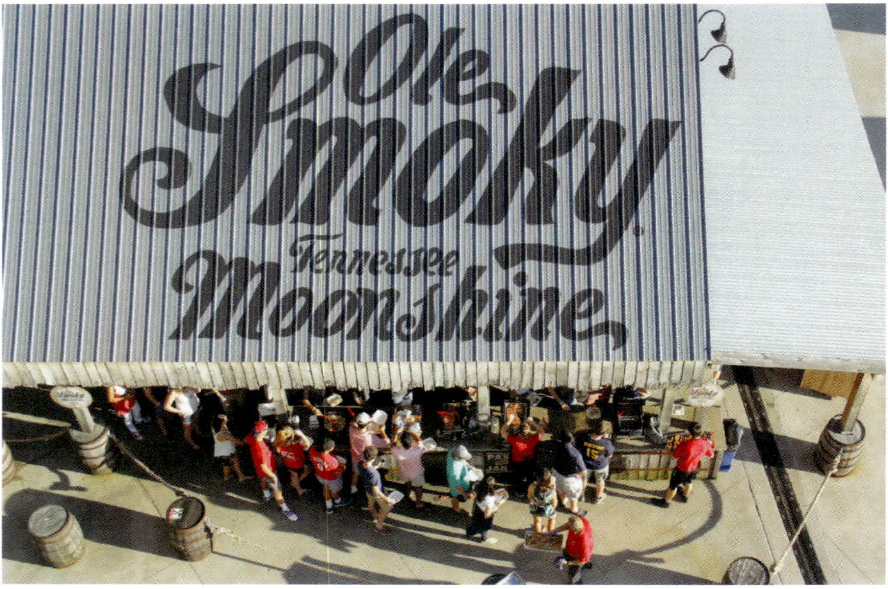

Painted script for Ole Smoky Tennessee Moonshine adorns this concession stand at Great American Ballpark. This feature was designed by Holthaus to evoke the nostalgic flair of hand-painted signs and can be seen only when looking down from one of the park's upper decks. *Photo by Ronny Salerno.*

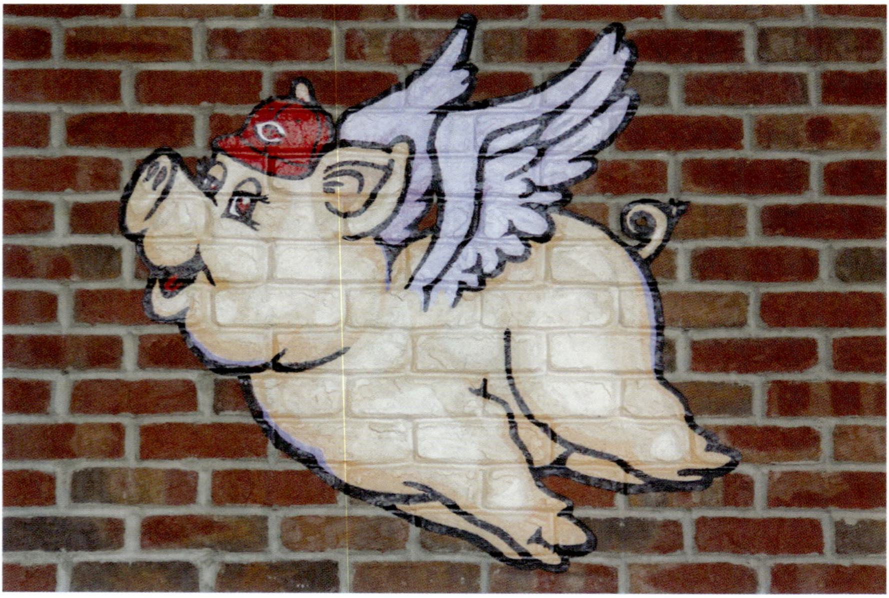

A hand-painted "flying pig" donning a Cincinnati Reds ball cap adorns the brickwork outside the Bootleggers bar. This feature was produced to give the bar its vintage feel and at the same time honors the sign-painting history behind the designs. *Photo by Ronny Salerno.*

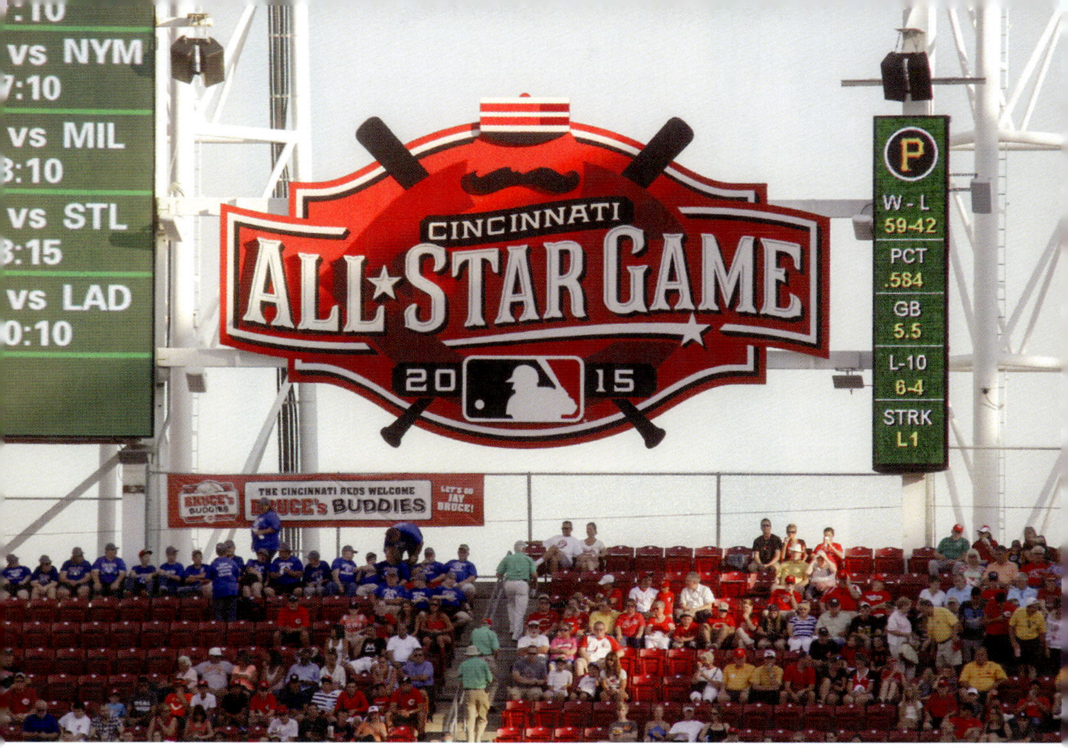

At the end of the 2014 Major League Baseball season, the Cincinnati Reds unveiled the logo for the following year's All-Star game, which they would be hosting. Designed by Holthaus Lackner, the sign is a dominating presence within the ballpark. *Photo by Ronny Salerno.*

an acknowledgement of history. The flying pig represents the city's "Flying Pig" marathon and nickname of "Porkopolis," while the handiwork behind their creation harkens back to the sign painters of days past. Kevin was in attendance for the All-Star game, sitting in a ballpark that's filled with his work and inspired by those who came before him. "I felt like an ambassador of the city," he says.

I had been searching for signs all over the city and started to instinctively look for Gus's signature, searching for proof that he had been there. His hand-painted works have a lifespan, and one day, despite how long they've held on to this point, they'll be gone. Whether they're covered up, knocked down, painted over or simply left alone, eventually they'll fade and be only memories like Arnold's mural. But Kevin and his family have kept the legacy alive in a different way. That's evident when you walk through the ballpark's mezzanine and look out above the right field stands, viewing the All-Star game logo. "It's a family legacy," says Kevin. "It's very fulfilling to look back and see where we're headed. It's a neat journey." There's also part of Gus there, memorialized in the fresh paint above a beer stand that evokes the city's history while at the same time honoring him. The Reds could be eliminated from the post season, barely staying out of the cellar in the league's standings, but as you grab your beer, you'll pass beneath a tribute to Gus, a small detail that most fans probably miss or ignore in the same way they do the fading advertisements around the city. From the walls of buildings to a modern ballpark and the legacy of his family, Gus's memory exists beyond the signature, and his legacy is worth tipping your glass to.

6

THE NEIGHBORHOODS

Cincinnati is composed of fifty-two individual neighborhoods. They each have their own reputations, identities and histories. You'll find them as you venture out of the downtown basin and into the dense neighborhoods, steep hills or streets along the river. Unlike the suburban communities and cross-border Kentucky cities that are often casually described as "Greater Cincinnati," these fifty-two geographic areas make up the actual city borders. In their diversity, they form a singular entity: the Queen City. They hold political and economic power, shaping the larger entity that created them. Across several of them, there are faded advertisements to be found that reflect their past, their stories, their personalities and their people.

There's Over-the-Rhine (OTR), where German immigrants created the name because the canal separating their neighborhood from downtown reminded them of the Rhine River. There's Clifton, a cultural hotbed of uptown that also houses the city's university; the East End, with its airport and curve along the Ohio River; East Price Hill, combining with the West and Lower variants as bastions of Roman Catholic heritage; the West End, a mixture of industry and population density that has been transformed by the highway built through it; Brighton, a quiet place where industrial buildings have become street art canvases; Evanston, where the affluent O'Bryonville business district still allows local history to shine through; Walnut Hills, home of the city's art museum; East Walnut Hills, where the ethnic and economic backgrounds are as diverse

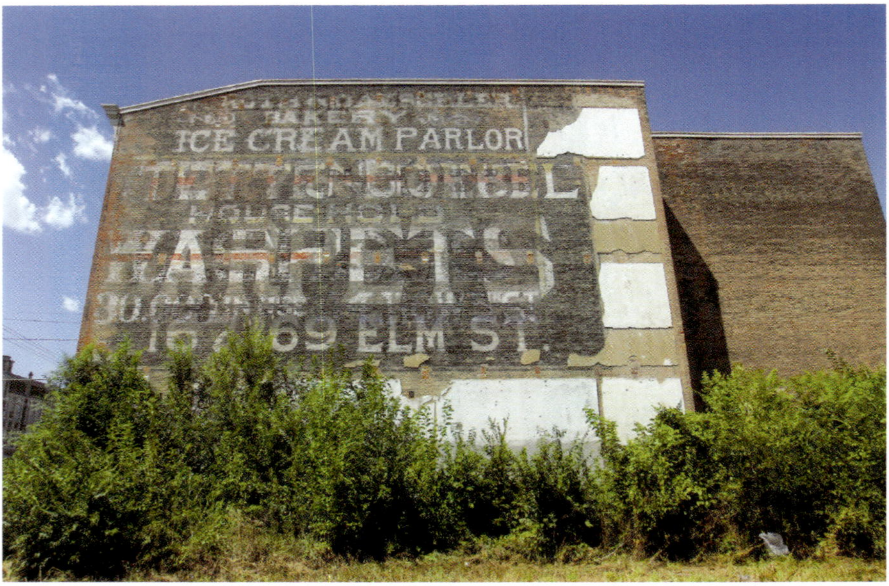

As the concrete chips and falls off the side of this brick building in the West End, several overlapping painted advertisements can be seen mentioning a bakery, an ice cream parlor, carpets and an address. *Photo by Ronny Salerno.*

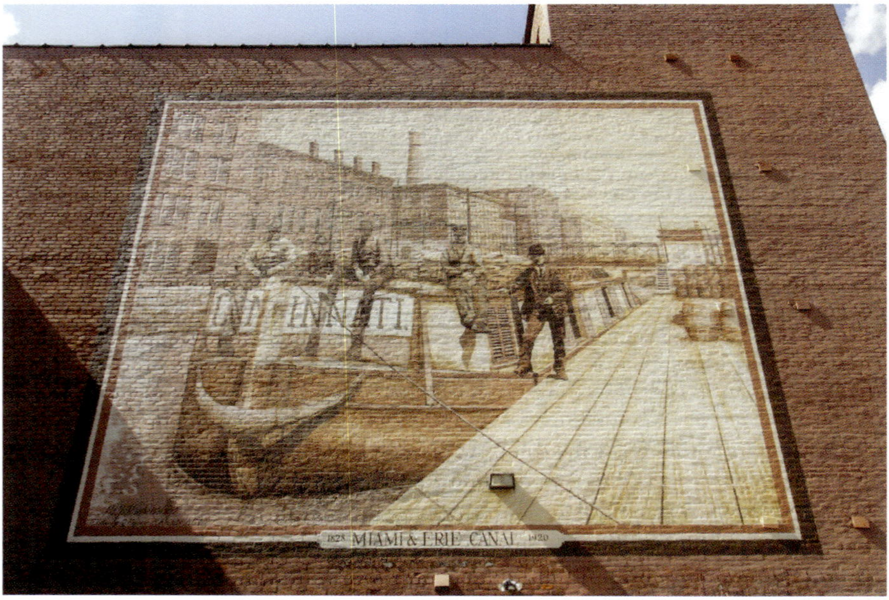

A mural at the edge of the city's Over-the-Rhine neighborhood depicts the canal that once separated the neighborhood from downtown. Resident German immigrants developed the neighborhood's name after jokingly referring to this canal as the Rhine River. *Photo by Ronny Salerno.*

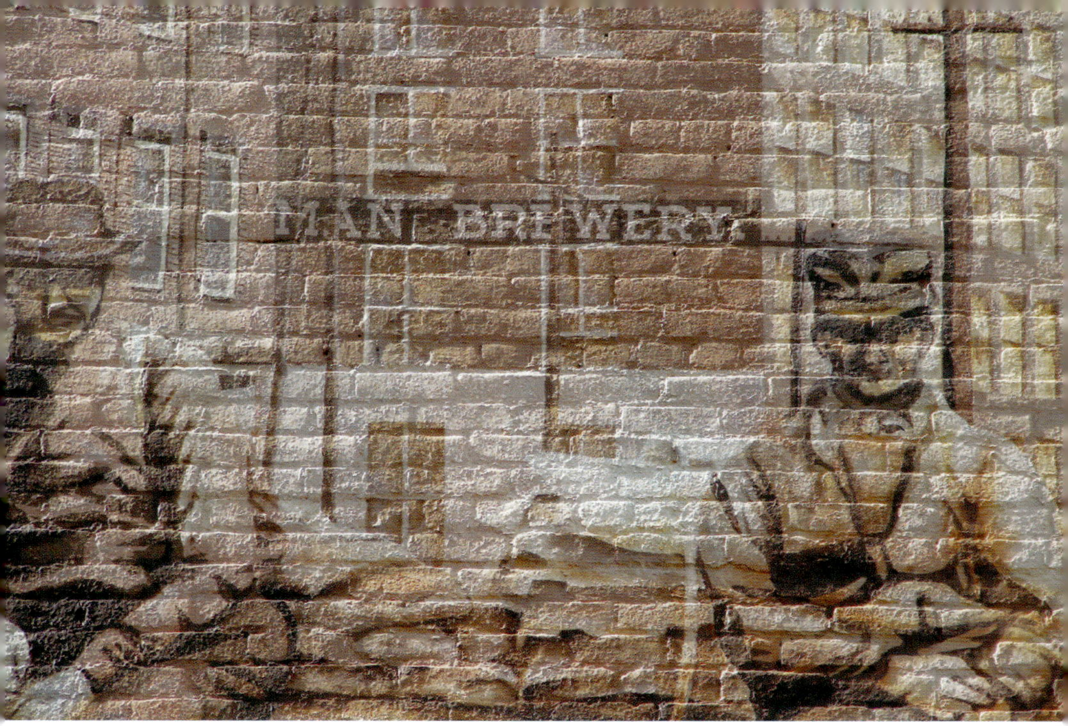

Above: A detail of the Over-the-Rhine mural depicts a hand-painted sign within a hand-painted mural. *Photo by Ronny Salerno.*

Below: Hanging over boarded-up doors barred by a padlock and chains, these hand-painted letters once signified a business's entrance. *Photo by Ronny Salerno.*

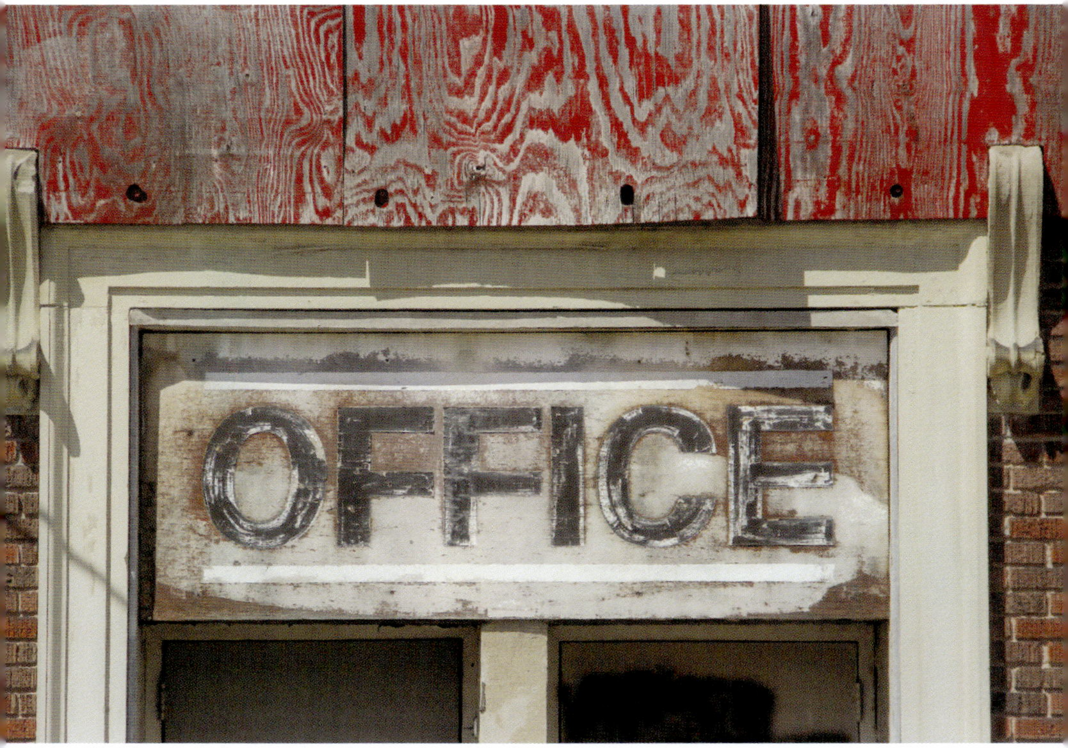

as the historic architecture; and Westwood, the neighborhood that quite possibly defines the city's "west side."

These particular neighborhoods are just a fraction, a sliver of the multiple identities that make up the city. Hidden among their buildings and down their streets are more of Cincinnati's fading advertisements. Featuring both national and local businesses, these signs help to tell the story of Cincinnati in a similar fashion to how the neighborhoods themselves shape it.

Elm Industries (Over-the-Rhine)

An advertisement of the former Elm Industries overlooking an empty lot is one of the gateways to the southern half of Over-the-Rhine on Race Street. Directly across from a streetcar stop, the painting encompasses nearly the entire side of a building that could one day be revitalized by the transit system's ushering in of new development. The statement is simple and to the point. Bold, black letters declare the business's various specialties in contrast to the more ornate advertisements found across the city. Yet even in its simplicity, the sign still has quirks and clues. A phone number near the bottom is painted in a different font over fresher white paint. Despite this updated feature, the number leads to a recorded "your call can not be completed as dialed" message. Aside from the phone number, one other feature stands out among the list of services offered: a detail of ornate, ironwork bars, an example of the company's product that can be placed over windows for security purposes. This part of the sign seems to imply that Elm Industries' products may have been more detailed than its advertising while at the same time reflecting the sign's previous host, "Elm Window," a name that can still be made out behind and beneath that of Elm Industries.

The Marburg Hotel (Clifton)

The picturesque, four-story brick building doesn't seem all that much different from the other residences and apartment buildings lining Ludlow Avenue near the University of Cincinnati. What probably once brightly stood out among the red bricks is now a faded, light shade of yellow with three simple words atop the building: "The Marburg Hotel."

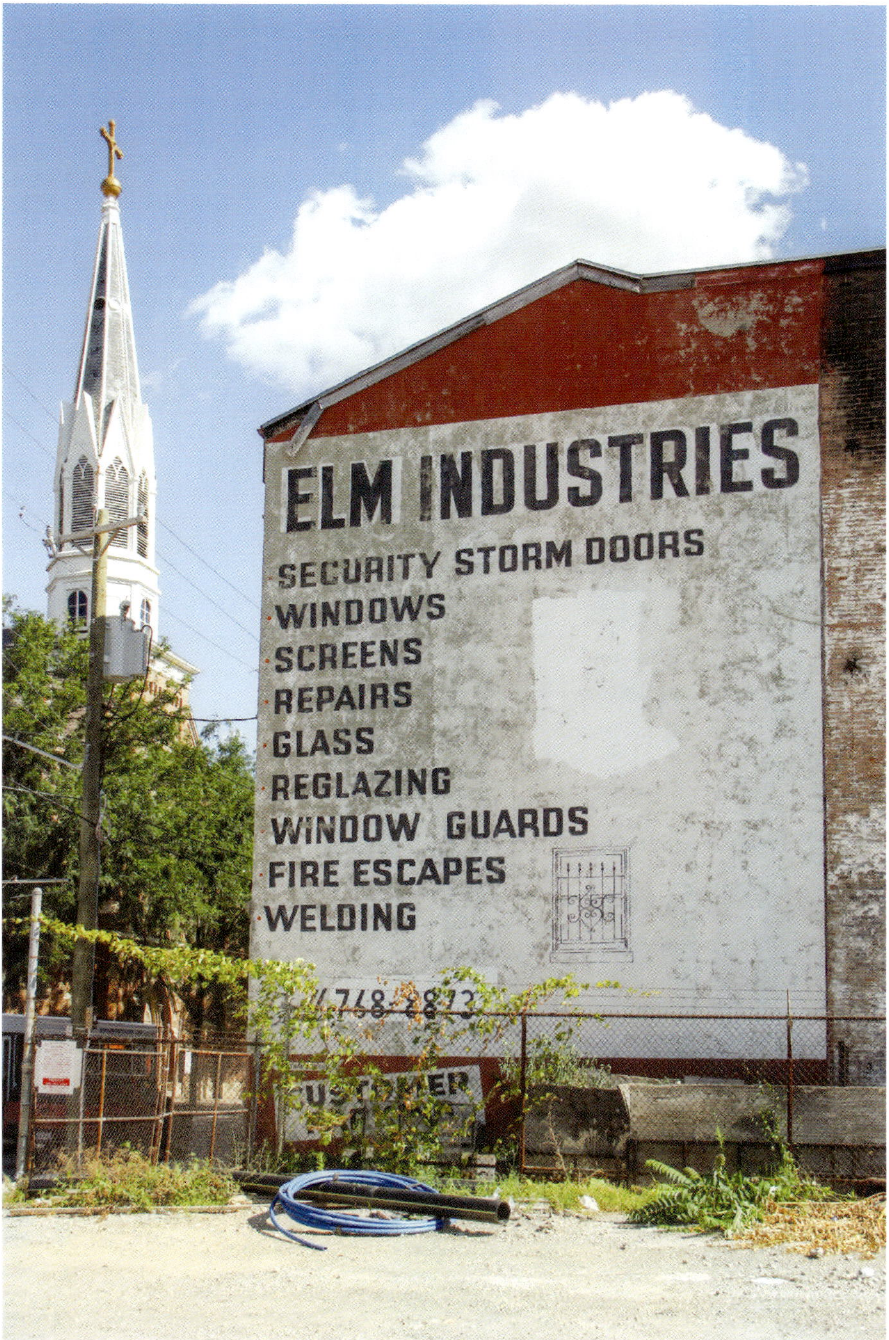

The sign for Elm Industries straightforwardly states the company's services in a monotone composition. One detail—a small painting of a window—contrasts the otherwise bland sign. *Photo by Ronny Salerno.*

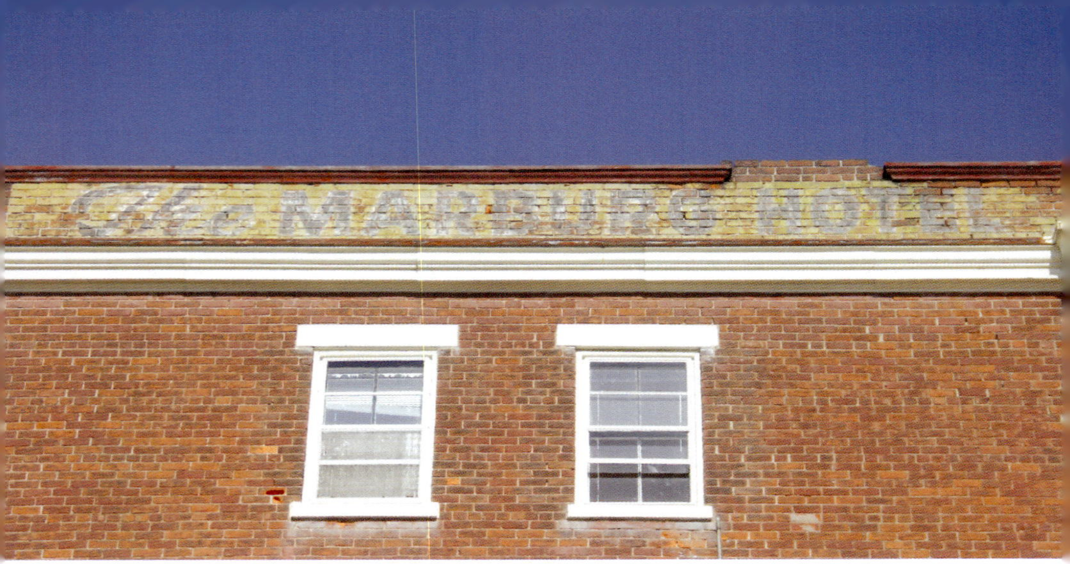

The Marburg Hotel would eventually become a University of Cincinnati dorm and then privately owned apartments. All the while, the former business's name has stood on the bricks. *Photo by Ronny Salerno.*

This particular structure shares a connection, besides proximity, to the nearby university.

The Marburg Hotel was built in 1900 in the city's Clifton neighborhood. Fifty-eight years later, the building was purchased by the University of Cincinnati to accommodate a large demand for student housing. The university quickly renovated the building into a women-only dorm and had it ready by the fall of 1960. In a series of letters sent to the University of Cincinnati's magazine, former students recounted how they heard rumors of the hotel being a place of "ill repute," claiming truck drivers would still honk as they passed in the night. Nevertheless, students seem to recall Ludlow Hall favorably, nostalgically noting that their rooms were often more spacious than those of their on-campus counterparts. Ludlow transitioned into a men's dorm and eventually received a basement ping pong table as well as a renovation in 1968. The "ladies of Ludlow" returned when things eventually switched back to women only.

The Marburg's transformation into forty-two rooms that housed approximately seventy-eight students temporarily helped the university meet the increasing demand. It was a quick fix to accommodate overflow students and late applicants. Despite having some advantages over traditional dorms, the off-campus location of the building presented challenges. Students had to be given free bus fare to use the city's transit system to get to class if they didn't want a long walk. The location would eventually no longer be a concern as the university constructed new dormitories, including the thirteen-floor, eight-hundred-occupant Calhoun Hall in 1967. According to the university,

Ludlow Hall was sold off in 1974, while county records show the Marburg Hotel Co. purchasing the property in 1970.

In the years since, as the university has grown exponentially, it's now just a little closer to the dormitory its students once reached by bus. The Marburg building is a private apartment complex today. It still houses students, with rooms available for rent along a tree-lined street across from a park. Although no longer a hotel, the Marburg name lives on in the form of the "Marburg Collective," a community of local artists and musicians who use the building as a venue and creative space in addition to a residence.

Queen City Flying Service (East End)

The main airport in and out of the Cincinnati metro area is known as "CVG," the reporting code typically found on airline baggage, which means: "Cincinnati/Northern Kentucky International Airport." As the name implies, the airport serves Cincinnati but is located across state lines in Kentucky. CVG rose out of a World War II–era training facility and began receiving commercial flights in 1947. By the modern era, CVG had become a hub for Delta airlines, and despite an often tumultuous airline industry, it remains today as the region's primary

The name Queen City Flying Service can still be found painted on a hangar at Lunken Airport. The building previously housed the company's fleet of charter aircraft. *Photo by Ronny Salerno.*

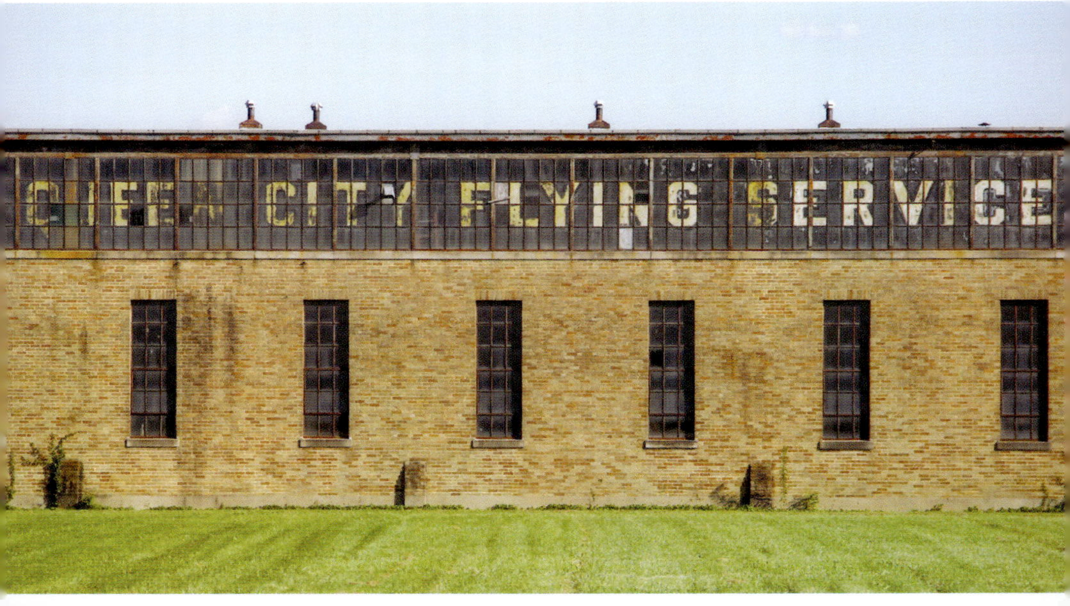

domestic airport, as well as the only international one. For Cincinnati, though, this was never the intended plan.

Lunken Airport sits on the city's east side. It opened in 1925, had a visit from Charles Lindbergh in 1927 and was completely under water ten years later. As the Ohio River reached twenty-five feet higher than flood stage, Cincinnati suffered the river's worst wrath in recorded history. Downtown streets were flooded, thousands were left displaced and the municipal airport was completely submerged, along with the baseball stadium. While the 1937 flood had been a disaster necessitating federal relief, Lunken was prone to water and fog issues even at lower river levels. Hesitations over the airport's proximity to the river and a lack of public investment gave CVG the upper hand. Commercial flights began heading there instead.

CVG hadn't gotten away with an overnight coup d'état, though. Lunken held on to a few commercial flights from airlines like TWA and an ambitious upstart company called Midwest Airways. Midwest had been the dream of Ebby Lunken, who, along with his head stewardess/eventual wife, Martha, got the airline and its four Lockheed propeller aircraft going in the early 1960s. Ebby had launched Midwest after he and a friend purchased Queen City Flying Service, a preexisting charter business whose name was emblazoned with paint on its hangar's windows. Midwest lasted a few years but struggled and eventually was relegated from a regional carrier to just straight charter service. Lunken's wife, Martha, would go on to start her own flight school at the airport as commercial flights ceased; meanwhile, CVG had become the dominant airline travel hub.

Today, Lunken is still quite active. A five-mile path around the perimeter gives recreationists plenty of space for cycling and running. There's a nearby golf course, too, and at anytime an aircraft can come quickly buzzing overhead. Local corporations maintain their private jets there, helicopter tours can be rented, flying lessons can be purchased and private pilots house their aircraft on the large tarmac. Ultimate Air Shuttle offers public charter flights often, the closest thing Lunken has to an active airline at the facility. Every now and then, rumors abound of national discount carriers coming in. Nothing ever seems to come of it, though, as locals draft letters to the paper reminding everyone about the noise ordinances. On hangar 3, the name of Queen City Flying Service remains. Queen City was founded by Lawrence Maxwell Schmidlapp, a man who had once won an air race between Miami, Key West and Havana. The paint used to proclaim his company's name predates his company's acquisition and Midwest Airways' bold plan but also outlived it.

A Super Cure (East Price Hill)

There's an intersection on the city's west side, one of many where you have to put your full faith in the traffic signals to know that you're truly allowed to make a wide, sweeping turn in front of so many stopped vehicles. A remnant of city planners past, this type of intersection is bordered by several indications of a neighborhood's ever-changing appearance. There's a large Kroger supermarket complete with a gas station and several spaces to accommodate hundreds of cars should it ever need to. The China Island restaurant sits on a parking lot peninsula jutting into the intersection and accommodating a bus stop. St. Lawrence, a Gothic-style Roman Catholic church, is nearby with its iconic spires dating back to their completion in 1894. Just down the block, past an empty lot and a patch of grass, there's a quaint three-story brick building. Sitting at the corner, it begins a string of similar buildings that continue down the avenue in historical contrast to the supermarket across the street. Some buildings have empty storefronts, others have been converted into Hispanic groceries, a few feature rolling garage doors and the three-story anchor is home to a discount cellular phone store. Despite so many buildings adapting to accommodate changing demographics and modern retail, one thing remains to tie it all in to a past life.

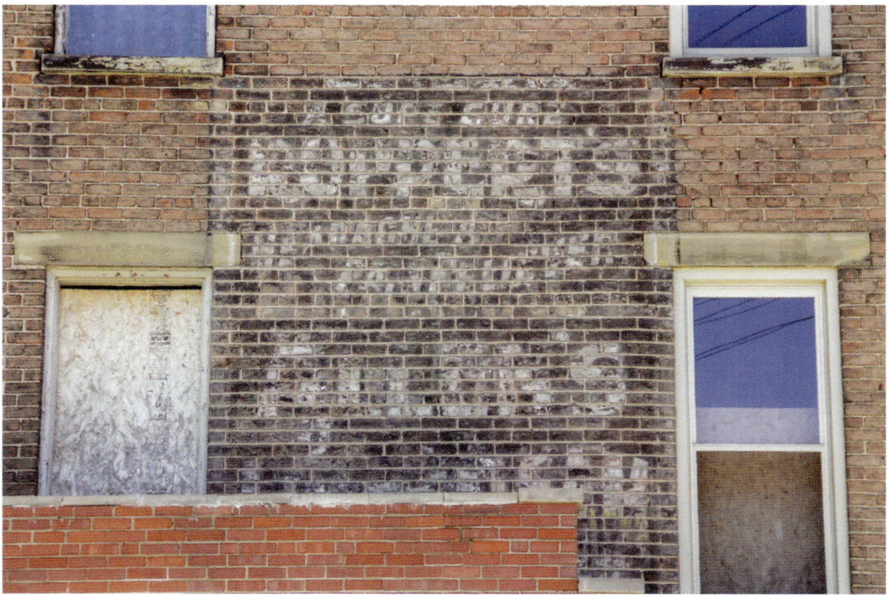

An ad for Roppert's Headache and Pain Relief touts the product as "A Sure Cure" near the top. Recognizable as a fading advertisement from the street, the letters and words become legible only when given a detailed look. *Photo by Ronny Salerno.*

On the red brick wall, completely exposed to the setting western sun, is a patch of black. It's obvious that it once was a sign, but the words can't be seen unless you take the time to really go up and look at them. Even then, a newer addition to the building partially blocks what's left of the faded words. You can step back, get up close, zoom in with a camera and dissect the image in Photoshop, and one phrase is certain: "A Sure Cure." A few more words flowing in the middle of the composition read, "Headache & Pain Relief." The other words seem too far gone to identify, but one of them might be "Roppert's." Was Roppert a proprietor of a previous business? Someone who offered his own headache remedy? One thing's for sure: the brand won't be found among the aisles of pills in the modern grocery store across the street.

A Tale of Two Hardware Signs (East Price Hill)

Meyer Hardware sits in a three-story building with a storefront quintessential of nostalgic America. Among the window signs advertising key copying, bed bug remedies and other hardware supplies is one that reads, "Proud to Be an

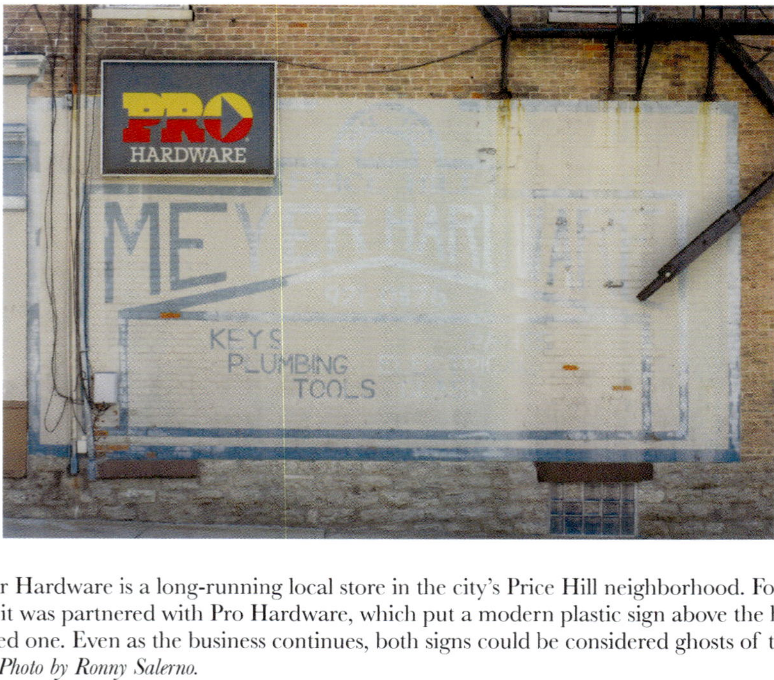

Meyer Hardware is a long-running local store in the city's Price Hill neighborhood. For a time, it was partnered with Pro Hardware, which put a modern plastic sign above the hand-painted one. Even as the business continues, both signs could be considered ghosts of the past. *Photo by Ronny Salerno.*

American," crowned with a waving fifty-star flag. The side of the building features two signs, one painted and nearly a full story high. It fades more as you look left to right, white paint mixed with the rust stains of the fire escapes above it. It proudly proclaims, "Meyer Hardware," with the business's home neighborhood of Price Hill displayed above it. The electrical wires running down the side of the building also received a coat of paint when the sign was made. In what would seem a sign of changing times, there's a modern and plastic "Pro Hardware" fixture placed over the hand-painted one, evoking how the local establishment once came to be under a national chain.

The Denver, Colorado–based PRO Group is a cooperative of retailers and distributors across the United States. Like many local hardware stores, Meyer seemed to join the PRO Group chain while retaining some independence. The partnership with PRO has ended, though, with Meyer returning to its independent status. In a twist, the only "ghost sign" on the side is the modern, plastic, backlit "PRO" symbol. The faded paint beneath it reflects a local mainstay still alive in the neighborhood.

Little Kings (West End)

Little Kings Cream Ale returned in 2009, just before I turned twenty-one. It was perfect timing. The seven-ounce bottles were sold in traditional six packs, as well as in cases featuring twelve or twenty-four of the distinctive green containers. Little Kings started becoming staples at parties my friends and I would attend. They were cheap, and even though they were physically small, they packed a punch with 5.5 percent alcohol by volume. Taste is subjective, and while it may not be the best beverage, it's definitely far from the worst. Not that you care when you're in the heat of a "Little Kings Race" with your roommate on a Saturday night. "You can still get 'Green Meanies'?" remarked a neighbor once as my roommates and I joined her on the elevator, each with a twenty-four case under our arms. She seemed surprised that the brand had returned but not that we planned to consume a copious amount.

Cream ale is considered a truly American form of beer, typically light in color, that gained a popular following after Prohibition ended. Little Kings debuted in 1958, a staple of the local Hudepohl-Schoenling Brewing Company. Around town, the beer was among local favorites, leading to advertising campaigns such as the one still holding on near Central Parkway.

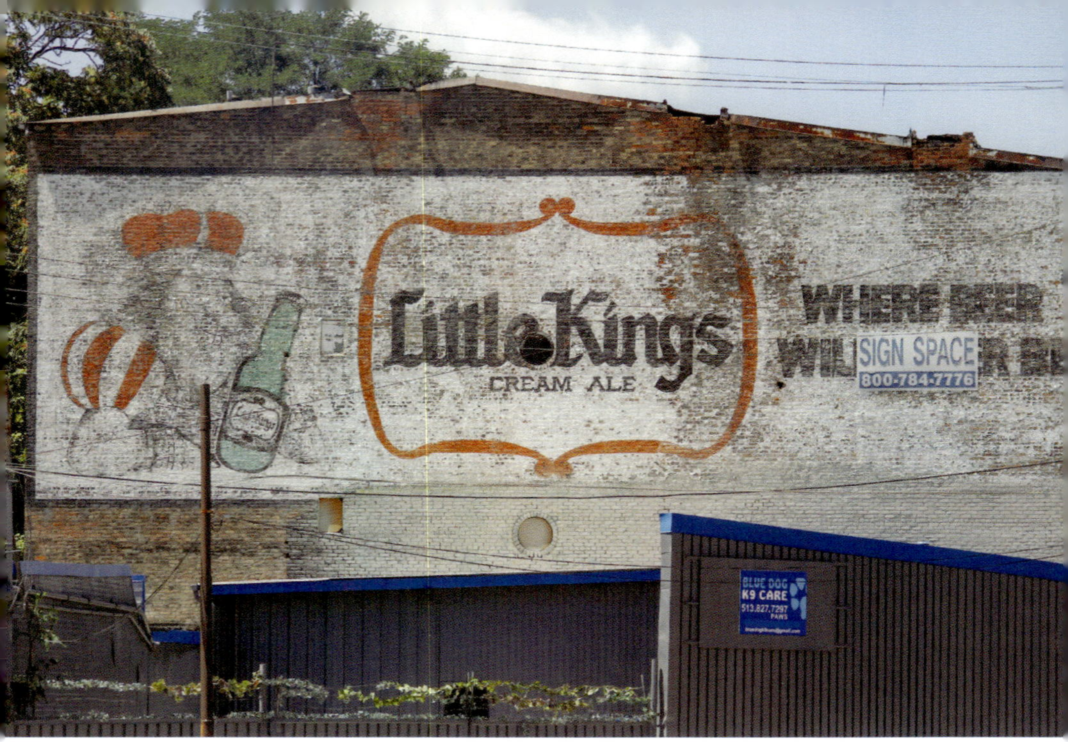

Little Kings Cream Ale has made a comeback along with several other local brands in recent years. This advertisement above Central Parkway reflects the drink's first incarnation. Its subsequent deterioration reflects the beverage's initial disappearance. *Photo by Ronny Salerno.*

The faded image of the king mascot grasping the green bottle and the partially obscured proclamation of "Where Beer Will Never Be" are examples of the beverage's vintage advertising. Nowadays, Little Kings still comes in its signature green bottles, as well as cans, although with slightly updated branding. It's one of many local brands that was purchased and consolidated under a revived Christian Moerlin brand and given a fresh makeover while retaining some hints of its older design style. The sign overlooking Central Parkway, one of the city's main thoroughfares, isn't proclaiming a business of days gone by. Rather, it's the older logo, the old catchphrase, a "retro" advertisement. While commissioned by different owners in years past, the advertisement works for the new guys in a way, even if the smiling face of a libation-touting king has faded.

Decorators Wall Paper Co. (Brighton)

There's a street of buildings in the city's Brighton neighborhood tucked just below the lanes of Central Parkway, the road that sits atop the city's never-completed subway system tunnels. A stop for that subway would have been located just a block away had it been completed, potentially shaping the neighborhood into something different than it's become. There's a mix of industrial buildings and locked storefronts advertising "insert your faith here" types of churches. The gritty buildings mesh with maintained residences all sitting below the hill that houses the university. This particular row of buildings has become a canvas. Murals and graffiti often complement the overgrowth of weeds and trees from the sidewalks. Brighton, just below the street and next to the forgotten subway tunnels, is a gallery of street art, often ignored by those a little wary of the neighborhood's tougher-looking exterior. Whereas graffiti are often viewed as a sign of nuisance and vandalism elsewhere, in Brighton, they're a sign of creativity among the neighborhood's grit.

One mural is particularly striking. It's a red-hued landscape featuring trees that have seemingly industrial pipes in place of branches. Alien-like figures descend from the sky and clutch barrels among waves of designs and color that would probably make both M.C. Escher and the members of Pink Floyd proud. The piece extends the entire side of the building aside from a rolling garage door, left untouched but used as another artist's canvas. At the

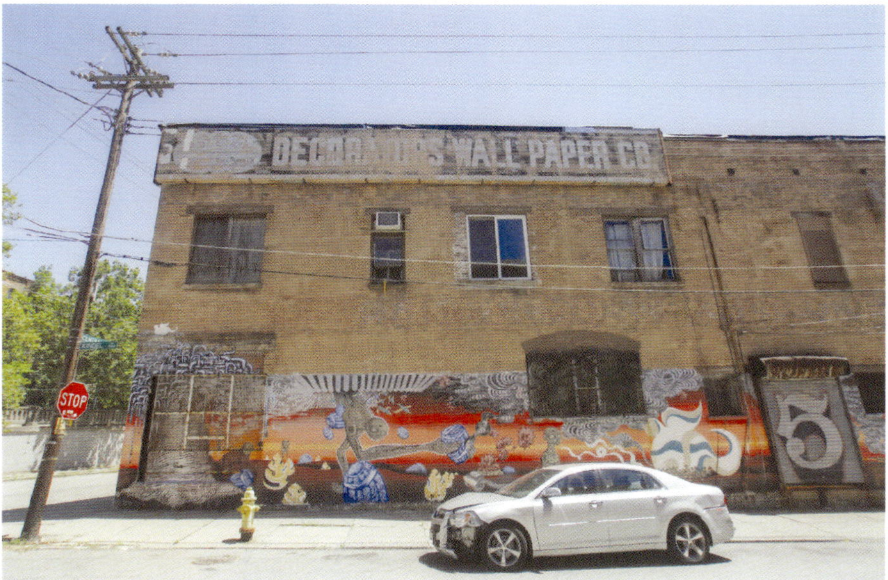

In the neighborhood of Brighton, this building's walls have become a canvas for street artists. Meanwhile, the name of Decorators Wall Paper Co. still remains painted at the top in a somewhat ironic twist. *Photo by Ronny Salerno.*

top of the building is a fading advertisement for Decorators Wallpaper Co., a business that was either never registered or left so long ago that there's no historic Yellow Pages listing or registry with the Better Business Bureau. No matter what became of the wallpaper proprietors, their remaining sign still works with the building's current state as artists decorate its walls.

Patented Tobacco (Brighton)

As a kid, I can remember the advertisements at Riverfront Stadium/ Cinergy Field, the ballpark where I grew up seeing the Reds play. For a time, there was a large "Channel 5 WLWT" logo hanging up that would rotate into other advertisements. There was also a large Marlboro ad, adorned in red and white echoing the popular cigarette brand casually called "Reds" and "Cowboy Killers." As I grew up, the tobacco companies were forced out of advertising by both government and consumer reactions. To me, that Marlboro ad sticks out—a piece of the ballpark where I grew up watching America's pastime. To other generations, there's a different nostalgia associated with tobacco advertising. "Chew Mail Pouch tobacco" is a common theme found painted on barns all across America. Mail Pouch ads are a staple of the American countryside. You can find souvenirs of the branding in nostalgia-peddling gift shops at your local highway off-ramp Cracker Barrel. The tobacco brand has become synonymous with rural culture. On thousands of barns, the instructions to "treat yourself to the best" and "chew Mail Pouch tobacco" can be found. In some places, the painted ads fade like the ones seen in this book. In other locations, they've been restored in an attempt to harken back to a "simpler time."

In urban Cincinnati, though, a tobacco advertisement adorns a brick wall. It's a curious case. The black background paint disappears in a sloping line across the building with hardly any trace of the advertisement above this line. Perhaps another building once stood here, preserving most of the ad and allowing the exposed parts to fade off. It proclaims, "Cool, sweet smoke," an obvious nod to tobacco, while referencing a patent date of May 25, 1886. On that date, the United States Patent Office has records of U.S. citizen W.B. Farrar and British citizen J.J. Thornton patenting a new method for curing tobacco. It's not quite clear which brand or company their patent evolved into, and the most telling part of the sign has disappeared over the years. Nevertheless, this advertisement is an example

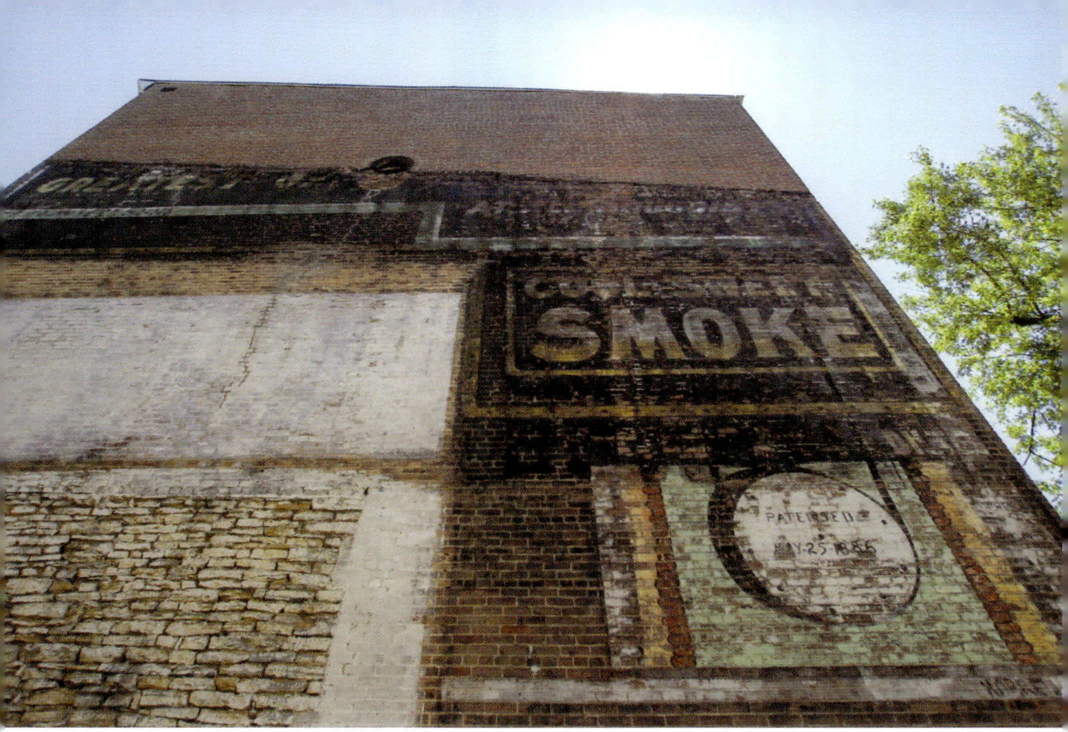

Above: A tobacco ad reads, "Cool, sweet smoke," along with a few other words and a statement claiming a patent on May 25, 1886. *Photo by Ronny Salerno.*

Below: On the front of the building housing the tobacco ad, traces of several colors of paint can still be seen, hinting that maybe there was once an advertisement here, too. *Photo by Ronny Salerno.*

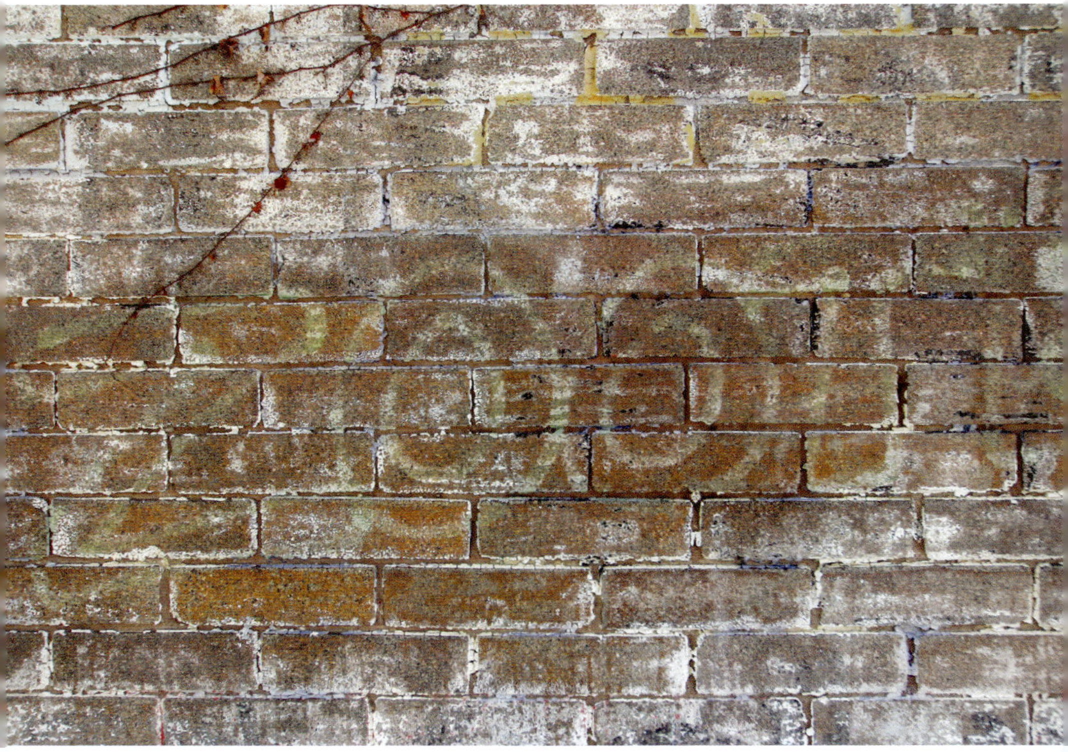

of tobacco-touting walls, a technique used by brands other than just Mail Pouch, although they may not have been as iconic or memorable or had their names preserved alongside country roads. On the front side of the building, traces of several paint colors can be seen. White, yellow and blue all seem to have once covered the brick. Like the name of a forgotten tobacco company, they seem to be gone as well.

Paramount Vodka (Over-the-Rhine)

Apparently, "anything goes" when Paramount Vodka is involved. Paramount may not be one of the more recognizable names on your local liquor store's shelf, but there's a good chance you've had it mixed into your "well drinks" on special. Reviewers don't seem to place Paramount in the upper echelons of vodka but don't put it down too hard either.

Despite three separate hand-painted ads around Cincinnati composed by the late Gus Holthaus, Paramount is local to Ohio but not the Queen City. Paramount distilleries was born out of Cleveland, five hours up the highway. According to a 2010 article by *Cleveland Scene* magazine, the distillery was responsible at the time for 10 percent of the state's liquor sales. Paramount offered liquor on a budget, its marquee products being flavored vodkas. You won't find Paramount held in the same regard as a name like Ketel One, but Newport, Kentucky's Party Source Liquor Store calls it "the perfect everyday vodka." Paramount Distillers Inc. purchased Meier's Wine Cellars of Cincinnati in 1976, bringing a production facility and presence to the Queen City, but its attempts to advertise vodka in the market seem to have faded with its signs. Although technically it still touts an active product, the bottle depicted isn't what you'll find on shelves today. The Germanic crest still exists but is now complemented by sleek blue packaging.

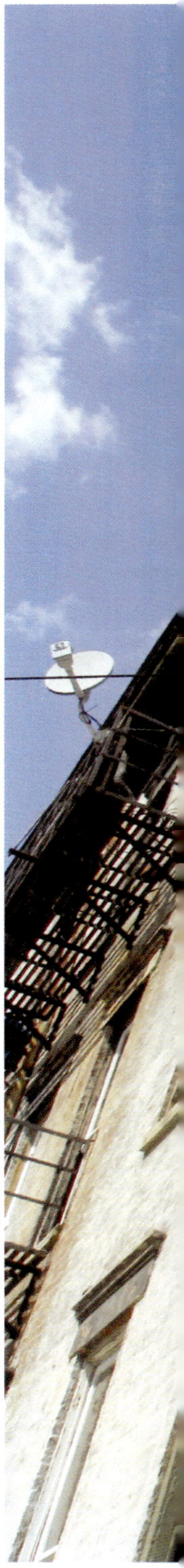

One of several fading Paramount Vodka ads touting the slogan: "anything goes." *Photo by Ronny Salerno.*

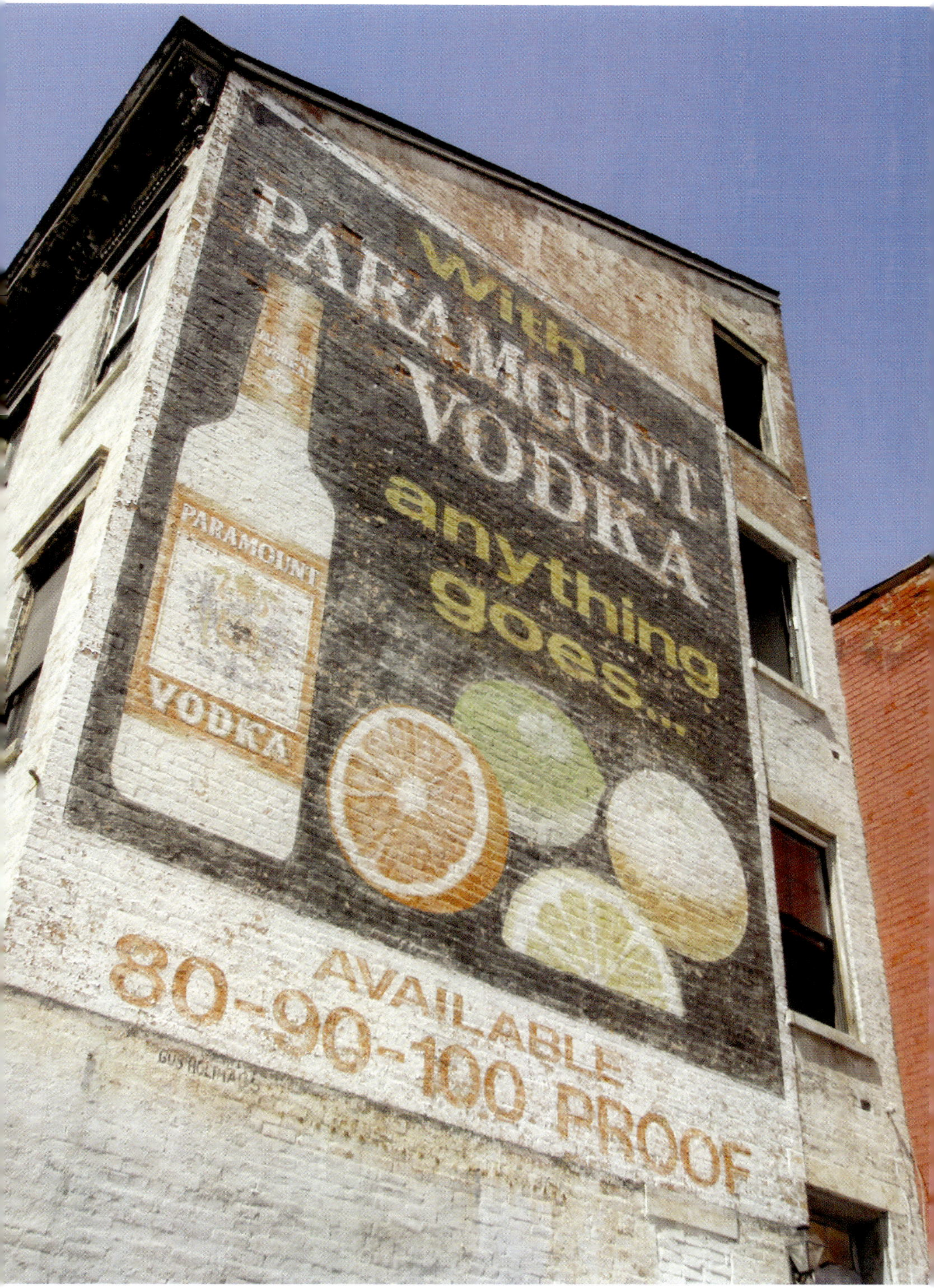
with
PARAMOUNT
VODKA
anything
goes...
PARAMOUNT
VODKA
AVAILABLE
80-90-100 PROOF

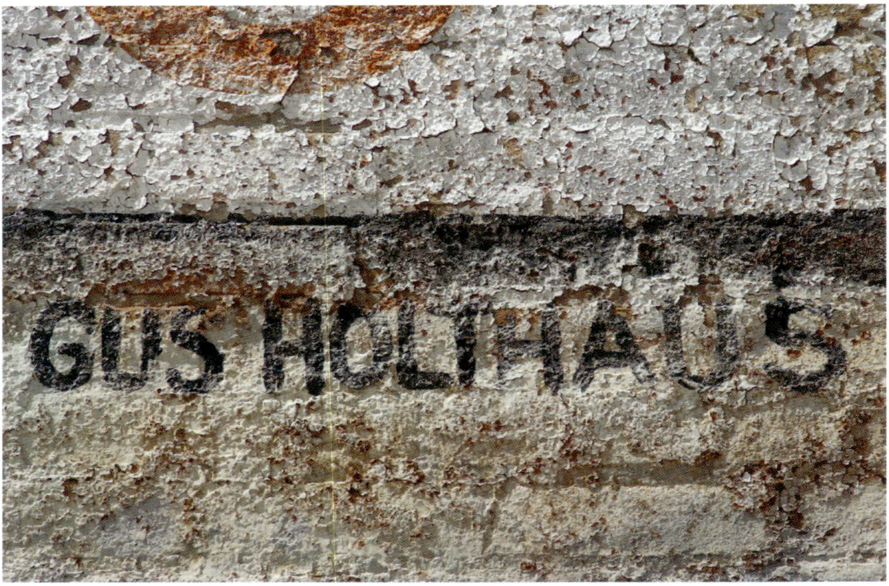

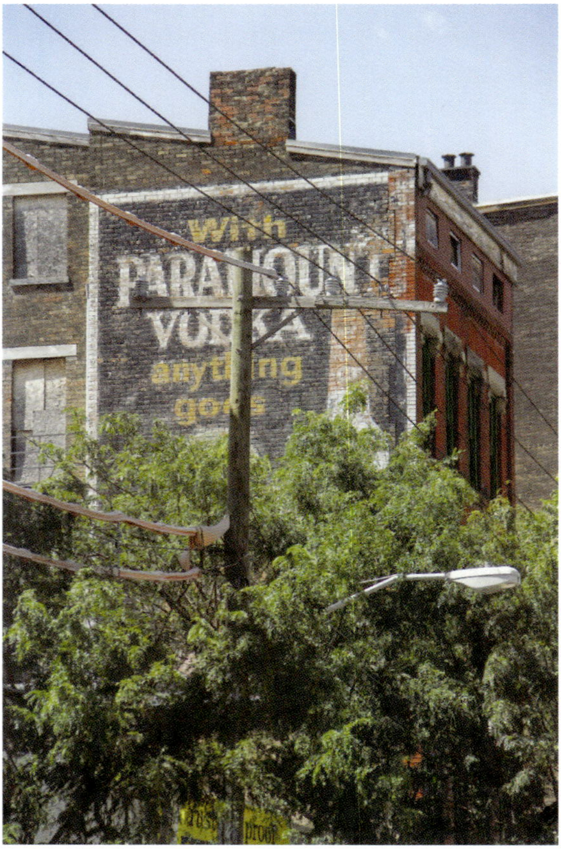

Above: The signature of Gus Holthaus as seen inscribed beneath an ad for Paramount Vodka. *Photo by Ronny Salerno.*

Left: Peering over trees and from behind electrical wires, this Paramount Vodka advertisement would have once been prominently seen by passing vehicles. *Photo by Ronny Salerno.*

In 2011, St. Louis–based Luxco Inc. purchased Paramount Distillers Inc. It has kept the Cleveland and Cincinnati facilities pumping along with several versions of its vodka. In addition to the standard, you'll find flavors such as blue raspberry, cherry, grape, orange and even bubblegum.

Globe Furniture (Over-the-Rhine)

Findlay Market is a city icon. Its existence on the National Register of Historic Places is due to its title as the state's oldest continuously operating public market. The market sits in the heart of Over-the-Rhine, offering everything from produce to fresh fish. Its interior shops and outdoor stalls have become a gathering place for people all over, while the neighborhood's Italianate buildings line the streets around it. One such building is that of Globe Furniture.

The four-story building adorned with a clock tower had long been a furniture supply outlet. Globe was founded in Cincinnati by the Meisel

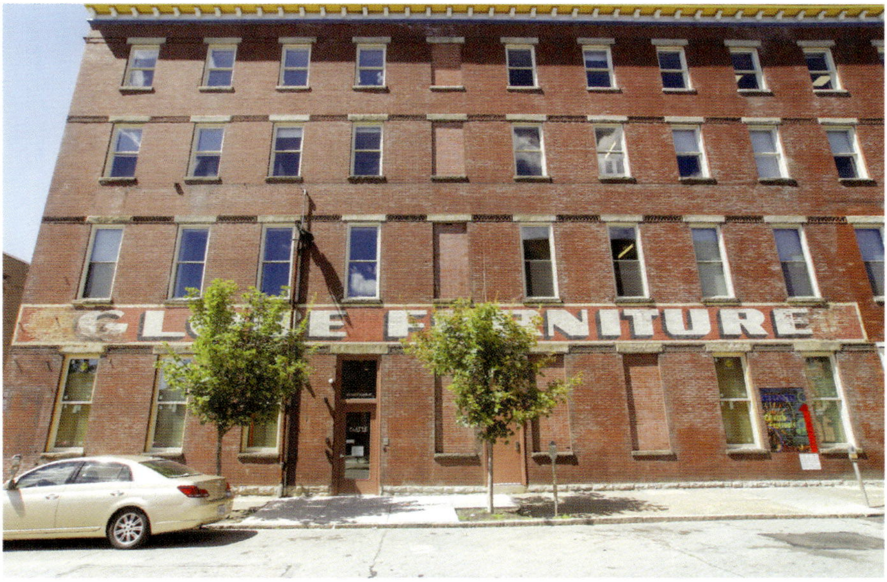

While the building itself has been renovated, this former location of Globe Furniture still has the company's name prominently displayed. Its style differs from a more contemporary one, also fading and documented earlier in the downtown chapter. *Photo by Ronny Salerno.*

family. If the name or concept of finding it in a fading sign sounds familiar, it may be because of another Globe furniture company mentioned in chapter two. However, the aforementioned Globe Furniture Rental wasn't affiliated with the Globe company found in Over-the-Rhine. In a January 1990 issue of *Cincinnati* magazine, an ad for Globe touted that consumers could "buy direct" from a forty-five-year-old Cincinnati furniture store. After some time, the company left its iconic location across from the market for another spot in the neighborhood. Eventually, it was complemented by a suburban location in nearby Symmes Township. Both locations went through brand changes under the Globe name, seemingly shifting toward the more upscale furniture market. Today, along with its aforementioned furniture rental neighbor downtown, Globe is gone.

The building is currently undergoing renovation, with initial plans calling for a restaurant space. Despite significant upgrades to the building, interior renovations, new tenants and updated paint on the trim, the name "Globe" still remains, free to fade on the side as it pleases—one of several furniture business ghost signs and one of two Globe ghost signs.

Apex (Over-the-Rhine)

The large building just off McMicken Avenue has great visibility. As you round the corner, its dominating presence is felt by the large words "Apex Furniture Manufacturing Company" imprinted on the side. Apex is gone; its only remaining local presence are the black letters against a yellow background. A website last updated in 2007 claims a Canadian company of the same name, and its only relation to Cincinnati is a hosted photograph of the same ghost sign. Its listed phone number now goes to a private number, someone operating as an independent travel agent.

While the possible modern remains of Apex may lead to dead ends, the company's history in Cincinnati is well known. Apex was founded by the late

Opposite, top: The name of Apex Furniture Manufacturing Company dominates the face of a building. Beneath the word "Apex," other fading letters can be seen hinting at former tenants. *Photo by Ronny Salerno.*

Opposite, bottom: Judging by how the paint transitions between surfaces, the concrete on this building began to deteriorate well before Gus Holthaus came along with his paintbrush. *Photo by Ronny Salerno.*

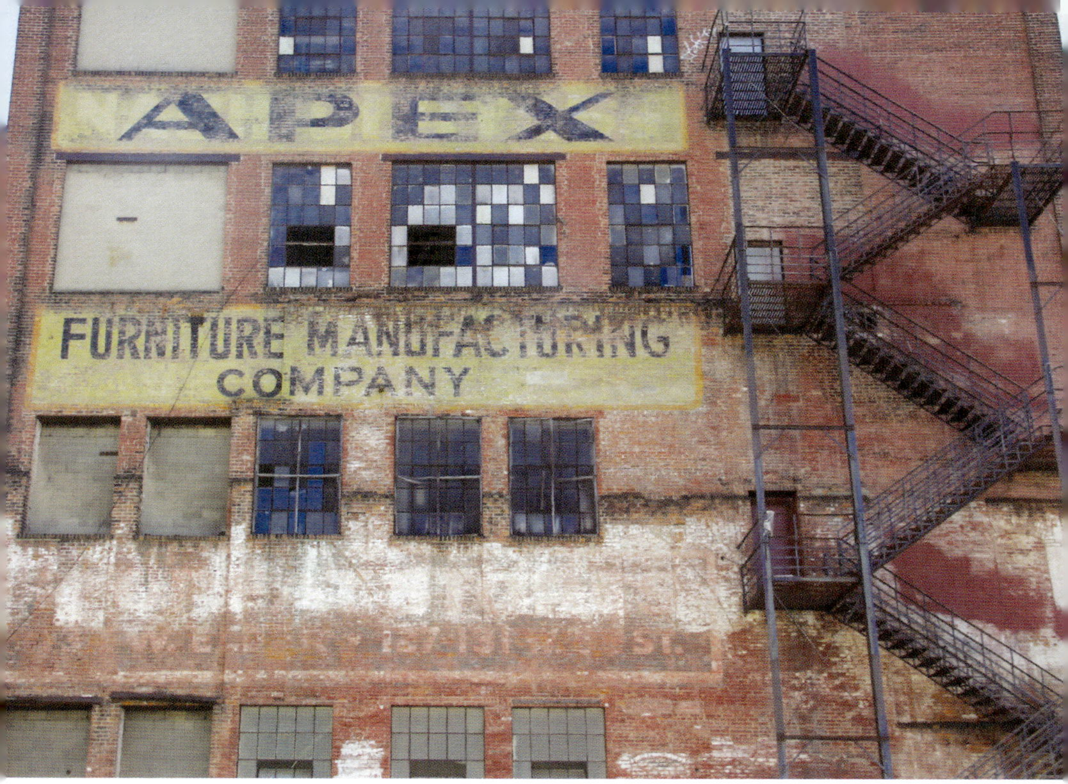
APEX
FURNITURE MANUFACTURING
COMPANY

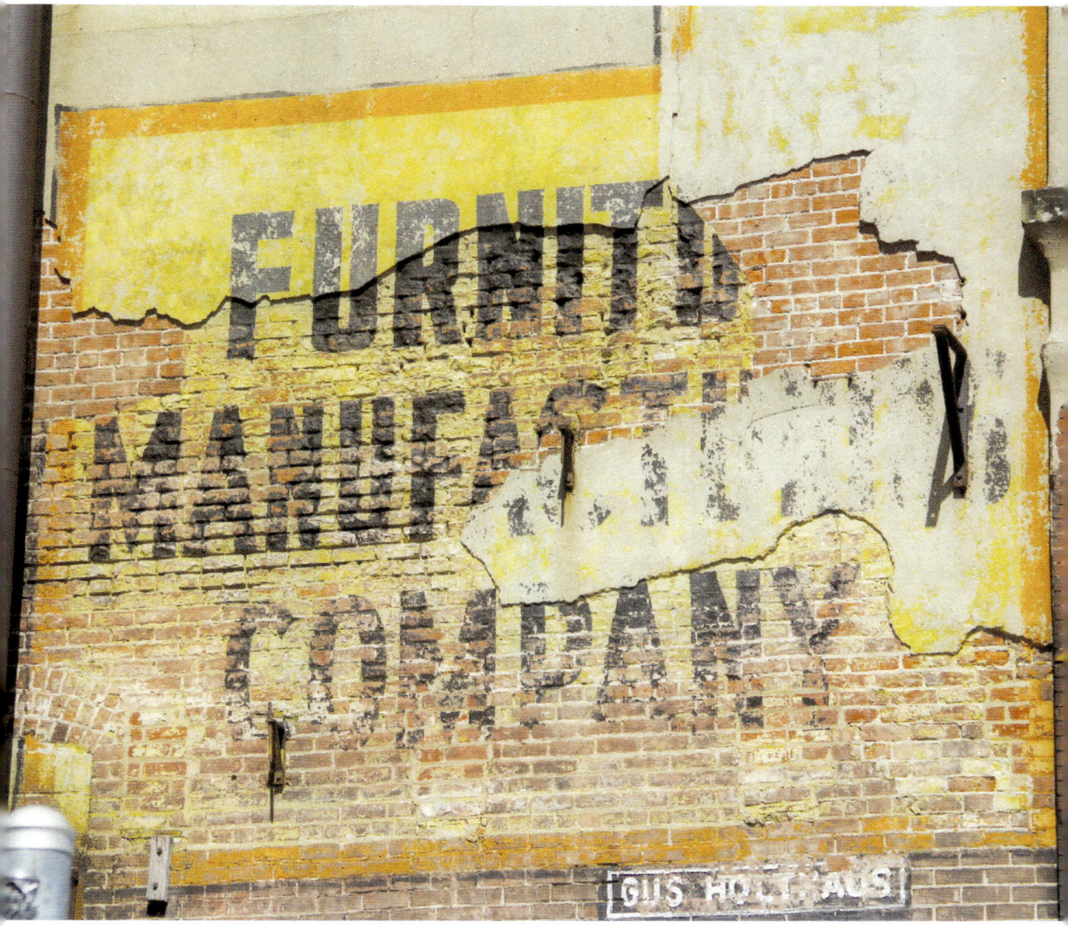
GUS HOLTHAUS

Israel Seibert. A man of Jewish descent, Seibert was born in Poland. During the Second World War, he found himself detained in concentration camps by Nazi occupiers. He would spend four years in the camps before being released. He made his way to Sweden, where he met his wife. The pair made their way to the United States by way of Ellis Island. According to Israel's son in an interview with the *Cincinnati Enquirer*, Israel chose to move to Cincinnati after finding local Hebrew Union College on a map. He went on to found Apex Furniture, which became a proprietor of upholstered products and sleeper sofas. The company's name was plastered all over the building via commissioned works from Gus Holthaus. Aside from the large, multi-story advertisement that faces the main thoroughfare, a block reading, "Furniture Manufacturing Company" in similar colors is also found.

There's another sign, though, just around the building's corner. It reads, "Solway's Furniture." It's quite a bit more eroded than the Apex name, painted in a different color scheme. Like the name it touts, this sign was here before Apex made its mark.

Carl Solway runs the Carl Solway Gallery a few blocks over from the large words of Apex and the fading print of his family's business. "It's interesting that somebody wants to know about it. It's been closed for over fifty years,"

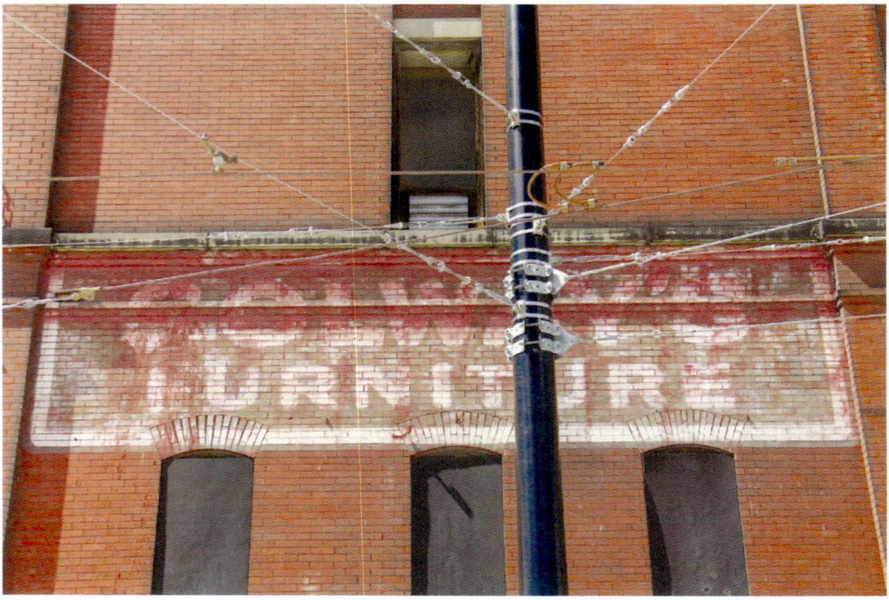

In addition to several Apex signs painted on the building, the name of Solway's Furniture can still be found. Solway's formerly used this location as a warehouse before Apex came into possession of it. *Photo by Ronny Salerno.*

he says on the phone while vacationing in Nevada. Carl and his gallery have long been a local institution, a leading name in the local art scene that was often mentioned in my university art classes. Before Carl became the proprietor of culture that he is today, he was a college kid who swooped in to take over the family business.

The building where "Solway's" can still be seen, along with the name of successor tenant Apex, is just up the road from the corner of Elder and Elm Streets, where the Solway Furniture Company had its showroom. The business was started by Carl's father, Harry Solway. The company provided installment plans for purchases and was a mainstay in the neighborhood of Over-the-Rhine. Carl recalls his father and the neighborhood fondly, especially their proximity to the historic Findlay Market. "The market house was surrounded by stands selling produce. I remember the metal oil cans; they were open all year round." Carl recalls how his father would often go to the market on Saturday nights, when it stayed open until nine o'clock: "All the kids would stay home because when he came home we'd have a feast!"

Harry Solway was a prominent figure among the neighborhood and the market's merchants. A member of the Findlay Market Association, he was among the men who began the annual tradition of the city's Opening Day Parade, commemorating the first Reds baseball game of the season. As the association's members walked down the street to deliver the American flag to the team, Carl would get to walk with his father onto the grass of Crosley Field. "It was the thrill of my life to be able to walk onto the ball field," he says. In addition to his business dealings, Harry was popular among his customers. His store offered installment plans and built a customer base among neighborhood residents. Folks might start out with some furniture for their homes and then come back to purchase high chairs and cribs as their families grew. The family business is also where Carl would cut his teeth as a salesman years before becoming an art dealer. During Christmas, Solway's sponsored a radio program featuring Santa Claus while the first floor started selling toys. There you'd find a twelve-year-old Carl: "Wouldn't you wanna buy toys from an actual kid that knew really cool toys?" Carl would eventually head off to college. In his senior year at the University of Pennsylvania in 1956, he was all set to graduate in June. His plans took a turn, though, when he received the news that his father had suffered a stroke at age fifty-eight. Carl returned home. His father, Harry, would pass away in August, before Carl returned to Pennsylvania to finish his degree.

After completing his program, Carl once again came back to Cincinnati to sort out the family business. "Nobody really wanted a furniture store in a

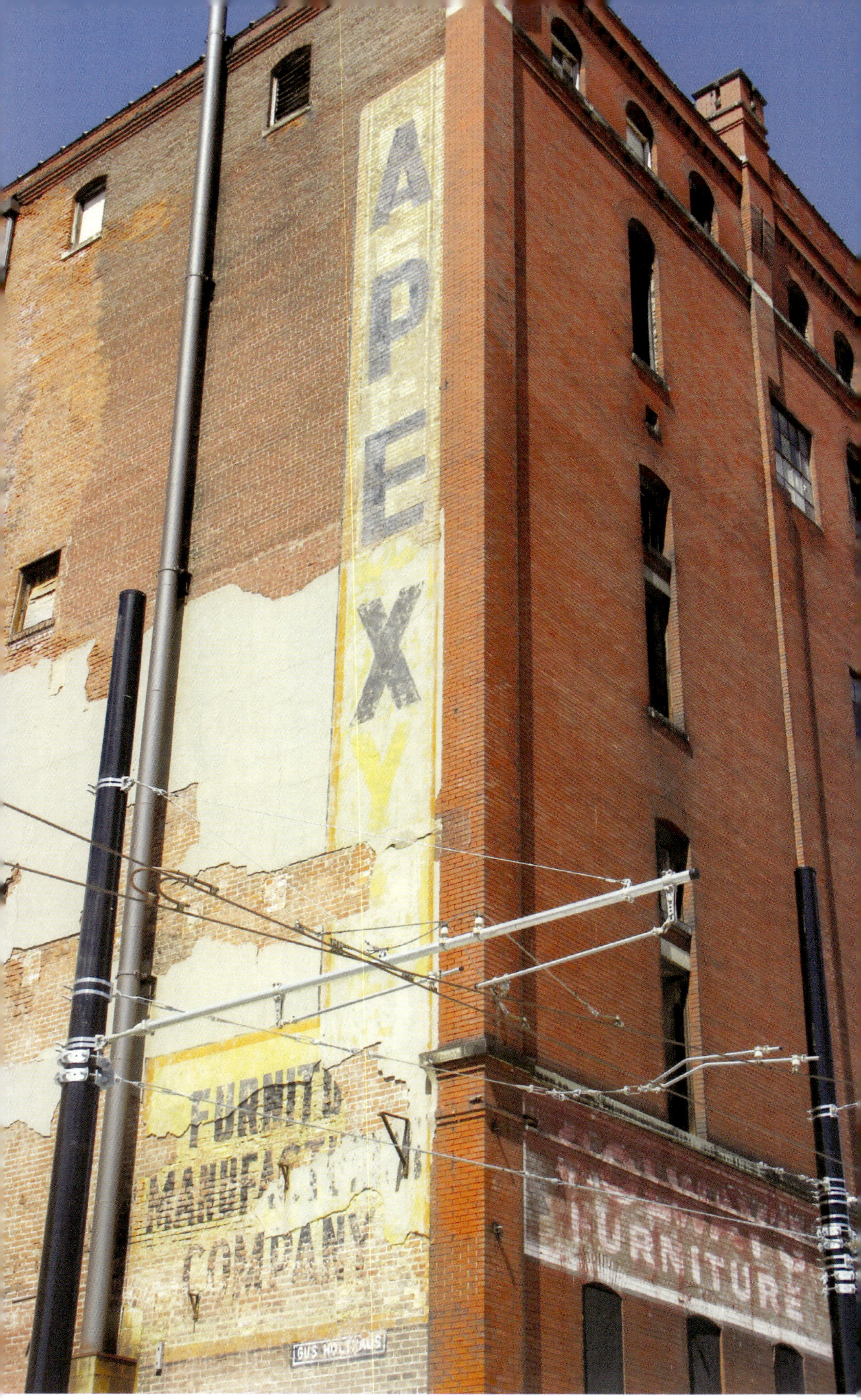
APEX
COMPANY

neighborhood that was changing while you had to compete with furniture stores in the suburbs," he recalls. OTR was going through a demographic shift; many of the original and prominent German families were now heading out to other neighborhoods. Carl and his cousin Louis Hellmann purchased the business from the rest of the family. "My job was to keep the store running but try and sell it," he says. Carl was taking all of this on at the age of twenty-one, with a wife and newborn baby at home. The store had fifty-five employees under two labor unions. For five years, Carl and his cousin were successful at running the business. They were helped by the financial arm of American Motors, which produced the then popular Kelvinator refrigerator brand, a popular item at Solway's. Carl and his cousin were very successful, helping American Motors turn around several furniture stores in New York by following the Solway company's lead. The agreement was twofold, though. In exchange for helping American Motors turn around its underperforming East Coast stores, American was to help find a buyer for the Solway Furniture Co. Eventually, it did, and Carl left the furniture business. "That was a tough thing to do," he says. "It's a shame; we had to leave behind a lot of employees."

The warehouse on Henry Street would eventually be sold to Apex for its manufacturing arm. Apex would add to the building's legacy and used its prominent location to heavily advertise the name. Yet Apex refrained from covering the Solway's sign on the front. It's a sign that Carl himself has stopped to photograph before. Even after his father's passing, he'd come across people who also shared fond memories of Harry: "I heard stories of people during the Depression who'd come in and say: 'Mr. Solway, we can't pay our five dollars this week.' Then Harry Solway would take out five dollars from his own pocket, hand it to them and tell them to go get groceries. That's the kind of person he was."

Carl speaks with a calm, soft voice, and it's clear that he cherishes the time he had with his father and the memories he has of the company. We trade stories about his times standing on the grass at Crosley Field and my times visiting the Astroturf of Riverfront Stadium. You can tell that Carl is proud of the family name, for what it stood for previously and what it stands for now. Down at the former warehouse on Henry, where the paint is fading, there are remnants of a "Y" under the Apex name. Perhaps it was another

Opposite: Looking at the corner of the building, both the Apex and Solway's names can been seen in their respective signs. Beneath the vertically running "Apex," the shape of a "Y" can be found, possibly where the name of Solway had been covered up. *Photo by Ronny Salerno.*

placement of the name Solway, featured prominently and running vertically down the building's side. After Carl sold off the company, he embarked on his own business venture. Today, the Carl Solway Gallery is regarded as one of the city's finest. He may not be in the furniture business anymore, but Carl has kept the Solway name going in Cincinnati.

Good Deals on Vine Street (Over-The-Rhine)

Go down Vine Street through OTR on a summer afternoon and you'll be hard pressed to find a parking spot. Every year it seems to get more crowded, with more people returning, coming down and enjoying the urban core.

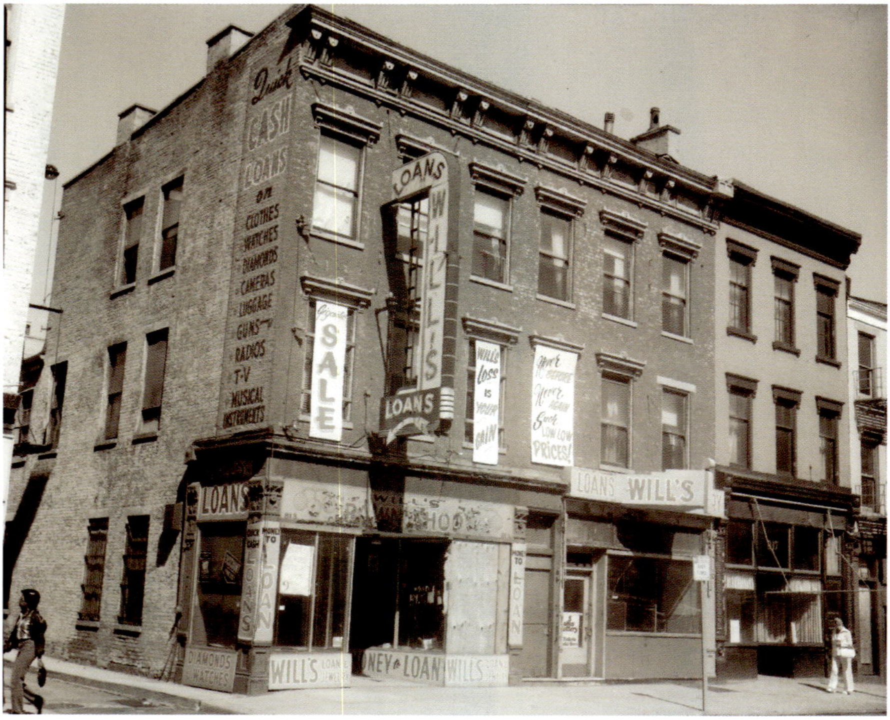

Demolished in 1981, this building on Vine Street for a "Will's Loans" features a vertically running wall painting that echoes ones still found on the street today. *Photograph by Historic American Buildings Survey, courtesy of the Library of Congress.*

Opposite: A multi-story ad for Barr's Loans lists the types of items available for pawn and trade at the former store. *Photo by Ronny Salerno.*

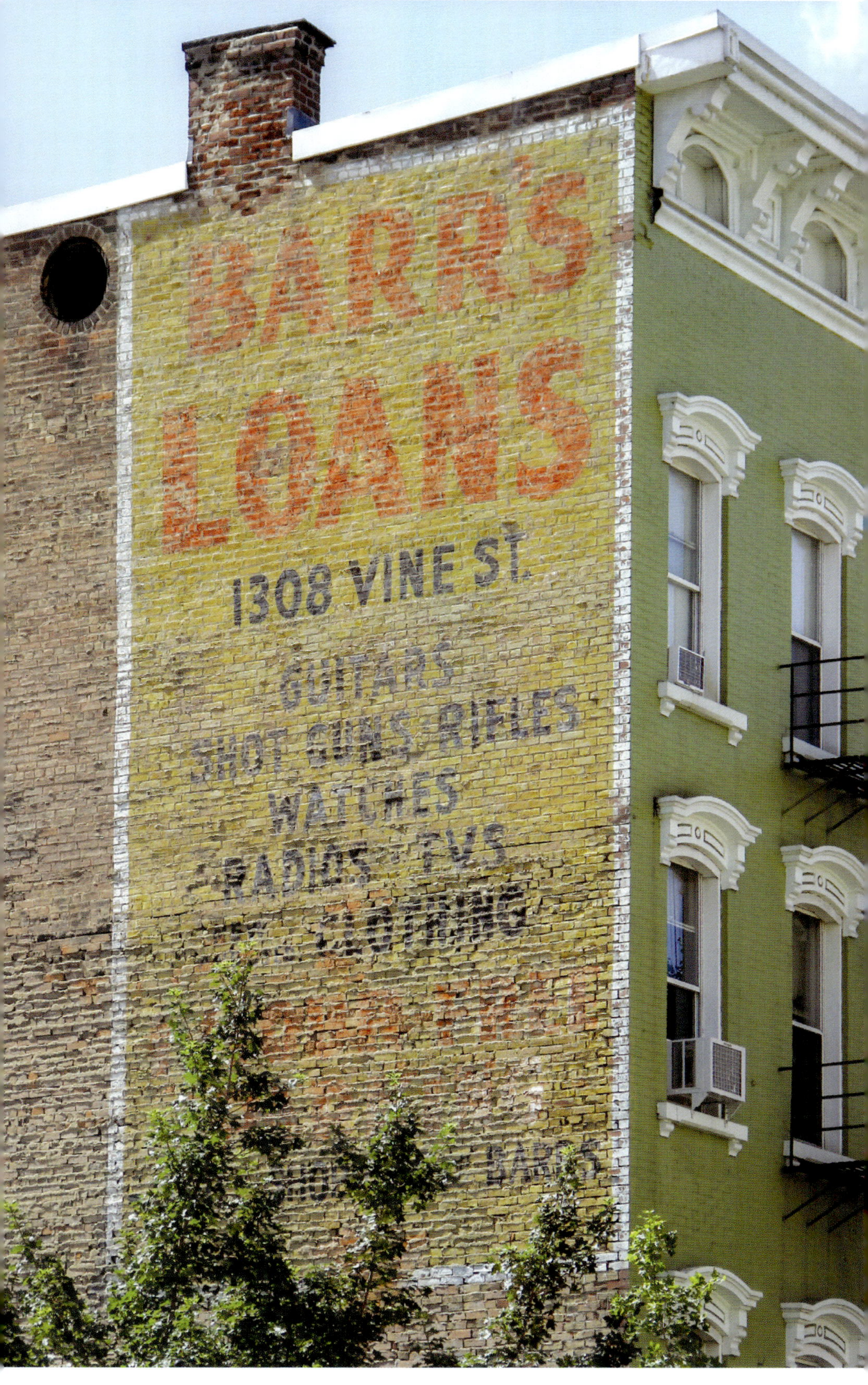
BARR'S
LOANS
1308 VINE ST.
GUITARS
SHOT GUNS RIFLES
WATCHES
RADIOS TVS
CLOTHING

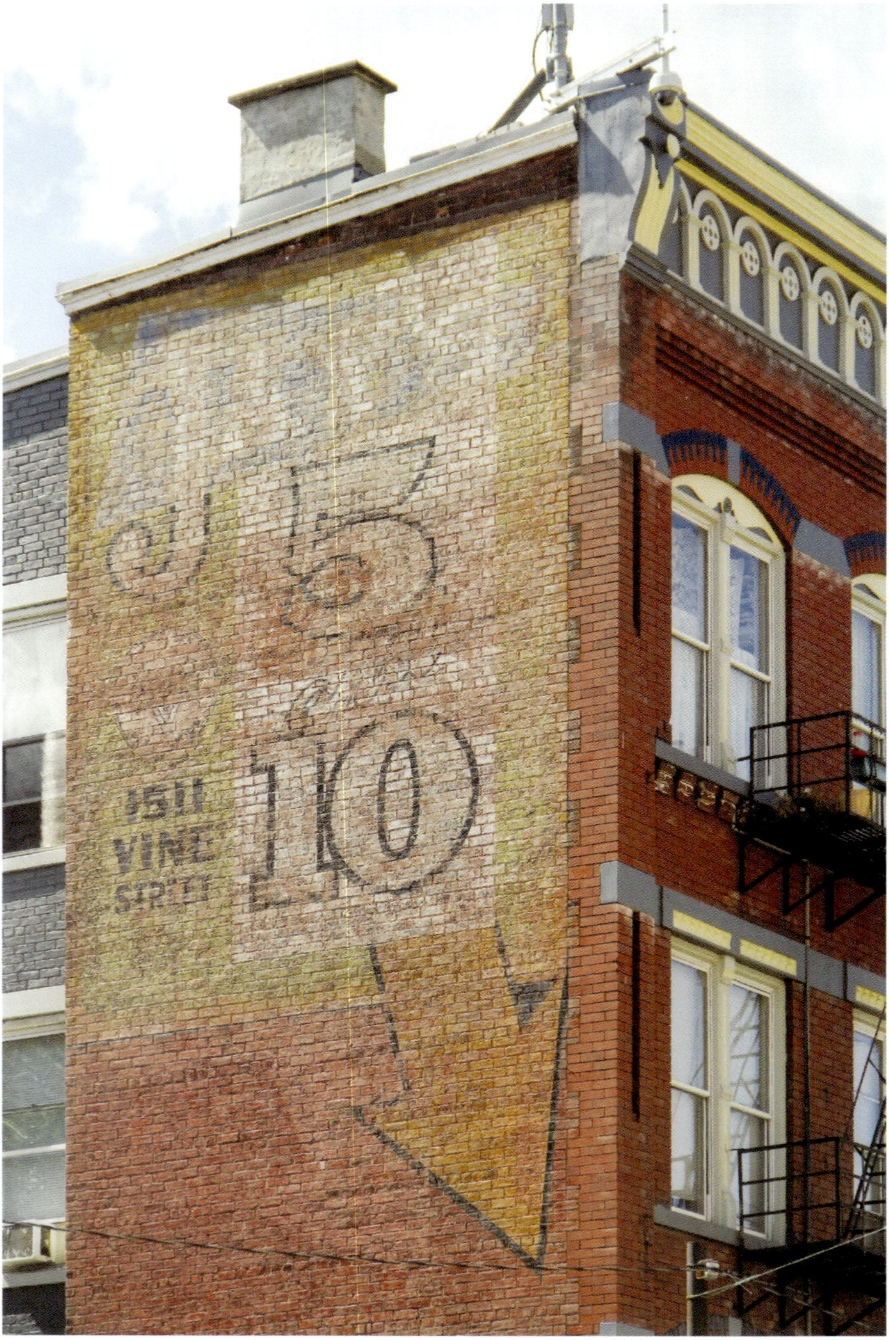

The large "5" and "10" hint that, at one point, a five-and-dime store may have existed below the painted arrow. *Photo by Ronny Salerno.*

Businesses have sprung up here again with the intense focus on economic development. The neighborhood is alive with people dining, ushering in and out of bars in search of happy hour deals and visiting the art galleries and shops. OTR is vibrant, with several of its preserved buildings donning bright colors in the wake of their renovations. OTR has shed its emptiness, its reputation, after so many years of vacant buildings. It's returning to its historic vibrancy. There are still remnants of the old days here, though, along the brick walls in fading paint that contrasts with the bright colors of economic vitality.

Throughout its history, OTR has been densely packed with row houses. The ones with storefronts competed for visibility. Some had an advantage, capitalizing on brick walls at street corners and alleyways or the walls that could be seen above smaller, neighboring structures. The signs in OTR were a mainstay for years on the neighborhood's main streets, like Vine.

Fire escapes and window air-conditioning units jump out from the bright lime green color of the building's façade. On the side, the brick is still natural, save for the advertisement running down its side. Guitars, shotguns, rifles, watches, radios, TVs, clothing—you name it, Barr's Loans wanted your business. It was located one block up the street from where it advertised but is gone now.

You'll find these days that OTR's storefronts seem to use smaller signs hanging over pedestrian walkways or embrace the trend of chalkboards placed out on the sidewalk. A sign vaguely stating the name "Jay's" and emblazoned with the numbers "5" and "10" harkens back to how some businesses used to take advantage of wall space. The advertisement is nostalgic not just for how it was made but also for advertising a five-and-dime store, types of stores that have since fallen out of economic fashion along with the paintings that proclaimed them.

F.H. Wilms (Evanston)

In the O'Bryonville Business District of Evanston, one ghost sign can be found at the edge of an alley. It's tucked away at the top of a building, hidden by trees and electrical wires. The building now houses a popular athletic and running outfitter. It's hard to make out the name, which has been cut off by newer electrical work, but it reads, "F.H. Wilms." City directories from 1922 and 1924 list the Wilms carpet cleaning and rug manufacturing

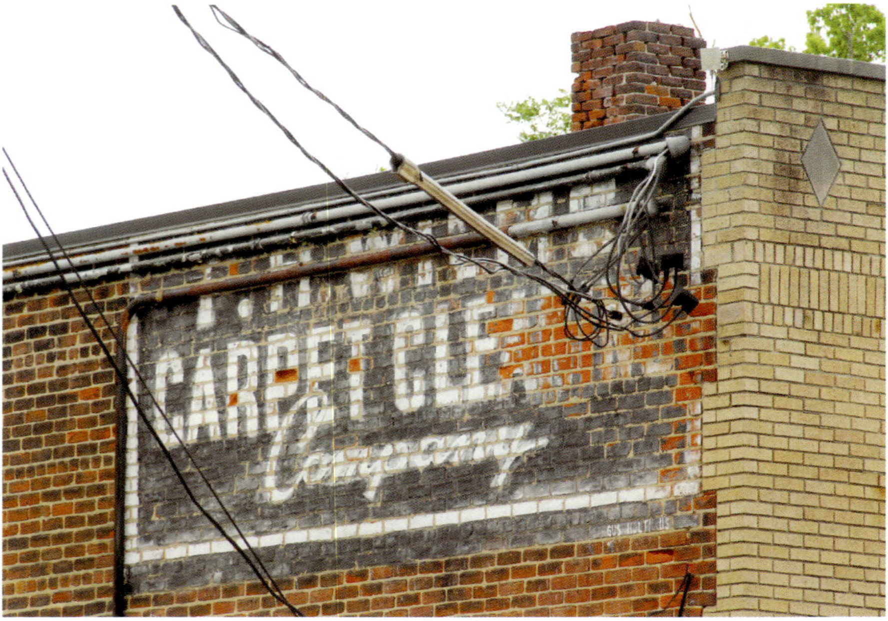

The ad for the F.H. Wilms carpet cleaning company has been partially covered by the building's addition of electrical wiring over the years. In some spots, paint has been so far washed away that the brick has been restored to its original color. *Photo by Ronny Salerno.*

business as being downtown on Plum Street. At some point, Wilms must have brought his practice into the neighborhood hills. Maybe it relocated, maybe it expanded. It's gone now, though, with only this sign and a few mentions from over ninety years ago in print. Like on so many other signs, at the bottom right, there's the signature of Gus Holthaus.

Deposits Guaranteed (Walnut Hills)

Between 1986 and 1995, 2,191 savings and loan institutions closed their doors. The savings and loan crisis in the United States stemmed from economic issues surrounding inflation and interest rates beginning in the late 1970s. These days, you'll be hard pressed to find a savings and loan

Opposite: An ad for Major Savings and Loans is now a mess of barely legible words, the most prominent of which echoed what was possibly the company's best feature: deposits were guaranteed. *Photo by Ronny Salerno.*

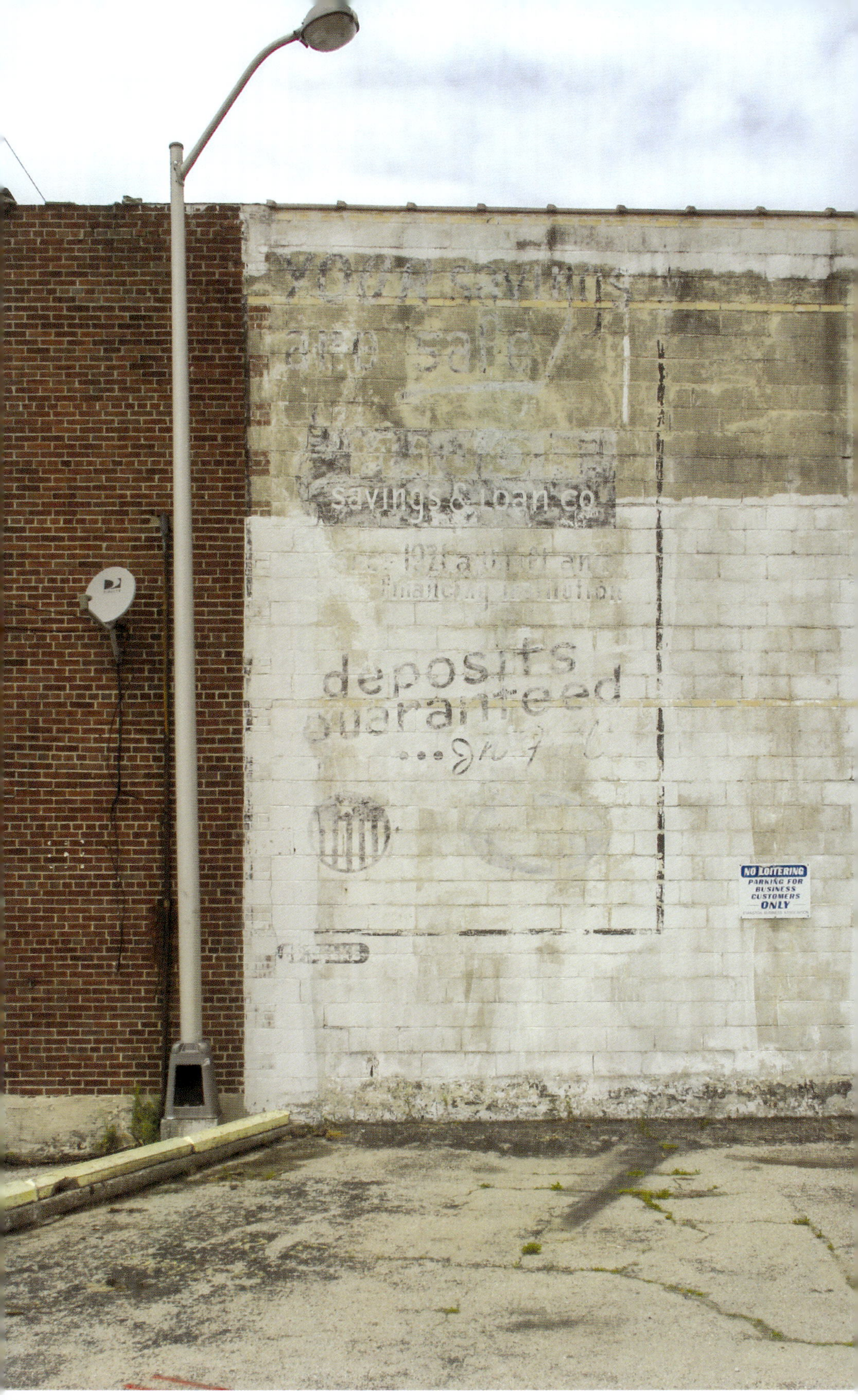
savings & loan co
deposits guaranteed
NO LOITERING
PARKING FOR BUSINESS CUSTOMERS ONLY

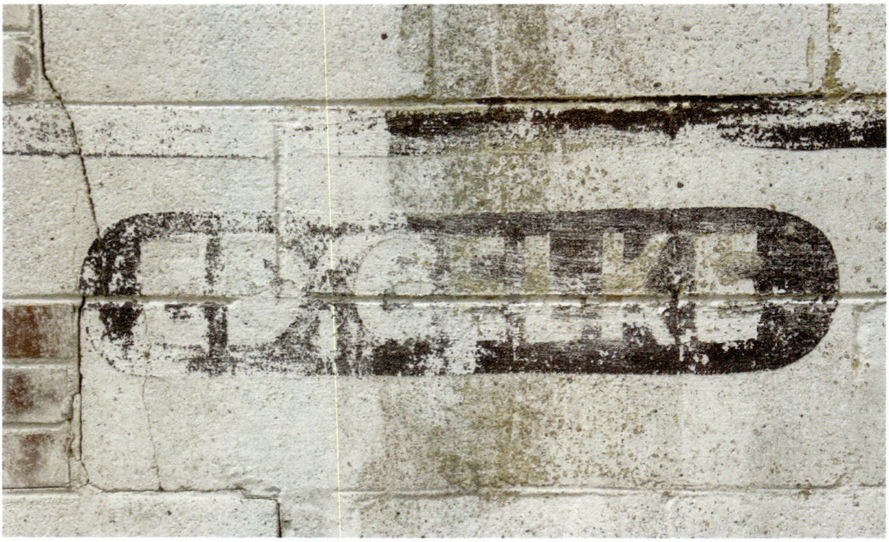

The faded signature of Ed Gelke beneath the Major Savings and Loan sign. Ed was another local sign painter. His business would eventually be bought out by Gus Holthaus. Ed was also responsible for the beer and burlesque ads seen in the historic image in this book's introduction. *Photo by Ronny Salerno.*

institution among the numerous locations of the country's big banks. For one savings and loan, though, its outlook in Cincinnati's Walnut Hills neighborhood once seemed hopeful just before the crisis took hold, and a painted wall sign advertised its name.

At one point, Pauline Strayhorne was the executive vice-president, secretary and chief operating officer of Major Savings and Loan. She started as a teller in 1947, working her way up from there. A 1983 interview with *Black Enterprise* outlined how she managed to keep up the company's performance in her ten years as managing officer. In the interview, Strayhorne is honest and blunt about the challenges facing the savings and loan industry and her own company's challenges within the African American community. The article also mentions Strayhorne's active role in volunteering with civic organizations.

There's no other substantial mention of Major Savings and Loans. Strayhorne's name popped up in 2014, when she was recognized for civil rights work by the local YWCA. It touted Strayhorne's thirty-eight-year-career at Major, meaning she would have left the company in 1985, two years after the exposé was published and roughly one year before the savings and loan crisis hit.

In a Walnut Hills parking lot, there's still a sign for Major Savings and Loan, even if its neighborhood location is gone. Facing a parking lot, it's barely noticeable to anyone who passes by in a car or on the bus. Phrases read: "Your savings are safe!" and "Deposits guaranteed...in full." The company's name isn't even recognizable in paint anymore. The word "Major" is outlined in fading black, while the letters are simply filled by the exterior of the wall with "Savings and Loan Co." hand painted beneath. The sign features the signature of Ed Gelke. It may be one of just a few, if not the only, signs that still have his name beneath it. Gelke would eventually be bought out by Holthaus. Also discernable are the numbers "1921"—the year the company was founded by Major Lee Zeigler, the man who would eventually hire Strayhorne.

Davis Furniture (Over-the-Rhine)

Often regarded as the Davis Furniture building, a landmark at the entrance to OTR gets its name from multiple painted signs that envelop it. Facing south, there's the most prominent: "Davis Furniture for over 100 years." The history is proudly proclaimed over the image of a man dropping a bowling ball onto a Simmons Beautyrest® mattress, a reference to the Simmons company's famous television ads. The north side simply states, "6 Months Same as Cash." Meanwhile, the back of the building facing east reiterates the company's name and lets passersby know that it's been there since 1902, takes cash or credit and is "the friendly store." The building is draped in black paint, allowing the yellow letters to stand out brightly. Around the front are two storefronts. Despite the appearance of the paint around the entire building, the Davis building is actually two separate properties that were conjoined.

The building traces its roots back to 1857, and over the years it housed a variety of tenants, both residential and business. Davis Furniture was born on Sycamore Street in 1902, the brainchild of David Davis. Sometime in the late 1930s or early '40s, the store relocated to its final location on Main Street, just inside the OTR neighborhood. David passed away in 1955, leaving the business to his two sons, Milton and Bertram. The brothers turned Davis into a retail powerhouse with huge showrooms and the latest in appliances, such as General Electric's first "no frost" refrigerator. Milton passed away in 1989 while Bertram kept at it. The store continued on, creating "loud" advertisements that

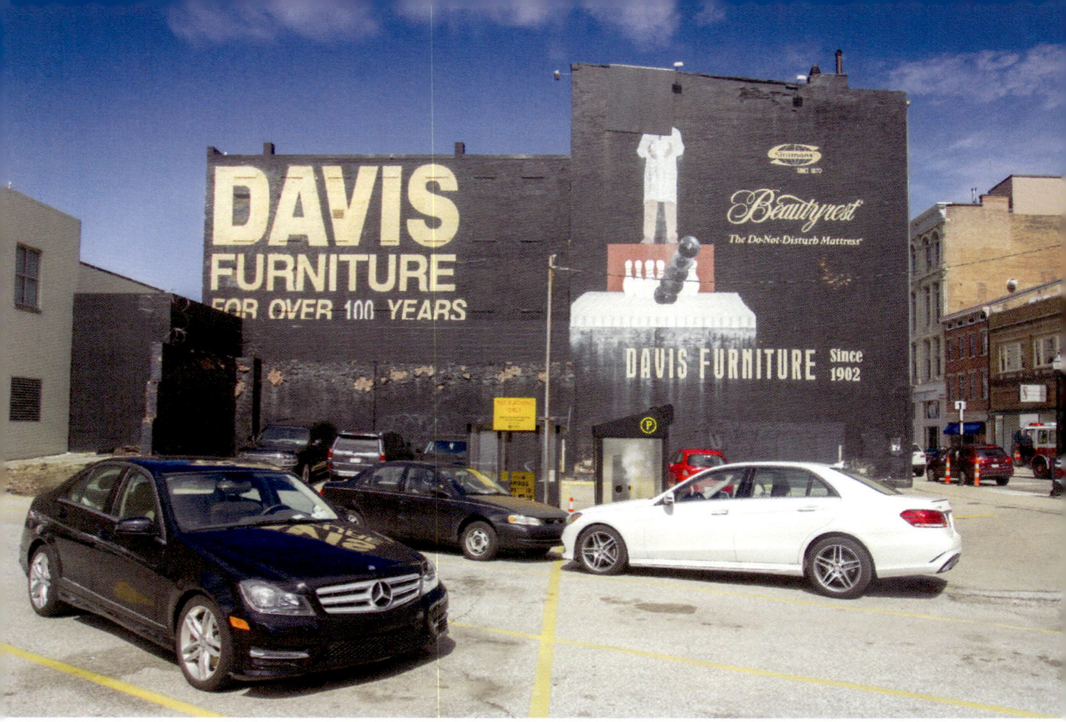

Above: The ad featuring a salesman dropping a bowling ball onto a mattress lined with bowling pins reflected a popular television commercial for Simmons Beautyrest® mattresses. The building's walls mark one of the recognizable entrances to the Over-the-Rhine neighborhood. *Photo by Ronny Salerno.*

Below: An ad for Davis Furniture touts its reputation as "the friendly store" while acknowledging the business's founding year and ability to accept both cash and credit. *Photo by Ronny Salerno.*

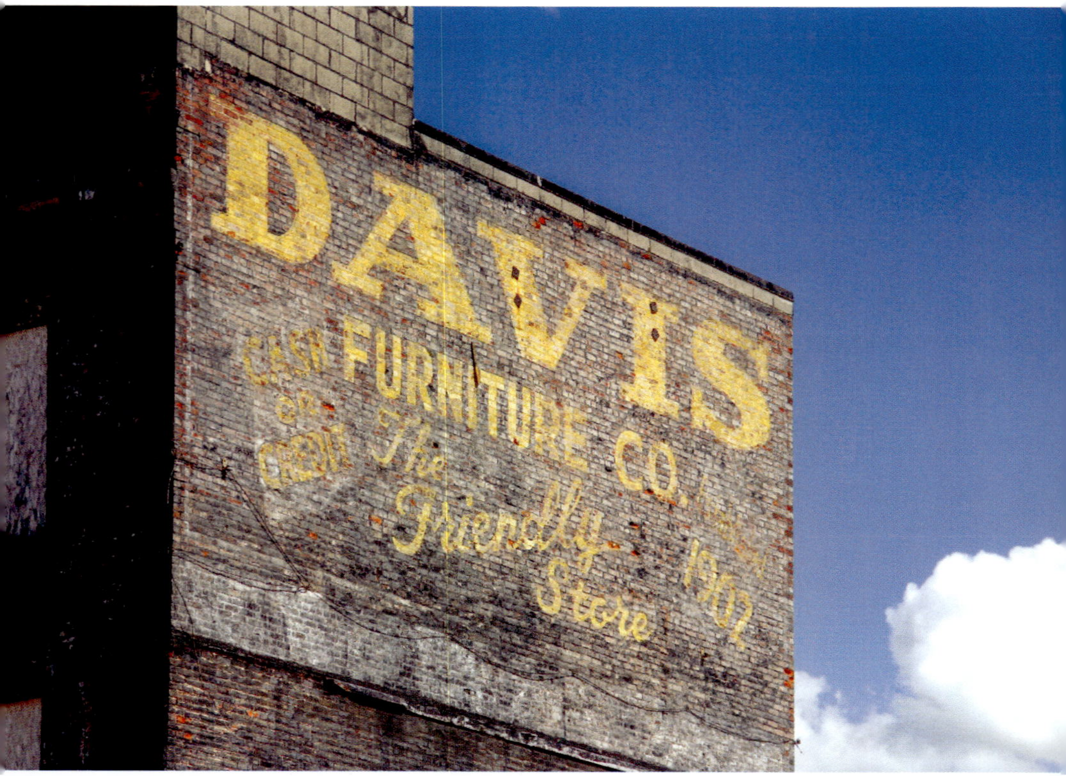

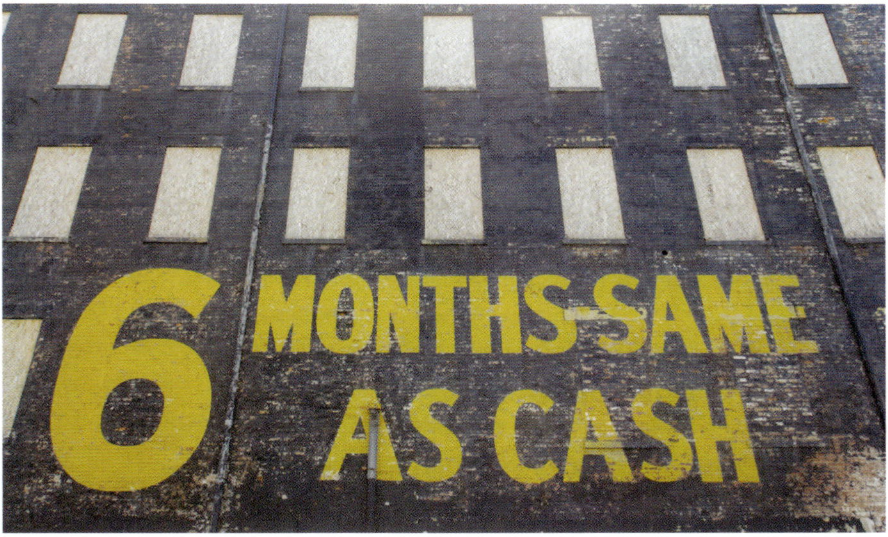

The boarded windows and peeling paint reflect the status of the former Davis Furniture Co., which at one time advertised financing options in bold yellow letters. *Photo by Ronny Salerno.*

encompassed the entire sides of the building. In a historic district, the building was preserved, but the all-black paint scheme stood out.

In the wake of the 2001 riots and after years of combating changing economic behaviors, Davis Furniture was having a hard time keeping up with the shopping malls and big box stores. From his nursing home bed, Bertram made the decision to close the store in 2004. As Davis Furniture exited, no new tenants entered.

In the years since, the two buildings have kept on the Davis name due to their physical paint scheme. As OTR began to emerge with a renaissance of revitalization and rehabilitation, many wondered when the Davis building would get some attention. After the structure was foreclosed on and purchased at a sheriff's auction, private developers picked up the property. After some inspections, though, the developers found the building to be beyond repair, outside the scope of economic feasibility. Permission was sought from the city to demolish the property, but the city declined, as it wanted to see the building preserved.

As of November 2014, the building's future remains uncertain. The windows are boarded up, and the glass storefronts warn everyone to stay out. The painted ads of Davis Furniture remain, still advertising a business that no longer exists. Although they're not original, these ads give the building its identity. If it is rehabbed, should the ads stay as a reminder of a time gone by? While the building would once again be habitable, should the paintings be left to fade like urban folk art? In a way, the bowling ball–dropping salesman gives the building its character. It's just as much a part of the neighborhood as the bricks that hold it up. Should the building come to life, perhaps the ads will be left to continue playing out their time on those walls. Or maybe a new tenant will use the space to advertise contemporary products. For now, the Davis building remains in flux.

Habig's (Westwood)

There was once an institution on the west side, in the aptly named neighborhood of Westwood, in the fashion of the prototypical mom and pop diners that now exist only on television shows and in pop culture realms. Sue Sena, a medical secretary still living in the neighborhood, recalls it fondly. Sena grew up as Sue Habig and was one of the nine family members who helped shape the family business, which served

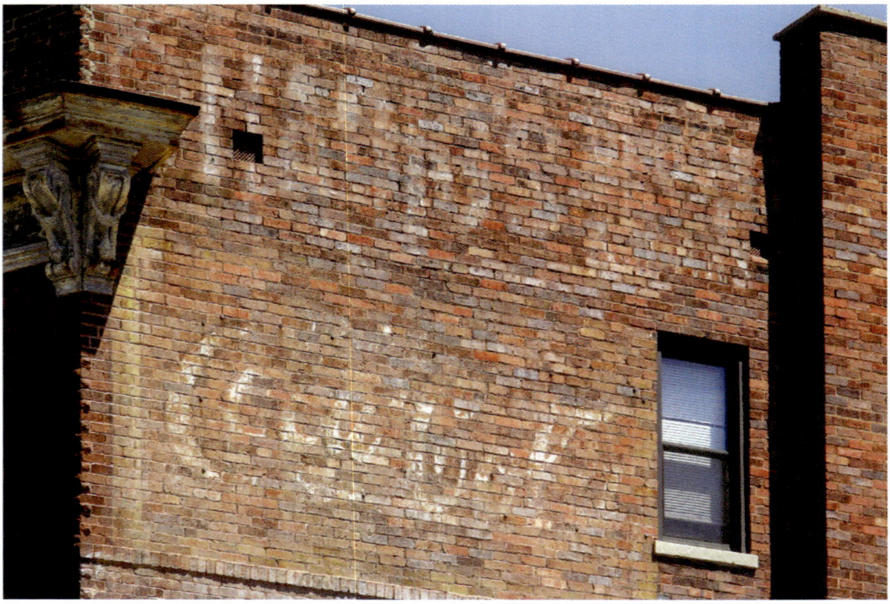

The name of Habig's pharmacy can be hard to read, along with the words "Drugs," "Films" and "Kodaks," but the Coca-Cola logo is still recognizable below. *Photo by Ronny Salerno.*

home-cooked meals derived from her grandmother's recipes. "My dad was so proud of that place," she says, recalling how her father opened the business while living in the apartment above.

Habig's had long been an institution as a local restaurant, but the Habig's name wasn't just known as a dining spot. Habig's drugstore could be found nearby. Just a few blocks away and at the old location, its sign still exists, keeping the family name that is proclaimed in Westwood. Drugs, film, Kodaks and Coca-Cola are all touted, the latter featuring a full logo. The pharmacy belonged to Sue's uncle.

In the later years, and with the pharmacy already closed, the last remaining Habig's business folded in 2004. The restaurant shut down amid changing demographics, aging regulars and increased competition throughout the area. "My dream is to open another one," Sena says. "Maybe one day, if I hit the lottery." If luck finds its way to Sue, maybe the Habig's name will return to Westwood just as her uncle's ghost sign finally fades away.

Coca-Cola (East Walnut Hills)

While rural landscapes are often dotted with barns proclaiming the high quality of Mail Pouch tobacco, urban environments have their own advertising mainstay: Coca-Cola. The soft drink giant was introduced to the country in 1886 and soon became the worldwide phenomenon it is today. The company had its logo created in the year before it debuted. The script lettering and bright red have become recognizable symbols in not just American culture but also across the world. As one of the world's most valuable brands, the Coca-Cola logo can be found on numerous souvenirs and collectibles around the world. The company even has its own museum, which draws over one million people per year to its Atlanta base of operations. The brand had to be built, though, and that started with advertising campaigns that were the historical equivalent of today's viral marketing buzz words.

Early on, the company embraced the idea of murals and hand-painted advertising. According to its own records, this started in the 1890s, and by 1910, the commissioning of wall signs accounted for 25 percent of the company's advertising budget. Coca-Cola murals became mainstays of wall advertising in cities, both big and small, all across the country. In several places, restoration projects have been brought forward to revive

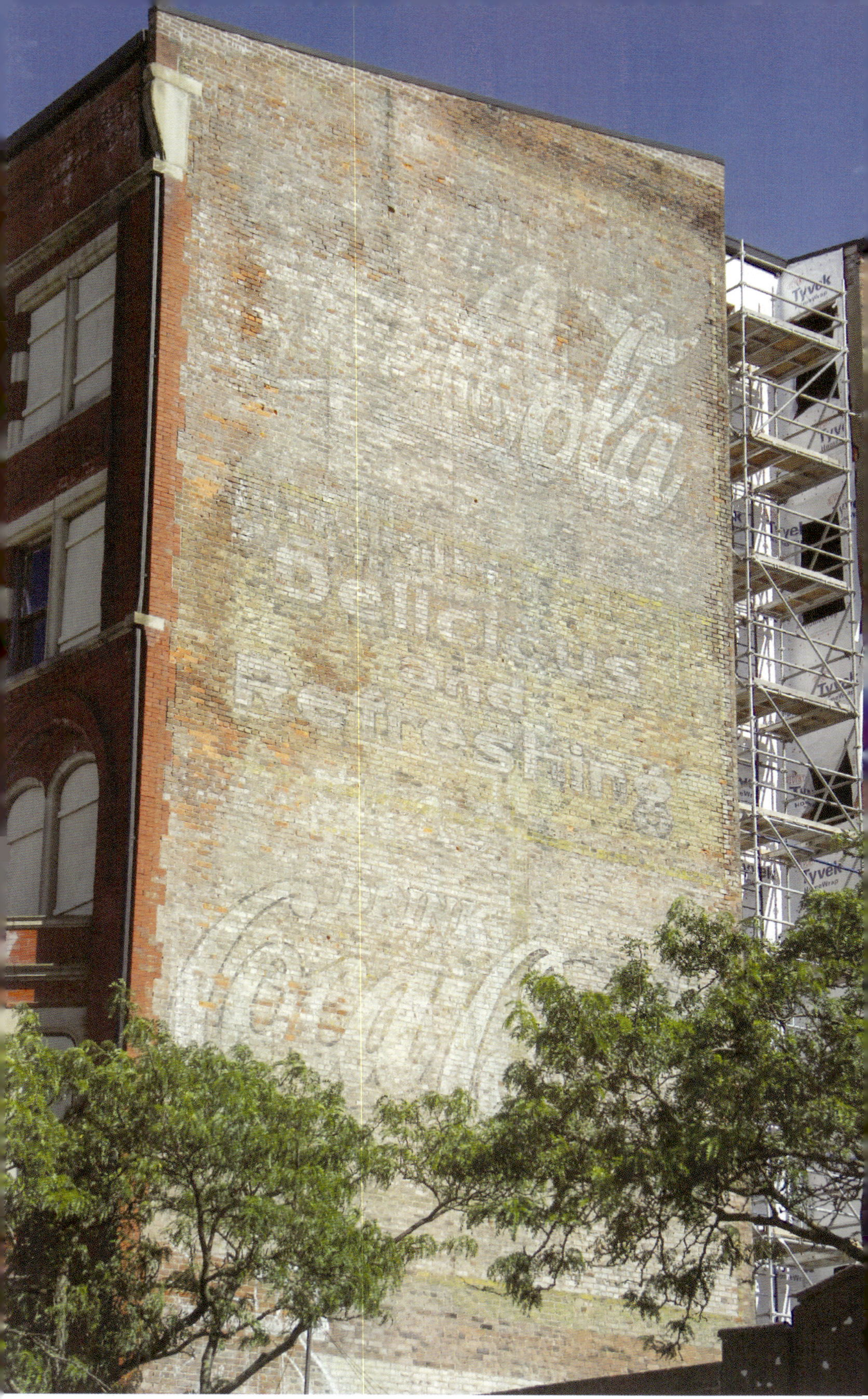
Delicious
and
Refreshing
Tyvek

some of the signs, cherishing them in the same way a collector seeks out Coca-Cola memorabilia.

While some of Coke's originally commissioned work has been restored to a glory worthy of an international press release, hundreds of signs can still be found fading away in cities all over the nation. The aforementioned Habig's drugstore had one just below its name, while over in Walnut Hills, Coke once dominated the entire side of a building.

It took years of advertising, clever marketing and tasty soda to push Coke into the giant it is today, but much of that was first promoted by the company's wall advertising. Even now, with much of a sign fading away into a blend of gray, yellow and original brick, the iconic script of the Coca-Cola lettering is easily recognizable. There are two logos—one at the top of the building and one near the lower half. Even with the word "Coca" missing from one, the script writing of "Cola" leaves no doubt about what product it is touting. The words "delicious and refreshing" can still be seen, part of a slogan originally introduced by the company in 1904. Despite distress and deterioration, the logo's familiarity is unparalleled.

The Mockbee (Brighton)

The Mockbee is a hulk of a building, or rather collection of buildings, built into the hillside. It is peppered with several ghost signs, specifically the one for C.M. Mockbee Co., a company that still exists within Cincinnati but is no longer at this space. The various fading signs can be seen from the highway nearby, the parkway below and the street out front. For years, the structure sat empty before the building's owner came together with a nonprofit to turn it and its several rooms into a massive art gallery. Several events were held there, ranging from performance art to concerts to gallery showings. The Mockbee gained a cult following as the place to see local art or an upcoming band. Its industrial interior was gutted and filled with creativity.

In 2005, rumors began to fly that the Mockbee would close down, just four years after the unique space opened. It persevered for a while longer, though, hosting anything it could from commercial shoots to poetry readings. By

Opposite: The Coca-Cola Company used to spend 25 percent of its advertising budget on painted signs. On this particular one, two of the company's iconic scripted logos can be seen fading away. *Photo by Ronny Salerno.*

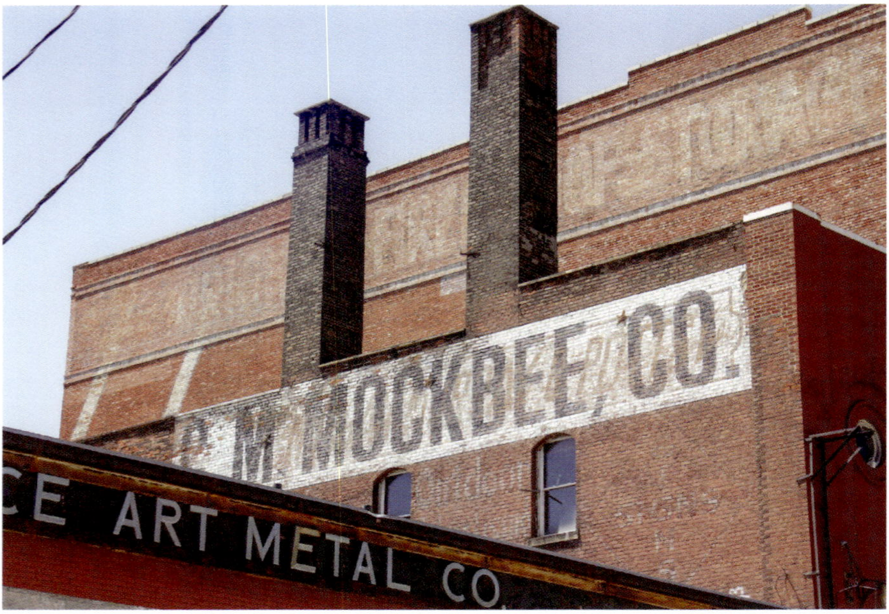

While the C.M. Mockbee Co. has moved elsewhere in the city, this prominent ghost sign atop the building helped lend to its name, "the Mockbee," when it was an arts venue. *Photo by Ronny Salerno.*

2011, things had taken a turn for the worst, and the facility could no longer keep the lights on. The Mockbee closed.

The faded sign out front may still represent an active business, but it has taken on new meaning. It no longer symbolizes a company but the former location of one of the city's most obscure art venues and unique dens of creativity.

Unlike the downtown collection, the neighborhood signs are less abundant, more infrequent. They're harder to come by and stick out a little more glaringly, contrasting with the more residentially suited areas. These fading ads are themselves indicative of the neighborhoods where they can be found. They tell the stories of the people who lived there, the people who existed there. They form snapshots of both individual and shared histories while at the same time offering a glimpse into the past. The signs and neighborhoods are multifaceted, interesting enough on their own and taking on common traits in a group. They're a collection of various ancestries, existing within borders and telling a story together.

7

CLINGING TO THE BRICKS

Let's say you wanted to open a business, and like so many others in Cincinnati, you're returning to the city's urban core to set up shop. You find a spot right on Main Street, where the building's side meets the street corner. You realize something: as pedestrians, cars, buses and the streetcar come your way, that exposed wall is prime real estate. You could tout your business's name, advertise products or specials and discern your location in a manner that other companies on the block can't. Maybe you want to go for a nostalgic feel, bring in some local artists and harken back to the day when painted walls were king. Sure, you could get the paint and hire the team to toil away at creating something unique, but there's a good chance someone might have a problem with that. There's a process that needs to be followed, and unlike in days past, it's simply not just up to the building's owner anymore.

There are lots of bureaucratic regulations to navigate when you set up shop in a building or area that is considered to be historic. From property purchasing to renovation to exterior changes, each move has to be overseen by the local government. There's constant maneuvering, submissions of plans and awaited approval. Signage is part of that process. The city itself wants to know exactly what you're planning to do before the sign goes up. For signage in the city, you need to obtain an "outdoor advertising sign permit." Even to reach that point, you must first have three complete drawings of what you intend to put up. Once all your ducks are in a row, your potential sign is subject to review according to the building, zoning and municipal codes. As the instructions state, "Any deficiencies will be noted and you will be required to revise your plans to comply with local code." If you violate this process, you'll face the consequences: escalating fines and potentially having your signage permanently removed.

Now, we're creating a hypothetical situation; the odds of being able to use your building as a billboard in a neighborhood, especially a historic district, are pretty slim. The local zoning laws seem to prefer signs above the door, near the street. They tend toward approving signage that's unobtrusive. Exceptions are made, though, especially for buildings that border highways or highly trafficked areas. Even then, you're more likely to see modern billboards that change out advertisers frequently. There's more money to be made in those situations, as you can continually rent out prime ad space to a variety of clients.

Let's pretend for a minute, though. Let's say that you got approved and you're going to continue the tradition of wall painting. You can't just paint the ad and then let it sit and fade away—not in a legal sense anyway. Section 895 of the city's municipal code calls for hand-painted signs to "be maintained, clean and in good repair, and the painted portions of such signs shall be periodically repainted and kept in good condition." Now, this book and these photographs are proof that this particular law isn't always enforced. Not that it could be effectively; many of the hand-painted signs were commissioned by companies that no longer exist. The local government also has bigger fish to fry, more pressing zoning battles to deal with. If you were to bring in a new hand-painted advertisement, though, you would be required, at least on paper, to comply. If you wanted to do this, to evoke history and create a nod back to the early days of advertising, you'd need someone to paint your ad. You'd need a "wall dog."

You're not likely to see many new painted advertisements in Cincinnati. As seen in this book, there are still a few active ones maintained, but it's certainly not the predominant form of reaching the public anymore. In larger metropolitan areas, however, they fill a niche. New York City especially is still fond of continuing the tradition of wall paintings. In 2014, media venture Voactiv produced a short documentary entitled *Wall Dogs*. The short film is titled after the nickname for the men and women who have put paint to brick in an effort to help clients reach consumers. There doesn't seem to be a clear indication of when the nickname started, but it has been

Opposite: A simple composition denotes the location of Campanello's, a still-active Italian restaurant highly regarded as a local "hole-in-the-wall" downtown. *Photo by Ronny Salerno.*

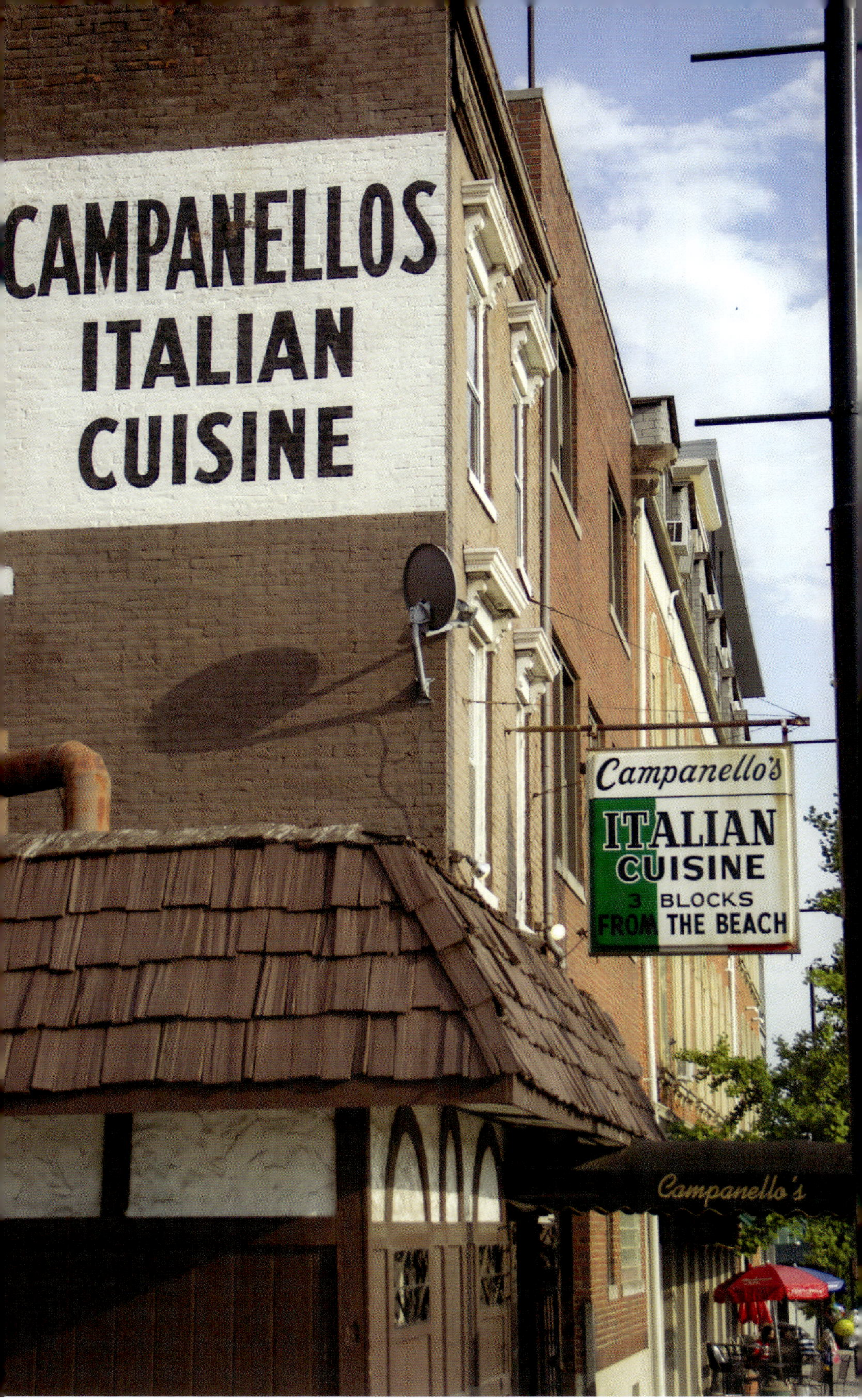
CAMPANELLOS
ITALIAN
CUISINE
Campanello's
ITALIAN
CUISINE
3 BLOCKS
FROM THE BEACH
Campanello's

recurring vernacular among anyone I've spoken to about the history of these pieces. In the film, modern painters accredit the nickname's origin to "old-timers." The harness keeping the painter safely connected to a backup plan is essentially viewed as a "chain," while the painter is a "dog." The artists shown seem to always be covered in specks of paint from their boots to their overalls to their jackets. They refer to the tradition behind their craft, to the permanence a wall painting brings and how their work is unique in the highly competitive, saturated advertising market of today. Indeed, their works have a subtlety that allows their presence to stand out in a city ripe with billboards of the vinyl and electronic variety. They start with a plan, a basic guideline of stencils, before moving on to using nothing but their hands and brushes. In a city with as much attention and people as New York, the wall dogs themselves often draw eyes to the advertisement. People stop and look, take a minute to glance up at the work being done. The hand-painted ad stands out but also has the benefit of being in a crowded city where demand is high. If you can have your product's placement be seen uniquely among the legions of potential attention grabbers, it could be worth the additional cost of commissioning a painting crew. And with an advertising demand like that found in one of the world's largest cities, many of these new wall paintings don't have the chance to fade before being covered up by the same brushes that gave them life. Oftentimes, the crews are shown painting works that reflect time-sensitive products such as concert dates and television show debuts, ads that become irrelevant after a certain point in time. They're in such high-exposure areas, though, that they'll quickly be replaced.

While Gus Holthaus's name is signed beneath so many of the old ads in the area, he certainly wasn't the only wall dog. There are Fred Lemon and Ed Gelke, too, as well as others who didn't add a personal touch at the bottom. And then there's Bob Carpenter. Like the late Gus Holthaus, Bob developed his sign painting into a larger business.

Based in nearby Cleves, Ohio, Carpenter Sign Services has worked with a variety of clients ranging from national chains to local institutions. Like Holthaus Lackner, Carpenter has evolved to accommodate more modern technologies. The Carpenter portfolio boasts billboards, mall shops, LED boards and backlit lettering among a variety of recognizable local landmarks. The company is able to assist in design work, help a client maintain signage and even help with the permit and zoning process. It all started with one man in 1959. Bob got his start as an apprentice painter. He would assist in creating posters and show cards. After five years, he broke out on his own. "It was all inside work. I liked working outside," he says. He hit the

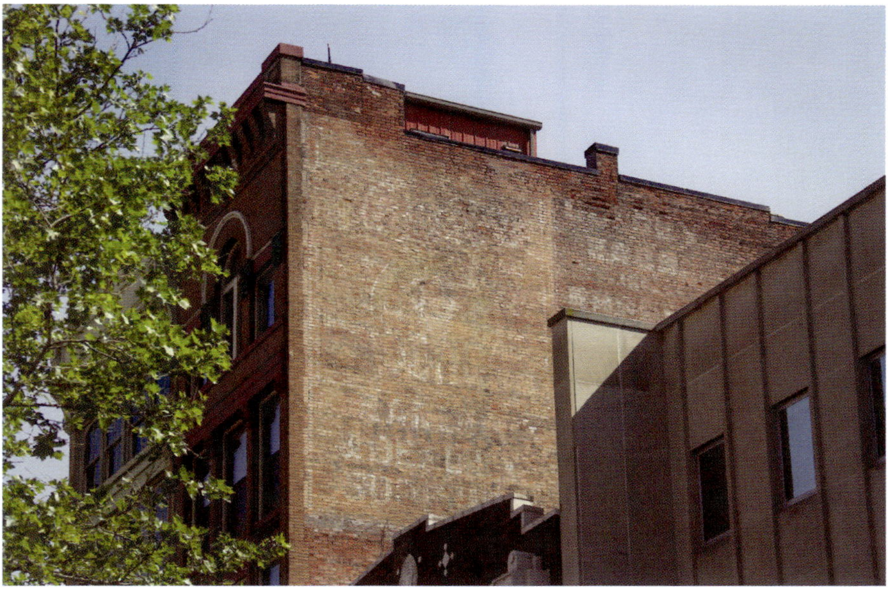

A nondescript advertisement off Main Street leaves a lot to the imagination. A circle can be seen in the center, leading one to wonder what product was once featured prominently on this wall. Gone with any legible words are also the potential signatures of any wall dogs. *Photo by Ronny Salerno.*

pavement in 1964, going door to door to solicit his services on Colerain Avenue, near where he lived. "We just did things as they came along and got a lot of referral business," he recalls. When working with a client, he was essential in executing plans or even sometimes building an idea from the ground up: "Sometimes they sent you exactly what they wanted, sometimes you had to draw it up for them." Bob was able to accommodate all kinds of orders, lending his creative talents when they were needed. He's a man who speaks matter-of-factly, straight to the point and short. However, when taking the time to answer questions or lay down some history, you get a sense of the pride he has. Bob's not boastful, but he has a lot of quality work to show for himself and his company. He was the quintessential wall dog. The enjoyment of working outside that led him to pursue wall advertisements was well suited to the working environments he'd be in: "We hung on ropes and scaffolds. You pulled yourself up by hand, lettered things and came back down at the end of the day."

As Bob's business grew, he began venturing into other forms of signage. He started working with billboard companies, painting their products before they were sent off to be hung near the highway. After awhile, he purchased a crane and bucket trucks so his company could perform billboard installation itself. Bob even worked closely with the Holthauses, fondly remembering Gus and Gus's father. The two companies would team up early on when Bob had trucks and Gus didn't.

Bob has had a wide array of clients that continue to use him to this day. He maintained business relationships all over town and would often return to touch up his hand-painted work: "Yeah, we'd repaint them every now and then. Or, you know, we'd update the signs for new merchandising, add phone numbers or even change the owner's name." Off the top of his head, he can rattle off old clients and local brands that are gone, companies that now exist only in the fond memories of locals. He'll tell you about doing the signage for all the Perkin's restaurants, Enterprise Rent-A-Cars and every Cincinnati-area Pizza Hut before the franchises became corporate. Carpenter Sign Services soon became a one-stop shop. You can come in and have years of experience ready to help you flesh out a design, professionals who know how to navigate the bureaucracy of zoning boards and a team that can physically create an ad for you. Once it's done, Bob and his group can even help install it. As the favor for wall advertisements faded out, Bob adapted and evolved much like the Holthauses, his professional colleagues.

You won't find Bob's signature beneath many signs, and he's not sure which, if any, signs of his still remain on the walls of the city. "Most of them are probably knocked down or covered up," he says. Nevertheless, Bob's mark on the city exists in a sign that's perhaps also a symbol of his company's growth. I see it every time I come down the expressway at night, heading across the bridge to home. One Lytle Place is a twenty-six-floor apartment structure, a hulking tower of concrete at the edge of the skyline that screams, "1970s." Breaking up its monotonous appearance are the lights running along the top. They border the building's roof all the way around in bright blue neon, a creation of Carpenter Sign Services. "I do very little painting anymore, except for painting the structures of electrical signs," says Bob. While wall-painted advertisements may no longer curry favor as they do among the buildings of New York City, and while Bob's hand-painted works may have been demolished, his contemporary pieces have become local landmarks imprinting his legacy on the city—a legacy that began when one man wanted to stop working inside and stepped out to become a wall dog.

"People want what their grandfathers had," says David Maley as we discuss the rising trend of consumers looking to the past. We discuss local beer and straight razors, old-school things that have gained a fresh popularity in recent years. David believes it's because people want craftsmanship, things that are hands on. This might explain why cities have embraced the surge in local art galleries, startups and the ever-growing "buy local" attitude. David is a visual communication designer. He Runs Cosette, a multi-disciplinary studio founded by himself and three other partners. They specialize in design and art direction across a multitude of physical and digital platforms. David and I both attended and graduated from Northern Kentucky University. He received a BFA in digital communication design. These days, he works in the heart of downtown, among the walls adorning the fading past of the city around him. "I think what's really great about the signs, what they represent, is the idea of hand lettering," he says. David specializes in typography, often designing his own typefaces. That's his "craft," and in his appreciation of the discipline, he can identify with what went into the hand-painted advertisements originally: "I look at them as a form of art, and I look at them as a point of craftsmanship. To know someone created it, that they were once up there painting."

This hand-painted ad for the still-active Shake It Records is a more modern take on painted wall advertising. It has managed to outlast the faded piece below it, an "Obey Giant" placed by renowned street artist Shepard Fairey. *Photo by Ronny Salerno.*

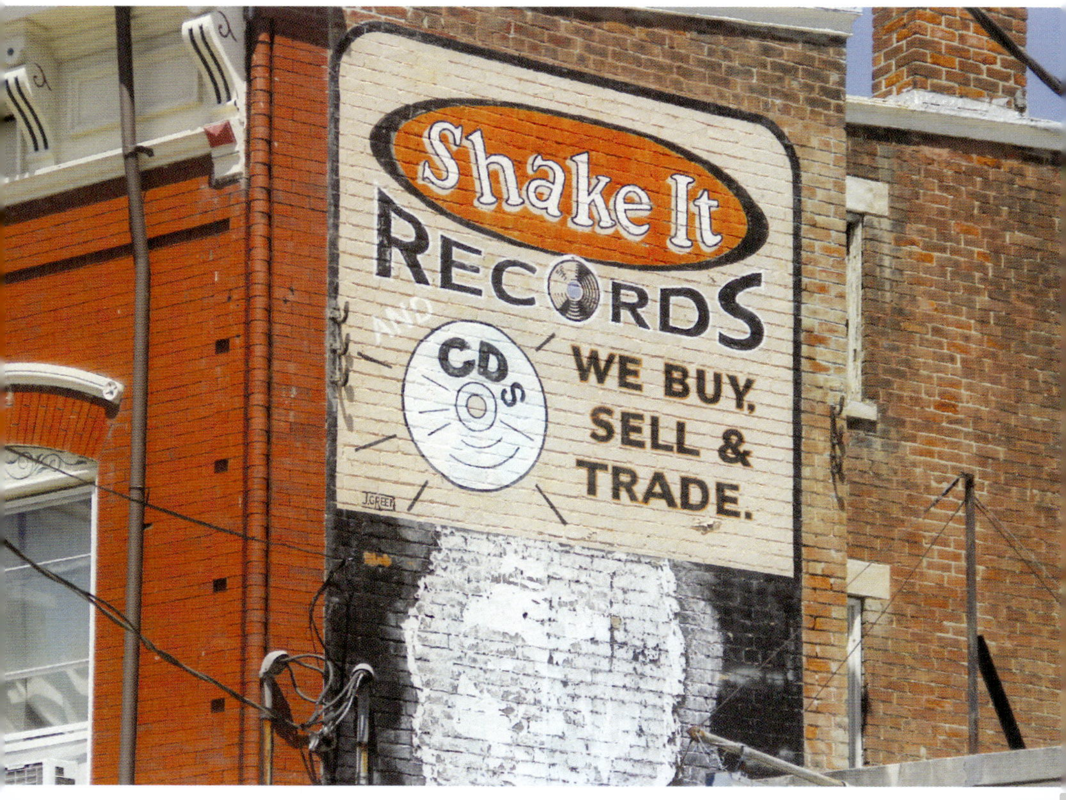

Dave sees the signs differently than I do. We have our own way of interpreting them, just like Bill Rinehart and I did. I see them as history, pieces on the wall of an art gallery, subjects that need to be photographed a certain way. I can respect the handiwork behind them, but I don't sense it the same way Dave does. Dave understands what it takes to create good design, to work with a client, to choose the right colors, to place the words, to make things pop and even to hand letter. He knows just how much it takes to create good design. He can see what makes these works so stylistically different from their contemporary successors. "You can do a good job replicating them, but these things have something," he says. "Their look will often be imitated in the digital realm, but you're not gonna be able to replicate forty years of the elements taking their tolls." He's right. While a synthetic distressed look may evoke feelings of age or nostalgia to a viewer, it's not quite the same as leaving paint on a wall for several decades. In that regard, these signs can have their various states imitated but never really duplicated. They're not just unique in what they represent but also how they've become a part of the landscape. In some respects, maybe they're no longer advertisements; maybe they're truly art whose creation is realized only with the physical influence of time.

8

CONSTANTLY FADING

The trip down I-75 was always special to me, even if we were sitting in traffic. As my father drove me to baseball games at Riverfront Stadium, that highway was the most direct route from our suburban home twenty miles out. We'd pass the entrances to the abandoned subway tunnels, historic buildings covered in graffiti, a barbed-wire lot of vehicles awaiting repossession auction, neighborhoods butting up right to the off-ramps, and then we'd round the bend. The skyline would appear, the Carew Tower at its peak. On the left was an old row house, its side exposed. At one point, it simply had "$1,000,000" painted on it with the logo of a local radio station. Other times, it would advertise local museum attractions and restaurants. Once, we passed by as a crew rolled large slabs of white paint onto it, preparing a new advertisement to fill the prime real estate. By the time I was driving on my own down to a new ballpark, the same building was advertising attractions for Kings Island, the local amusement park where I worked. The paint was gone, though, replaced with a vinyl canvas that could easily be changed. Whatever new roller coaster, water slide or promotional deal we had going on, my employer had it plastered there. Even now, as the fall approaches, it's touting the great deal you can get on next year's season passes when you "buy right now." That wall never fades; there's not enough time before a new ad takes the place of a former one, before a contract is up or a new promotion starts.

There's another advertising spot like it, down in the city's core. This one touts CincyFavorites.com, a website that will send your preferred local dish

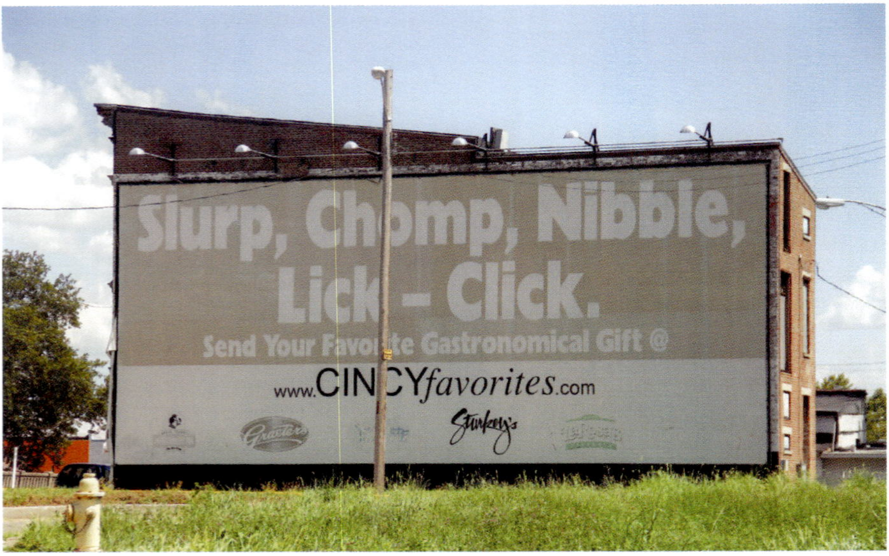

A strung-up vinyl advertisement fades in the sun, aging less gracefully than its painted-brick historical counterparts. *Photo by Ronny Salerno.*

to acquaintances abroad. That website still does business, but you wouldn't guess it from its advertisement—vinyl strung up across an entire building's side like the one I often see out of my car window. Rust from the metal supports has dripped down onto it, the vibrant red background has faded to pink and all the company logos have been bleached by the sun. It's a fading ad, like so many others in this book, but there's something it lacks. It's more of an eyesore—like something someone neglected to take down. As it ages, it will simply bleach to complete white. There's no mystery about it, no hint of craftsmanship or handiwork behind it. Even the graphic designer who put it together, his or her work doesn't translate like those of the hand-painted signs—the ones you can truly appreciate, the ones still hanging on, the ones whose permanence was implanted directly onto a building, not strung up beside it.

Over the years, the things I've photographed have been a reflection of myself, stories I wanted to tell. Cincinnati may be called a "flyover" city, just another midwestern pocket of moderately high buildings and surrounding "McMansions." Like all those other cities, though, there are individual histories, things to truly be appreciated when you take the time to explore and open your mind to the surroundings. The city is surging, an urban rebirth of culture, art, food, development and progress. It's a city with a mind for history and an appreciation of where it has come from. Even for all the good being done, there are things overlooked and stories that have been forgotten. I see the fading ads as more than just hidden, "vintage" historical markers. They let you dial into the past while reflecting artists and craftsmen who poured sweat and grit into their creations. They have a finite life, just as humans do. Unlike so many other historic artifacts, there's no true organized effort to preserve them, and maybe that's just fine.

I made these photographs in the summer of 2015, documenting these signs as I saw them at that point. Even as these words are being laid to print, some of those signs have disappeared. When left undisturbed by the forces of man, they're constant victims to the forces of nature. Their constant erosion forms their identities, bringing them a distinctive look and awarding them the nickname of "ghost sign" or "fading ad," depending on how you view what constitutes their life cycle. Each second, they near their true mortality—just as we do. One day, they'll be completely gone. In essence, though, isn't that what makes them so unique? The fact that they're evolving new identities while devolving physically, ghosts of forgotten names, products and advertising techniques. Or the fact that they're largely ignored, surviving often due to indifference, allowed to mostly play out their days as the elements see fit. Combined with their physical characteristics, their primary goals of hawking a product, discerning locations and

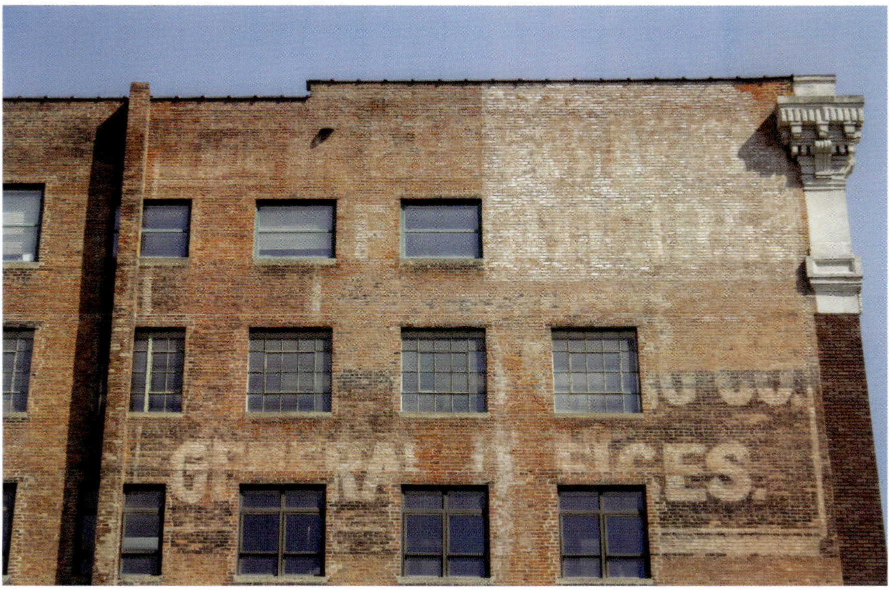

"General Offices," as seen from Main Street. *Photo by Ronny Salerno.*

giving direction—they're reflections. They hold weight. They hold stories behind them, stories of people like Gus Holthaus, Carl Solway and Bob Carpenter. These fading ads represent a lot more than just the words in their compositions. They soldier on among construction, weather and the distress of time, all the while carrying stories behind them, reflecting. Even if one day they're gone completely, at least this book will act as a way to prolong their stories and their reflections—just as it has been a reflection of me.

WORKS CITED

ABC WCPO-TV Channel 9. "Fortune 500 List Has 10 Companies from Greater Cincinnati." May 6, 2013, updated August 24, 2013. http://www.wcpo.com/money/local-business-news/fortune-500-list-has-ten-companies-from-greater-cincinnati (accessed summer 2015).

Beer Judge Certification Program. "Cream Ale." http://www.bjcp.org/2008styles/style06.php (accessed summer 2015).

Better Business Bureau. "Apollo Heating Cooling & Plumbing BBB Business Review File." January 1, 1969. http://www.bbb.org/cincinnati/business-reviews/heating-and-air-conditioning/apollo-heating-cooling-plumbing-in-cincinnati-oh-159/ (accessed summer 2015).

———. "Polinsky Office Furniture Co BBB Business Review." November 22, 2006. http://www.bbb.org/cincinnati/business-reviews/office-furniture-and-equipment/polinsky-office-furniture-co-in-cincinnati-oh-11029528 (accessed summer 2015).

Biank Fasig, Lisa. "Down for the Count." *Cincinnati Enquirer*, March 9, 1997.

———. "Globe Furniture Sells Stores." *Cincinnati Enquirer*, September 13, 2000.

Blount, Jim. "After 164 Years, Papermaking Scheduled to End in Hamilton." *Hamilton Journal News*, republished by Lane Public Library, 2011.

Carpenter, Bob. Interview with author, August 28, 2015.

Cincinnati Herald. "Gerhardstein, Strayhorne Recognized for Civil Rights Work by YWCA." April 10, 2014. http://thecincinnatiherald.com/news/2014/apr/10/gerhardstein-strayhorne-recognized-civil-rights-wo (accessed summer 2015).

Cincinnati magazine. "Dining Guide: Thai Taste." March 2000, 109.

———. Gibson and Perin advertisement, November 1985, 122; May 1984, 33.

———. Globe Furniture advertisement. January 1990.

Cincinnati Views. "Checker Stores Postcards." http://www.cincinnativiews.net/department_stores.htm#department%20stores%20top (accessed summer 2015).

City of Cincinnati. *Cincinnati: A Guide to the Queen City and Its Neighbors*. N.p.: U.S. History Publishers, 1943.

———. "Cincinnati, Ohio—Code of Ordinances Chapter 895." https://www.municode.com/library/oh/cincinnati/codes/code_of_ordinances?nodeId=TITVIIIBURE_CH895OUADSI (accessed summer 2015).

———. "Outdoor Advertising Sign Construction Permit." http://www.cincinnati-oh.gov/planning/linkservid/13913728-959F-36A7-0934F1DBD5E64F21/showMeta/0 (accessed summer 2015).

———. "Signs." http://www.cincinnati-oh.gov/planning/linkservid/13A55FA6-0275-DEF6-CC03E7127F32C4D7/showMeta/0 (accessed summer 2015).

City of Covington Economic Development Department. "Covington Kentucky Design Guidelines." N.d.

City of Newport. "History of Newport, Kentucky." http://www.newportky.gov/Newport-Info/History.aspx (accessed summer 2015).

City Population. "State of Kentucky Population (as Sourced from U.S. Census Bureau)." http://www.citypopulation.de/USA-Kentucky.html (accessed summer 2015).

Coca-Cola Company. "Coca-Cola Murals Make a Comeback." October 23, 2012. http://www.coca-colacompany.com/history/coca-cola-murals-make-a-comeback#TCCC (accessed summer 2015).

———. "A History of Coca-Cola Advertising Slogans." January 1, 2012. http://www.coca-colacompany.com/stories/coke-lore-slogans#TCCC (accessed summer 2015).

Coolidge, Sharon. "Historic OTR Building: Demolish or Rehab?" *Cincinnati Enquirer*, June 7, 2014.

Coston, Casey. "Updated Insider's Guide to OTR and Downtown." *Soapbox Cincinnati*, May 26, 2015. http://www.soapboxmedia.com/features/052615-insider-guide-otr-downtown-casey-coston.aspx (accessed summer 2015).

Curnutte, Mark. "What's Best for Downtown." *Cincinnati Enquirer*, May 20, 1999.

Dean, Adam. Interview with author, August 9, 2015.

"Digging Cincinnati History" blog. "Before Davis Furniture—1119–1123 Main Street, Over-the-Rhine." June 12, 2014. http://www.

diggingcincinnati.com/2014/06/before-davis-furniture-1119-1123-main.html (accessed summer 2015).

———. "Before Sam Caldwell & Co.—118 East 9th." April 20, 2013. http://www.diggingcincinnati.com/2013/04/before-sam-caldwell-co-118-east-9th_20.html (accessed summer 2015).

———. "The Dennison Hotel." May 7, 2015. http://www.diggingcincinnati.com/2015/05/the-dennison-hotel.html (accessed summer 2015).

———. "Globe Furniture Building—Findlay Market." June 15, 2013. http://www.diggingcincinnati.com/2013/06/globe-furniture-building-findlay-market.html (accessed summer 2015).

Dodds, Eric. "Mad Men: A Brief History of the Real-World Burger Chef." *TIME*, May 19, 2014. http://time.com/104799/burger-chef-mad-men-history (accessed summer 2015).

Drozdz, Maya. "Schuster Electric Co. Ghost Sign in Cincinnati." "VisuaLingual" blog, April 3, 2012. https://visualingual.wordpress.com/2012/04/03/schuster-electric-co-ghost-sign-in-cincinnati (accessed summer 2015).

Exhibit City News. "CORT Chairman and CEO to Retire." June 26, 2012.

Faherty, John, and Sharon Coolidge. "After 7-Hour 'Kabuki,' 'Sham,' OTR Building Stays." *Cincinnati Enquirer*, November 4, 2014.

Farrar. "US Patent 342591." May 25, 1886. http://www.google.com.na/patents/US342591 (accessed summer 2015).

Forest History Society, Durham, NC. "Inventory of the Champion International Corporation Image Collection, 1950–1979." Library and Archives. http://foresthistory.org/ead/Champion_International_Corporation.html (accessed summer 2015).

Gen Lookups. "Florence Seibert Obituary." January 11, 2000. http://www.genlookups.com/oh/webbbs_config.pl/read/721 (accessed summer 2015).

Gill, Michael. "The Paramount Pledge." *Cleveland Scene*, December 29, 2010.

Guilford County Archives. "Greensboro Business Directory 1886." October 10, 2007. http://files.usgwarchives.net/nc/guilford/directories/business/1886/greensbo112gms.txt (accessed summer 2015).

Happy Cow Healthy Eating Guide. "Spatz Natural Life Health Foods." July 16, 2008. http://www.happycow.net/reviews/spatz-natural-life-health-food-cincinnati-2384 (accessed summer 2015).

Helbig, Don. E-mail to author, June 15, 2015.

Holthaus, Kevin. Interview with author, July 31, 2015.

Industrial Commission of Ohio. *Bulletin* 5, no. 1 (1918): 28.

Jernigan, Meg. "History of the Metropole Hotel in Cincinnati." *USA Today*. http://traveltips.usatoday.com/history-metropole-hotel-cincinnati-62135.html (accessed summer 2015).

John R. Green Company. "About Us." http://www.johnrgreenco.com/index.php?main_page=index&main_page=page&id=5&zenid=ivrcd8v0sbbnt7jp15o3pu1q14 (accessed summer 2015).

Johnson, Stephen, and Cheryl Bauer. *Images of America: Lunken Airfield*. Charleston, SC: Arcadia Publishing, 2012.

Kiesewetter, John. E-mail to author, September 2, 2015.

Knight, Cameron. Interview with author, September 1, 2015.

———. "Provident Camera Closes Its Shutters." *City Beat*, April 7, 2009.

Kornegay, Sharon. "Pauline Strayhorne Is Major Federal's Prime Asset." *Black Enterprise*, June 1983, 129.

Levingston, Chelsey. "Inside Hamilton History: A Tour of Former SMART/Champion Paper Mill." *Hamilton Journal News*, May 19, 2015.

Lunken, Martha. "Unusual Attitude: Once I Built an Airline." *Flying Magazine*, April 27, 2012. http://www.flyingmag.com/pilots-places/pilots-adventures-more/once-i-built-airline-part-i?page=0,0 (accessed summer 2015).

Macy's Inc. "Macy's Inc. History." https://www.macysinc.com/press-room/macysinc-history/overview/default.aspx (accessed summer 2015).

Maley, David. Interview with author, July 1, 2015.

National Park Service. "National Register of Historic Places Registration Form for Monmouth Street Historic District." June 19, 1996. http://focus.nps.gov/pdfhost/docs/NRHP/Text/96000794.pdf (accessed summer 2015).

Office of Hamilton County Auditor Dusty Rhodes. "Parcel ID: 079-0004-0082-00." N.d.

Office Space. "212–214 E Eighth Street." http://www.officespace.com/cincinnati-oh/building/42791-212-e-eighth-street (accessed summer 2015).

Party Source. "Paramount 100 Vodka." https://www.thepartysource.com/express/item.php?id=2445 (accessed summer 2015).

Pro Hardware. "Store Locator: Cincinnati." http://www.prohardware.com/Pages/Locate/StoreLocatorProcess.asp (accessed summer 2015).

Quaker Oats. "Quaker History." http://www.quakeroats.com/about-quaker-oats/content/quaker-history.aspx (accessed summer 2015).

Ramos, Steve. "Lights Out at Mockbee." *City Beat*, October 5, 2005.

Rhiney, Sean. "Dennison Hotel Gets New Life as Historic Ironworks Apartments." *Soapbox Cincinnati*, March 1, 2011., http://www.

soapboxmedia.com/devnews/0301dennisonhotelbecomesironworks.aspx (accessed summer 2015).
Rieselman, Deborah. "Former House of Ill Repute?" *UC Magazine*, April 2013.
———. "Ludlow Hall: Cause to Shudder Twice." *UC Magazine*, April 2013.
———. "Ludlow Hall: 'Makeshift Dorm.'" *UC Magazine*, September 2012.
———. "Memories of UC Dorm on Ludlow Avenue in 1960s." *UC Magazine*. http://magazine.uc.edu/issues/0413/ludlow.html (accessed summer 2015).
———. "Remembering Ludlow Hall." *UC Magazine*, July 2003.
———. "Search for RA Bob Deddens." *UC Magazine*, April 2013.
Rinehart, Bill. Interview with author, May 28, 2015.
Schuster Electronics. "Schuster History." http://schusterusa.com/about/schuster-history (accessed summer 2015).
Sena, Sue. Interview with author, August 8, 2015.
Sobel, Robert. *ITT: The Management of Opportunity*. N.p.: Beard Books, 2000, 202–04.
Society for Cincinnati Sports Research. "Cincinnati Stingers Team History." http://www.scsr.org/CHA/Teams/CS1.htm (accessed summer 2015).
Solway, Carl. Interview with author, September 1, 2015.
Stinson, Tamia. "Pale as a Ghost Sign." *City Beat*, April 3, 2013, 1.
Sullivan, Jack. "Sam'l Klein Risked the Risqué." "Those Pre-Pro Whiskey Men" blog, October 22, 2011. http://pre-prowhiskeymen.blogspot.com/2011/10/saml-klein-risked-risque.html (accessed summer 2015).
Supreme Court of Ohio. *Williams, Appellee v. Aetna Finance Company, d.b.a. ITT Financial Services, Appellant.* November 4, 1998
Suttell, Scott. "Luxco Inc. of St. Louis Buys Paramount Distillers Inc." *Crain's Cleveland Business*, September 21, 2011.
Sweeney, Michael R. "Bavarian Brewery Survived Prohibition, but Not the Big Beer Makers." *Cincinnati Enquirer*, August 4, 2008.
Tenkotte, Paul A., and James C. Claypool. *The Encyclopedia of Northern Kentucky*. Lexington: University Press of Kentucky, 2009, 1,023.
Thompson, Richelle. "Holocaust Education: Teach and Don't Forget." *Cincinnati Enquirer*, August 29, 2000.
Tier One Asset Management Group. "Marx Cromer Warehouse Lofts." http://tier1amg.com/showDetails.asp?id=271 (accessed summer 2015).
Transit Authority of Northern Kentucky. "History." http://www.tankbus.org/about-tank/history.aspx (accessed summer 2015).
Tucker, Randy, and Ken Alltucker. "Downtown Lazarus Last of Its Kind." *Cincinnati Enquirer*, January 17, 2004.

21c Museum & Hotel. "Condé Nast Traveler Readers Vote 21c Museum Hotels to Top 100 Hotels in World." Press release, October 15, 2013. http://www.21cmuseumhotels.com/cincinnati/visit/news/2013/conde-nast-traveler-readers-vote-21c-museum-hotels-to-top-100-hotels-in-the-world (accessed summer 2015).

U.S. Department of Commerce, Bureau of the Census, Geography Division. *Census and You*. Washington, D.C.: U.S. Department of Commerce, Bureau of the Census, Geography Division, 1993.

United States Census Bureau. "Maps of Metropolitan and Micropolitan Statistical Areas." February 2013. http://www.census.gov/population/metro/files/metro_micro_Feb2013.pdf (accessed summer 2015).

———. "Population of the 100 Largest Cities, 1790–1990." http://www.census.gov/population/www/documentation/twps0027.html (accessed summer 2015).

United States Court of Appeals Sixth Circuit. *Anheuser-Busch, Inc., Appellant and Cross-Appellee, v. Bavarian Brewing Company, Appellee and Cross-Appellant.* February 26, 1959.

Williams Directory Company. *Cincinnati (Hamilton County, OH) City Directory*. Cincinnati, OH, 1922.

Williams, Ginger. "Nothing But the Facts: Here's to Your Health." *Cincinnati Magazine*, November 1982, 174.

ABOUT THE AUTHOR

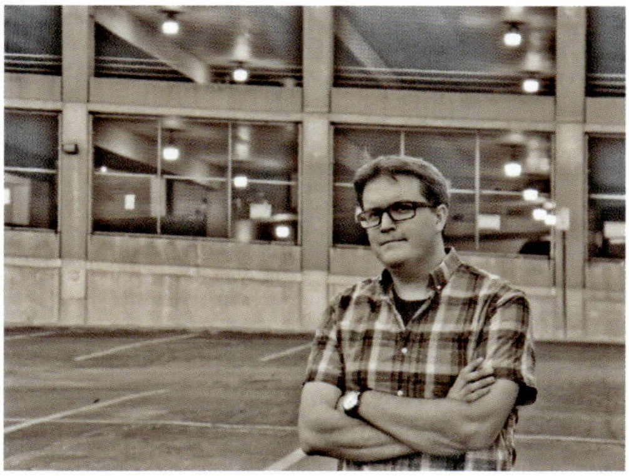

Ronny Salerno was born in Cincinnati in 1989. He graduated from Northern Kentucky University in 2013 with a BA in studio arts focused on photography and a concentration in journalism. Since 2007, he has produced "Queen City Discovery," an ongoing photographic and editorial collection documenting urban exploration, history, people, places and things across the midwestern United States and beyond. He also authors the series "Suburbia Lost" and "Kings Waffle," documentations of suburban building abandonment and the regulars at a local diner, respectively. He has been featured in local art galleries as part of the Forgotten Cincinnati and Urban Landscapes shows throughout the years. In 2013, he published *The Future Is One of Mighty Ducks T-Shirts and Discmen*, a collection of photographs comprising five years of work. His editorial work has been featured in outlets such as *ABC World News*, *NBC Nightly News*, the *Daily Mail* and the *Cincinnati Enquirer*. When he's not wandering around the city with his camera, he enjoys Cincinnati Reds baseball and sipping Waffle House coffee.

queencitydiscovery.com
ronnysalerno.com

Visit us at
www.historypress.net

This title is also available as an e-book